The Great Transformation

Karl Polanyi

Foreword by Robert M. MacIver

Beacon Press   Boston

Copyright 1944 by Karl Polanyi
First Beacon Paperback edition published in 1957
by arrangement with Rinehart & Company, Inc.
Beacon Press books are published under the auspices
of the Unitarian Universalist Association
Printed in the United States of America

International Standard Book Number: 0–8070–5679–0
Eleventh printing, November 1971

To my beloved wife
Ilona Duczynska
I dedicate this book
which owes all to her help and criticism

AUTHOR'S ACKNOWLEDGMENTS

THIS BOOK was written in America during the Second World War. But it was begun and finished in England, where the author was Lecturer for the Extramural Delegacy of the University of Oxford and the corresponding institutions of the University of London. Its main thesis was developed during the academic year 1939–40 in conjunction with his work in Tutorial Classes, organized by the Workers' Educational Association, at Morley College, London, at Canterbury and at Bexhill.

The story of this book is a story of generous friendships. Very much is due to the author's English friends, notably Irene Grant, with whose group he was associated. Common studies linked him to Felix Schafer of Vienna, an economist, at present in Wellington, New Zealand. In America John A. Kouwenhoven helped as a trusted friend with reading and editing; many of his suggestions have been incorporated in the text. Among other helpful friends were the author's Bennington colleagues, Horst Mendershausen and Peter F. Drucker. The latter and his wife were a source of sustained encouragement, notwithstanding their wholehearted disagreement with the author's conclusions; the former's general sympathy added to the usefulness of his advice. The author also owes thanks for a careful reading to Hans Zeisel of Rutgers University. The book was seen through the press entirely by Kouwenhoven, with the help of Drucker and Mendershausen, for which act of friendship the author feels deeply grateful.

To the Rockefeller Foundation he is indebted for a two-year Fellowship, 1941–43, which permitted him to complete the book at Bennington College, Vermont, following an invitation extended to him by Robert D. Leigh, then president of that college. Plans for the work were advanced by a series of public lectures and a seminar held during the academic year 1940–41. Research facilities were kindly granted by the Library of Congress in Washington, D. C., as well as by the Seligman Library of Columbia University, New York. To all of them his thanks are due.

K. P.

Shoreham, Sevenoaks, Kent.

TABLE OF CONTENTS

PART THREE

TRANSFORMATION IN PROGRESS

NOTES ON SOURCES

FOREWORD

HERE IS A BOOK that makes most books in its field seem obsolete or outworn. So rare an event is a portent of the times. Here, at a crucial hour, is a fresh comprehension of the form and the meaning of human affairs. Mr. Polanyi does not profess to be writing history—he is rewriting it. He is not bringing a candle light into one of its dark corners, nor is he plausibly making it the public scripture of his private faith; instead, with insight as well as with knowledge, he is shedding a new illumination on the processes and revolutions of a whole age of unexampled change.

Mr. Polanyi's immediate objective is to bring out, as he does with remarkable discernment, the social implications of a particular economic system, the market economy that grew to its full stature in the nineteenth century. The time has come when retrospective wisdom may assess it all, for, as Aristotle said, we can learn the nature of anything only when it has reached—and passed—its maturation. Events and processes, theories and actions, appear in a new perspective. Much that to the pedestrian writer of history seems merely episodic becomes invested with a deeper significance; much that seems merely bizarre is given a juster estimate. The reduction of man to labor and of nature to land under the impulsion of the market economy turns modern history into a high drama in which society, the chained protagonist, at last bursts its bonds.

This new orientation, suggested in other works but not developed before, confers new proportions on men and ideas. Take, for example, the Chartist Movement and the prophetic spirit of Robert Owen. Or take the famous recommendation of Speenhamland—how much deeper Mr. Polanyi cuts into its historic meaning! How intelligible becomes the picture of the judicial squires prescribing armchair principles to a force that neither they nor the most enlightened of their age could yet comprehend. With new understanding we witness the battle of ideologies around the inexorably growing economy, some blindly opposing, some seeking to retard its more ruthless thrusts into the social fabric, some single-mindedly—or simple-mindedly—hailing its every advance. We witness the rearguard action of the champions of the old order, the impotent discomfiture of the upholders of a tradition-bound Christianity, the easy triumph of the orthodox economists who neatly explain it all. But the advancing front leaves ruin in its train, and the hastily built defences crumble before it. We see how with a new liberation went a new servitude, and we measure the challenge that now faces our own age.

Mr. Polanyi leaves far behind alike the dogmatics of Karl Marx and the apologetics of the reaction. He is concerned with the economic process in modern civilization but he offers no doctrine of economic determinism. He gives instead a penetrating analysis of a particular historical transformation in which the supersession of one economic system by another played the decisive role. This happened not because the economic relation is always primary but because in this instance, and in this instance alone, the "ideal system" of the new economics demanded a ruthless abnegation of the social status of the human being. Skillfully he adduces the colonial situation and the industrially invaded societies of primitive people in order to show, not what this "ideal system" meant for them but what it also imported for us. The "satanic mills" were heedless of all human needs but one; relentlessly they began to grind society itself into its atoms. Therefore men had to discover society. For Mr. Polanyi the last word is society. The major tragedy attendant on the Industrial Revolution was brought about not by the callousness and greed of profit-seeking capitalists—though there was inhumanity enough in the record—but by the social devastation of an uncontrolled *system*, the market economy. Men failed to realize what the cohesion of society meant. The inner temple of human life was despoiled and violated. The tremendous problem of the social control of a revolutionary change was unappreciated; optimistic philosophies obscured it, shortsighted philanthropies conspired with power interests to conceal it, and the wisdom of time was still unborn.

But in presenting this argument Mr. Polanyi is not casting wistful eyes on some happier past; he is not pleading the cause of reaction. There is no way back and no solution can come through the search for one. What our age needs is the reaffirmation, for its own conditions and for its own needs, of the essential values of human life. Tradition fails us and will betray us if we trust to it. We must not abandon the principle of individual freedom but we must re-create it. We cannot restore a past society, even if the haze of history hides its evils from us; we must rebuild society for ourselves, learning from the past what lessons and what warnings we are capable of learning. Perhaps in doing so we might also bear in mind that the causation of human affairs is too deeply tangled to be wholly unraveled by the wisest minds. There is always a point where we must trust our values in action, so that the urgent forces of the present world may release themselves in new directions towards new goals.

A book so stimulating and so deep-probing is bound to excite controversy and to be questioned at various points. Some may doubt whether the role of the market economy was so absolute, whether the logic of the system was in itself so rigorous and compelling. They may not be willing to go as far as the author when at one point he ways that "nations and peoples were mere puppets in a show utterly beyond their control." Some may wish that the different forms of "protection" against the self-regulating market were given different valuations and they may be a little uneasy that the tariff promoter and social legislator seem to appear as brothers-in-arms. And so forth. But they must all surely recognize the clear cogency of the total argument. We stand at a new vantage point, looking down, after the earthquake, on the ruined temples of our cherished gods. We see the weakness of the exposed foundations—perhaps we can learn how, and where, to rebuild the institutional fabric so that it may better withstand the shocks of change.

Of primary importance today is the lesson it carries for the makers of the coming international organization. For one thing it shows that such liberal formulas as "world peace through world trade" will not suffice. If we are content with such formulas we are the victims of a dangerous and deceptive simplification. Neither a national nor an international system can depend on the automatic regulants. Balanced budgets and free enterprise and world commerce and international clearinghouses and currencies maintained at par will not guarantee an international order. Society alone can guarantee it; international society must also be discovered. Here too the institutional fabric must maintain and control the economic scheme of things.

So the message of this book is not only for the economist, though it has a powerful message for him; not only for the historian, though it opens for him new paths; not only for the sociologist, though it conveys to him a deepened sense of what society means; not only for the political scientist, though it will help him to restate old issues and to evaluate old doctrines—it is for every intelligent man who cares to advance beyond his present stage of social education, for every man who cares to know the society in which he lives, the crisis it has passed through, and the crises that are now upon us. Here he may gain new glimpses of a deeper faith. Here he can learn to look beyond the inadequate alternatives that are usually offered to him, the thus far and no farther of liberalism, the all or nothing of collectivism, the sheer negation of individualism, for these all tend to make some economic system the primary desideratum, and it is only as we discover the primacy of society, the inclusive coherent unity of human interdependence, that we can hope to transcend the perplexities and the contradictions of our times.

R. M. MacIver

PART ONE

The International System

1

THE HUNDRED YEARS' PEACE

NINETEENTH CENTURY civilization has collapsed. This book is concerned with the political and economic origins of this event, as well as with the great transformation which it ushered in.

Nineteenth century civilization rested on four institutions. The first was the balance-of-power system which for a century prevented the occurrence of any long and devastating war between the Great Powers. The second was the international gold standard which symbolized a unique organization of world economy. The third was the self-regulating market which produced an unheard-of material welfare. The fourth was the liberal state. Classified in one way, two of these institutions were economic, two political. Classified in another way, two of them were national, two international. Between them they determined the characteristic outlines of the history of our civilization.

Of these institutions the gold standard proved crucial; its fall was the proximate cause of the catastrophe. By the time it failed most of the other institutions had been sacrificed in a vain effort to save it.

But the fount and matrix of the system was the self-regulating market. It was this innovation which gave rise to a specific civilization. The gold standard was merely an attempt to extend the domestic market system to the international field; the balance-of-power system was a superstructure erected upon and, partly, worked through the gold standard; the liberal state was itself a creation of the self-regulating market. The key to the institutional system of the nineteenth century lay in the laws governing market economy.

Our thesis is that the idea of a self-adjusting market implied a stark utopia. Such an institution could not exist for any length of time without annihilating the human and natural substance of society; it would have physically destroyed man and transformed his surroundings into a wilderness. Inevitably, society took measures to protect itself, but whatever measures it took impaired the self-regulation of the market, disorganized industrial life, and thus endangered society in yet another

3

way. It was this dilemma which forced the development of the market system into a definite groove and finally disrupted the social organization based upon it.

Such an explanation of one of the deepest crises in man's history must appear all too simple. Nothing could seem more inept than the attempt to reduce a civilization, its substance and ethos, to a hard and fast number of institutions; to select one of them as fundamental and proceed to argue the inevitable self-destruction of civilization on account of some technical quality of its economic organization. Civilizations, like life itself, spring from the interaction of a great number of independent factors which are not, as a rule, reducible to circumscribed institutions. To trace the institutional mechanism of the downfall of a civilization may well appear as a hopeless endeavor.

Yet it is this we are undertaking. In doing so we are consciously adjusting our aim to the extreme singularity of the subject matter. For the civilization of the nineteenth century was unique precisely in that it centered on a definite institutional mechanism.

No explanation can satisfy which does not account for the suddenness of the cataclysm. As if the forces of change had been pent up for a century, a torrent of events is pouring down on mankind. A social transformation of planetary range is being topped by wars of an unprecedented type in which a score of states crashed, and the contours of new empires are emerging out of a sea of blood. But this fact of demoniac violence is merely superimposed on a swift, silent current of change which swallows up the past often without so much as a ripple on the surface! A reasoned analysis of the catastrophe must account both for the tempestuous action and the quiet dissolution.

Ours is not a historical work; what we are searching for is not a convincing sequence of outstanding events, but an explanation of their trend in terms of human institutions. We shall feel free to dwell on scenes of the past with the sole object of throwing light on matters of the present; we shall make detailed analyses of critical periods and almost completely disregard the connecting stretches of time; we shall encroach upon the field of several disciplines in the pursuit of this single aim.

First we shall deal with the collapse of the international system. We shall try to show that the balance-of-power system could not ensure peace once the world economy on which it rested had failed. This accounts for the abruptness with which the break occurred, the inconceivable rapidity of the dissolution.

But if the breakdown of our civilization was timed by the failure of world economy, it was certainly not caused by it. Its origins lay more than a hundred years back in that social and technological upheaval from which the idea of a self-regulating market sprang in Western Europe. The end of this venture has come in our time; it closes a distinct stage in the history of industrial civilization.

In the final part of the book we shall deal with the mechanism which governed social and national change in our time. Broadly, we believe that the present condition of man is to be defined in terms of the institutional origins of the crisis.

The nineteenth century produced a phenomenon unheard of in the annals of Western civilization, namely, a hundred years' peace—1815–1914. Apart from the Crimean War—a more or less colonial event—England, France, Prussia, Austria, Italy, and Russia were engaged in war among each other for altogether only eighteen months. A computation of comparable figures for the two preceding centuries gives an average of sixty to seventy years of major wars in each. But even the fiercest of nineteenth century conflagrations, the Franco-Prussian War of 1870–71, ended after less than a year's duration with the defeated nation being able to pay over an unprecedented sum as an indemnity without any disturbance of the currencies concerned. This triumph of a pragmatic pacifism was certainly not the result of an absence of grave causes for conflict. Almost continuous shifts in the internal and external conditions of powerful nations and great empires accompanied this irenic pageant. During the first part of the century civil wars, revolutionary and anti-revolutionary interventions were the order of the day. In Spain a hundred thousand troops under the Duc d'Angoulême stormed Cadiz; in Hungary the Magyar revolution threatened to defeat the Emperor himself in pitched battle and was ultimately suppressed only by a Russian army fighting on Hungarian soil. Armed interventions in the Germanies, in Belgium, Poland, Switzerland, Denmark, and Venice marked the omnipresence of the Holy Alliance. During the second half of the century the dynamics of progress was released; the Ottoman, Egyptian, and the Sheriffian empires broke up or were dismembered; China was forced by invading armies to open her door to the foreigner and in one gigantic haul the continent of Africa was partitioned. Simultaneously, two powers rose to world importance: the United States and Russia. National unity was achieved by Germany and Italy; Belgium, Greece, Roumania,

Bulgaria, Serbia, and Hungary assumed, or reassumed, their places as sovereign states on the map of Europe. An almost incessant series of open wars accompanied the march of industrial civilization into the domains of outworn cultures or primitive peoples. Russia's military conquests in Central Asia, England's numberless Indian and African wars, France's exploits in Egypt, Algiers, Tunis, Syria, Madagascar, Indo-China, and Siam raised issues between the Powers which, as a rule, only force can arbitrate. Yet every single one of these conflicts was localized, and numberless other occasions for violent change were either met by joint action or smothered into compromise by the Great Powers. Regardless of how the methods changed, the result was the same. While in the first part of the century constitutionalism was banned and the Holy Alliance suppressed freedom in the name of peace, during the other half—and again in the name of peace—constitutions were foisted upon turbulent despots by business-minded bankers. Thus under varying forms and ever-shifting ideologies—sometimes in the name of progress and liberty, sometimes by the authority of the throne and the altar, sometimes by grace of the stock exchange and the checkbook, sometimes by corruption and bribery, sometimes by moral argument and enlightened appeal, sometimes by the broadside and the bayonet—one and the same result was attained: peace was preserved.

This almost miraculous performance was due to the working of the balance of power, which here produced a result which is normally foreign to it. By its nature that balance effects an entirely different result, namely, the survival of the power units involved; in fact, it merely postulates that three or more units capable of exerting power will always behave in such a way as to combine the power of the weaker units against any increase in power of the strongest. In the realm of universal history balance of power was concerned with states whose independence it served to maintain. But it attained this end only by continuous war between changing partners. The practice of the ancient Greek or the Northern Italian city-states was such an instance; wars between shifting groups of combatants maintained the independence of those states over long stretches of time. The action of the same principle safeguarded for over two hundred years the sovereignty of the states forming Europe at the time of the Treaty of Münster and Westphalia (1648). When, seventy-five years later, in the Treaty of Utrecht, the signatories declared their formal adherence to this principle, they thereby embodied it in a *system*, and thus established mutual guarantees of survival for the strong and the weak alike through the medium of war. The fact that in the nineteenth century the same mechanism resulted in peace rather than war is a problem to challenge the historian.

The entirely new factor, we submit, was the emergence of an acute peace interest. Traditionally, such an interest was regarded as outside the scope of the state system. Peace with its corollaries of crafts and arts ranked among the mere adornments of life. The Church might pray for peace as for a bountiful harvest, but in the realm of state action it would nevertheless advocate armed intervention; governments subordinated peace to security and sovereignty, that is, to intents that could not be achieved otherwise than by recourse to the ultimate means. Few things were regarded as more detrimental to a community than the existence of an organized peace interest in its midst. As late as the second half of the eighteenth century, J. J. Rousseau arraigned trades people for their lack of patriotism because they were suspected of preferring peace to liberty.

After 1815 the change is sudden and complete. The backwash of the French Revolution reinforced the rising tide of the Industrial Revolution in establishing peaceful business as a universal interest. Metternich proclaimed that what the people of Europe wanted was not liberty but peace. Gentz called patriots the new barbarians. Church and throne started out on the denationalization of Europe. Their arguments found support both in the ferocity of the recent popular forms of warfare and in the tremendously enhanced value of peace under the nascent economies.

The bearers of the new "peace interest" were, as usual, those who chiefly benefited by it, namely, that cartel of dynasts and feudalists whose patrimonial positions were threatened by the revolutionary wave of patriotism that was sweeping the Continent. Thus, for approximately a third of a century the Holy Alliance provided the coercive force and the ideological impetus for an active peace policy; its armies were roaming up and down Europe putting down minorities and repressing majorities. From 1846 to about 1871—"one of the most confused and crowded quarter centuries of European history" [1]—peace was less safely established, the ebbing strength of reaction meeting the growing strength of industrialism. In the quarter century following the Franco-Prussian War we find the revived peace interest represented by that new powerful entity, the Concert of Europe.

[1] Sontag, R. J., *European Diplomatic History, 1871–1932*, 1933.

Interests, however, like intents, necessarily remain platonic unless they are translated into politics by the means of some social instrumentality. Superficially, such a vehicle of realization was lacking; both the Holy Alliance and the Concert of Europe were, ultimately, mere groupings of independent sovereign states, and thus subject to the balance of power and its mechanism of war. How then was peace maintained?

True, any balance-of-power system will tend to prevent such wars as spring from one nation's failure to foresee the realignment of powers which will result from its attempt to alter the *status quo*. Famous instances were Bismarck's calling off of the press campaign against France, in 1875, on Russian and British intervention (Austria's aid to France was taken for granted). This time the Concert of Europe worked against Germany who found herself isolated. In 1877–78 Germany was unable to prevent a Russo-Turkish War, but succeeded in localizing it by backing up England's jealousy of a Russian move towards the Dardanelles; Germany and England supported Turkey against Russia—thus saving the peace. At the Congress of Berlin a long-term plan for the liquidation of the European possessions of the Ottoman Empire was launched; this resulted in averting wars between the Great Powers in spite of all subsequent changes in the *status quo,* as the parties concerned could be practically certain in advance of the forces they would have to meet in battle. Peace in these instances was a welcome by-product of the balance-of-power system.

Also, wars were sometimes avoided by deliberately removing their causes, if the fate of small powers only was involved. Small nations were checked and prevented from disturbing the *status quo* in any way which might precipitate war. The Dutch invasion of Belgium in 1831 eventually led to the neutralization of that country. In 1855 Norway was neutralized. In 1867 Luxembourg was sold by Holland to France; Germany protested and Luxembourg was neutralized. In 1856 the integrity of the Ottoman Empire was declared essential to the equilibrium of Europe, and the Concert of Europe endeavored to maintain that empire; after 1878, when its disintegration was deemed essential to that equilibrium, its dismemberment was provided for in a similarly orderly manner, though in both cases the decision meant life and death to several small peoples. Between 1852 and 1863 Denmark, between 1851 and 1856 the Germanies threatened to disturb the balance; each time the small states were forced by the Great Powers to conform. In these instances, the liberty of action offered to them by the system was used by the Powers to achieve a joint interest—which happened to be peace.

But it is a far cry from the occasional averting of wars either by a timely clarification of the power situation or by the coercing of small states to the massive fact of the Hundred Years' Peace. International disequilibrium may occur for innumerable reasons—from a dynastic love affair to the silting of an estuary, from a theological controversy to a technological invention. The mere growth of wealth and population, or, eventually, their decrease, is bound to set political forces in motion; and the external balance will invariably reflect the internal. Even an organized balance-of-power system can ensure peace without the permanent threat of war only if it is able to act upon these internal factors directly and prevent imbalance *in statu nascendi*. Once the imbalance has gathered momentum only force can set it right. It is a commonplace that to insure peace one must eliminate the causes of war; but it is not generally realized that to do so the flow of life must be controlled at its source.

The Holy Alliance contrived to achieve this with the help of instruments peculiar to it. The kings and aristocracies of Europe formed an international of kinship; and the Roman Church provided them with a voluntary civil service ranging from the highest to the lowest rung of the social ladder in Southern and Central Europe. The hierarchies of blood and grace were fused into an instrument of locally effective rule which needed only to be supplemented by force to ensure continental peace.

But the Concert of Europe, which succeeded it, lacked the feudal as well as the clerical tentacles; it amounted at the best to a loose federation not comparable in coherence to Metternich's masterpiece. Only on rare occasions could a meeting of the Powers be called, and their jealousies allowed a wide latitude to intrigue, crosscurrents, and diplomatic sabotage; joint military action became rare. And yet what the Holy Alliance, with its complete unity of thought and purpose, could achieve in Europe only with the help of frequent armed interventions was here accomplished on a world scale by the shadowy entity called the Concert of Europe with the help of a very much less frequent and oppressive use of force. For an explanation of this amazing feat, we must seek for some undisclosed powerful social instrumentality at work in the new setting, which could play the role of dynasties and episcopacies under the old and make the peace interest effective. This anonymous factor was *haute finance*.

No all-around inquiry into the nature of international banking in the nineteenth century has yet been undertaken; this mysterious institution has hardly emerged from the chiaroscuro of politico-economic mythology.[2] Some contended that it was merely the tool of governments; others, that the governments were the instruments of its unquenchable thirst for gain; some, that it was the sower of international discord; others, that it was the vehicle of an effeminate cosmopolitanism sapping the strength of virile nations. None was quite mistaken. *Haute finance*, an institution *sui generis*, peculiar to the last third of the nineteenth and the first third of the twentieth century, functioned as the main link between the political and the economic organization of the world in this period. It supplied the instruments for an international peace system, which was worked with the help of the Powers, but which the Powers themselves could neither have established nor maintained. While the Concert of Europe acted only at intervals, *haute finance* functioned as a permanent agency of the most elastic kind. Independent of single governments, even of the most powerful, it was in touch with all; independent of the central banks, even of the Bank of England, it was closely connected with them. There was intimate contact between finance and diplomacy; neither would consider any long-range plan, whether peaceful or warlike, without making sure of the other's good will. Yet the secret of the successful maintenance of general peace lay undoubtedly in the position, organization, and techniques of international finance.

Both the personnel and the motives of this singular body invested it with a status the roots of which were securely grounded in the private sphere of strictly business interest. The Rothschilds were subject to no one government; as a family they embodied the abstract principle of internationalism; their loyalty was to a firm, the credit of which had become the only supranational link between political government and industrial effort in a swiftly growing world economy. In the last resort, their independence sprang from the needs of the time which demanded a sovereign agent commanding the confidence of national statesmen and of the international investor alike; it was to this vital need that the metaphysical extraterritoriality of a Jewish bankers' dynasty domiciled in the capitals of Europe provided an almost perfect solution. They were anything but pacifists; they had made their fortune in the financing of wars; they were impervious to moral consideration; they had no objection to any number of minor, short, or localized wars. But their business would be impaired if a general war between the Great Powers

[2] Feis, H., *Europe, the World's Banker, 1870–1914*, 1930, a work we have often textually followed.

should interfere with the monetary foundations of the system. By the logic of facts it fell to them to maintain the requisites of general peace in the midst of the revolutionary transformation to which the peoples of the planet were subject.

Organizationally, *haute finance* was the nucleus of one of the most complex institutions the history of man has produced. Transitory though it was, it compared in catholicity, in the profusion of forms and instruments, only with the whole of human pursuits in industry and trade of which it became in some sort the mirror and counterpart. Besides the international center, *haute finance* proper, there were some half dozen national centers hiving around their banks of issue and stock exchanges. Also, international banking was not restricted to the financing of governments, their adventures in war and peace; it comprised foreign investment in industry, public utilities, and banks, as well as long-term loans to public and private corporations abroad. National finance again was a microcosm. England alone counted half a hundred different types of banks; France's and Germany's banking organization, too, was specific; and in each of these countries the practices of the Treasury and its relations to private finance varied in the most striking, and, often, as to detail, most subtle way. The money market dealt with a multitude of commercial bills, overseas acceptances, pure financial bills, as well as call money and other stockbrokers' facilities. The pattern was checkered by an infinite variety of national groups and personalities, each with its peculiar type of prestige and standing, authority and loyalty, its assets of money and contact, of patronage and social aura.

Haute finance was not designed as an instrument of peace; this function fell to it by accident, as historians would say, while the sociologist might prefer to call it the law of availability. The motive of *haute finance* was gain; to attain it, it was necessary to keep in with the governments whose end was power and conquest. We may safely neglect at this stage the distinction between political and economic power, between economic and political purposes on the part of the governments; in effect, it was the characteristic of the nation-states in this period that such a distinction had but little reality, for whatever their aims, the governments strove to achieve them through the use and increase of national power. The organization and personnel of *haute finance*, on the other hand, was international, yet not, therefore, altogether independent of national organization. For *haute finance* as an activating center of bankers' participation in syndicates and consortia, investment groups, foreign loans, financial controls, or other transactions of an ambitious scope, was bound to seek the co-operation of national banking, national capital, national finance. Though national finance, as a rule, was less subservient to government than national industry, it was still sufficiently so to make international finance eager to keep in touch with the governments themselves. Yet to the degree to which—in virtue of its position and personnel, its private fortune and affiliations—it was actually independent of any single government, it was able to serve a new interest, which had no specific organ of its own, for the service of which no other institution happened to be available, and which was nevertheless of vital importance to the community: namely, peace. Not peace at all cost, not even peace at the price of any ingredient of independence, sovereignty, vested glory, or future aspirations of the powers concerned, but nevertheless peace, if it was possible to attain it without such sacrifice.

Not otherwise. Power had precedence over profit. However closely their realms interpenetrated, ultimately it was war that laid down the law to business. Since 1870 France and Germany, for example, were enemies. This did not exclude noncommittal transactions between them. Occasional banking syndicates were formed for transitory purposes; there was private participation by German investment banks in enterprises over the border, which did not appear in the balance sheets; in the short-term loan market there was a discounting of bills of exchange and a granting of short-term loans on collateral and commercial papers on the part of French banks; there was direct investment as in the case of the marriage of iron and coke, or of Thyssen's plant in Normandy, but such investments were restricted to definite areas in France and were under a permanent fire of criticism from both the nationalists and the socialists; direct investment was more frequent in the colonies, as exemplified by Germany's tenacious efforts to secure high-grade ore in Algeria, or by the involved story of participations in Morocco. Yet it remains a stern fact that at no time after 1870 was the official though tacit ban on German securities at the Bourse of Paris lifted. France simply "chose not to risk having the force of loaned capital" [3] turned upon herself. Austria also was suspect; in the Moroccan crisis of 1905–06 the ban was extended to Hungary. Financial circles in Paris pleaded for the admission of Hungarian securities, but industrial circles supported the government in its staunch opposition to any concession to a possible military antagonist. Politico-diplomatic

[3] Feis, H., op. cit., p. 201.

rivalry continued unabated. Any move that might increase the presumptive enemy's potential was vetoed by the governments. Superficially, it more than once appeared as if the conflict had been quashed, but the inside circles were aware that it had been merely shifted to points even more deeply hidden under the amicable surface.

Or take Germany's Eastern ambitions. Here also politics and finance intermingled, yet politics was supreme. After a quarter of a century of perilous bickering, Germany and England signed a comprehensive agreement on the Baghdad railway, in June, 1914—too late to prevent the Great War, it was often said. Others argued that, on the contrary, the signing of the agreement proved conclusively that the war between England and Germany was *not* caused by a clash of economic expansionism. Neither view is borne out by the facts. The agreement actually left the main issue undecided. The German railway line was still not to be carried on beyond Basra without the consent of the British government, and the economic zones of the treaty were bound to lead to a head-on collision at a future time. Meanwhile, the Powers would continue to prepare for The Day, which was even nearer than they reckoned.[4]

International finance had to cope with the conflicting ambitions and intrigues of the great and small powers; its plans were thwarted by diplomatic maneuvers, its long-term investments jeopardized, its constructive efforts hampered by political sabotage and backstairs obstruction. The national banking organizations without which it was helpless often acted as the accomplices of their respective governments, and no plan was safe which did not carve out in advance the booty of each participant. However, *power finance* just as often was not the victim, but the beneficiary of *Dollar diplomacy* which provided the steel ribs to the velvet glove of finance. For business success involved the ruthless use of force against weaker countries, wholesale bribing of backward administrations, and the use of all the underhand means of gaining ends familiar to the colonial and semicolonial jungle. And yet by functional determination it fell to *haute finance* to avert general wars. The vast majority of the holders of government securities, as well as other investors and traders, were bound to be the first losers in such wars, especially if the currencies were affected. The influence that *haute finance* exerted on the Powers was consistently favorable to European peace. And this influence was effective to the degree to which the governments themselves depended upon its co-operation in more than one

[4] Cf. Notes on Sources, page 264.

direction. Consequently, there was never a time when the peace interest was unrepresented in the councils of the Concert of Europe. If we add to this the growing peace interest inside every nation where the investment habit had taken root, we shall begin to see why the awful innovation of an armed peace of dozens of practically mobilized states could hover over Europe from 1871 to 1914 without bursting forth in a shattering conflagration.

Finance—this was one of its channels of influence—acted as a powerful moderator in the councils and policies of a number of smaller sovereign states. Loans, and the renewal of loans, hinged upon credit, and credit upon good behavior. Since, under constitutional government (unconstitutional ones were severely frowned upon), behavior is reflected in the budget and the external value of the currency cannot be detached from the appreciation of the budget, debtor governments were well advised to watch their exchanges carefully and to avoid policies which might reflect upon the soundness of the budgetary position. This useful maxim became a cogent rule of conduct once a country had adopted the gold standard, which limited permissible fluctuations to a minimum. Gold standard and constitutionalism were the instruments which made the voice of the City of London heard in many smaller countries which had adopted these symbols of adherence to the new international order. The Pax Britannica held its sway sometimes by the ominous poise of heavy ship's cannon, but more frequently it prevailed by the timely pull of a thread in the international monetary network.

The influence of *haute finance* was ensured also through its unofficial administration of the finances of vast semicolonial regions of the world, including the decaying empires of Islam in the highly inflammable zone of the Near East and North Africa. It was here that the day's work of financiers touched upon the subtle factors underlying internal order, and provided a *de facto* administration for those troubled regions where peace was most vulnerable. That is how the numerous prerequisites of long-term capital investments in these areas could often be secured in the face of almost insuperable obstacles. The epic of the building of railways in the Balkans, in Anatolia, Syria, Persia, Egypt, Morocco, and China is a story of endurance and of breathtaking turns reminiscent of a similar feat on the North American Continent. The chief danger, however, which stalked the capitalists of Europe was not technological or financial failure, but war—not a war between small countries (which could be easily isolated) nor war upon a small country by a Great Power (a frequent and often convenient occurrence), but a general war between the Great Powers themselves. Europe was not an empty continent, but the home of teeming millions of ancient and new peoples; every new railroad had to thread its way across boundaries of varying solidity, some of which might be fatally weakened, others vitally reinforced, by the contact. Only the iron grip of finance on the prostrate governments of backward regions could avert catastrophe. When Turkey defaulted on its financial obligations in 1875, military conflagrations immediately broke out, lasting from 1876 to 1878 when the Treaty of Berlin was signed. For thirty-six years thereafter peace was maintained. That astounding peace was implemented by the Decree of Muharrem of 1881, which set up the Dette Ottomane in Constantinople. The representatives of *haute finance* were charged with the administration of the bulk of Turkish finance. In numerous cases they engineered compromises between the Powers; in others, they prevented Turkey from creating difficulties on her own; in others again, they acted simply as the political agents of the Powers; in all, they served the money interests of the creditors, and, if at all possible, of the capitalists who tried to make profits in that country. This task was greatly complicated by the fact that the Debt Commission was *not* a body representative of the private creditors, but an organ of Europe's public law on which *haute finance* was only unofficially represented. But it was precisely in this amphibious capacity that it was able to bridge the gap between the political and the economic organization of the age.

Trade had become linked with peace. In the past the organization of trade had been military and warlike; it was an adjunct of the pirate, the rover, the armed caravan, the hunter and trapper, the sword-bearing merchant, the armed burgesses of the towns, the adventurers and explorers, the planters and conquistadores, the manhunters and slave traders, the colonial armies of the chartered companies. Now all this was forgotten. Trade was now dependent upon an international monetary system which could not function in a general war. It demanded peace, and the Great Powers were striving to maintain it. But the balance-of-power system, as we have seen, could not by itself ensure peace. This was done by international finance, the very existence of which embodied the principle of the new dependence of trade upon peace.

We have become too much accustomed to think of the spread of capitalism as a process which is anything but peaceful, and of finance capital as the chief instigator of innumerable colonial crimes and expansionist aggressions. Its intimate affiliation with heavy industries made Lenin assert that finance capital was responsible for imperialism, notably for the struggle for spheres of influence, concessions, extraterritorial rights, and the innumerable forms in which the Western Powers got a stranglehold on backward regions, in order to invest in railways, public utilities, ports, and other permanent establishments on which their heavy industries made profits. Actually, business and finance were responsible for many colonial wars, but also for the fact that a general conflagration was avoided. Their affiliations with heavy industry, though really close only in Germany, accounted for both. Finance capital as the roof organization of heavy industry was affiliated with the various branches of industry in too many ways to allow one group to determine its policy. For every one interest that was furthered by war, there were a dozen that would be adversely affected. International capital, of course, was bound to be the loser in case of war; but even national finance could gain only exceptionally, though frequently enough to account for dozens of colonial wars, as long as they remained isolated. Every war, almost, was organized by financiers; but peace also was organized by them.

The precise nature of this strictly pragmatic system, which guarded with extreme rigor against a general war while providing for peaceful business amidst an endless sequence of minor ones, is best demonstrated by the changes it brought about in international law. While nationalism and industry distinctly tended to make wars more ferocious and total, effective safeguards were erected for the continuance of peaceful business in wartime. Frederick the Great is on record for having "by reprisal" refused, in 1752, to honor the Silesian loan due to British subjects.[5] "No attempt of this sort has been made since," says Hershey. "The wars of the French Revolution furnish us with the last important examples of the confiscation of the private property of enemy subjects found in belligerent territory upon the outbreak of hostilities." After the outbreak of the Crimean War enemy merchantmen were allowed to leave port, a practice which was adhered to by Prussia, France, Russia, Turkey, Spain, Japan, and the United States during the fifty following years. Since the beginning of that war a very large indulgence in commerce between belligerents was allowed. Thus, in the Spanish-American War, neutral vessels, laden with American-owned cargoes

[5] Hershey, A. S., *Essentials of International Public Law and Organization,* 1927, pp. 565-69.

other than contraband of war, cleared for Spanish ports. The view that eighteenth century wars were in *all* respects less destructive than nineteenth century ones is a prejudice. In respect to the status of enemy aliens, the service of loans held by enemy citizens, enemy property, or the right of enemy merchantmen to leave port, the nineteenth century showed a decisive turn in favor of measures to safeguard the economic system in wartime. Only the twentieth century reversed this trend.

Thus the new organization of economic life provided the background of the Hundred Years' Peace. In the first period, the nascent middle classes were mainly a revolutionary force endangering peace as witnessed in the Napoleonic upheaval; it was against this new factor of national disturbance that the Holy Alliance organized its reactionary peace. In the second period, the new economy was victorious. The middle classes were now themselves the bearers of a peace interest, much more powerful than that of their reactionary predecessors had been, and nurtured by the national-international character of the new economy. But in both instances the peace interest became effective only because it was able to make the balance-of-power system serve its cause by providing that system with social organs capable of dealing directly with the internal forces active in the area of peace. Under the Holy Alliance these organs were feudalism and the thrones, supported by the spiritual and material power of the Church; under the Concert of Europe they were international finance and the national banking systems allied to it. There is no need to overdo the distinction. During the Thirty Years' Peace, 1816–46, Great Britain was already pressing for peace and business, nor did the Holy Alliance disdain the help of the Rothschilds. Under the Concert of Europe, again, international finance had often to rely on its dynastic and aristocratic affiliations. But such facts merely tend to strengthen our argument that in every case peace was maintained not simply through the chancelleries of the Great Powers but with the help of concrete organized agencies acting in the service of general interests. In other words, only on the background of the new economy could the balance-of-power system make general conflagrations avoidable. But the achievement of the Concert of Europe was incomparably greater than that of the Holy Alliance; for the latter maintained peace in a limited region in an unchanging Continent, while the former succeeded in the same task on a world scale while social and economic progress was revolutionizing the map of the globe. This great political feat was the result of the emergence of a specific entity, *haute finance*, which was the given link between the political and the economic organization of international life.

It must be clear by this time that the peace organization rested upon economic organization. Yet the two were of very different consistency. Only in the widest sense of the term was it possible to speak of a political peace organization of the world, for the Concert of Europe was essentially not a system of peace but merely of independent sovereignties protected by the mechanism of war. The contrary is true of the economic organization of the world. Unless we defer to the uncritical practice of restricting the term "organization" to centrally directed bodies acting through functionaries of their own, we must concede that nothing could be more definite than the universally accepted principles upon which this organization rested and nothing more concrete than its factual elements. Budgets and armaments, foreign trade and raw material supplies, national independence and sovereignty were now the functions of currency and credit. By the fourth quarter of the nineteenth century, world commodity prices were the central reality in the lives of millions of Continental peasants; the repercussions of the London money market were daily noted by businessmen all over the world; and governments discussed plans for the future in light of the situation on the world capital markets. Only a madman would have doubted that the international economic system was the axis of the material existence of the race. Because this system needed peace in order to function, the balance of power was made to serve it. Take this economic system away and the peace interest would disappear from politics. Apart from it, there was neither sufficient cause for such an interest, nor a possibility of safeguarding it, in so far as it existed. The success of the Concert of Europe sprang from the needs of the new international organization of economy, and would inevitably end with its dissolution.

The era of Bismarck (1861–90) saw the Concert of Europe at its best. In two decades immediately following Germany's rise to the status of a Great Power, she was the chief beneficiary of the peace interest. She had forced her way into the front ranks at the cost of Austria and France; it was to her advantage to maintain the *status quo* and to prevent a war which could be only a war of revenge against herself. Bismarck deliberately fostered the notion of peace as a common venture of the Powers, and avoided commitments which might force Germany out of the position of a peace power. He opposed expansionist ambitions in the Balkans or overseas; he used the free trade weapon consistently against Austria, and even against France; he thwarted Russia's and

Austria's Balkan ambitions with the help of the balance-of-power game, thus keeping in with potential allies and averting situations which might involve Germany in war. The scheming aggressor of 1863–70 turned into the honest broker of 1878, and the deprecator of colonial adventures. He consciously took the lead in what he felt to be the peaceful trend of the time in order to serve Germany's national interests.

However, by the end of the seventies the free trade episode (1846–79) was at an end; the actual use of the gold standard by Germany marked the beginnings of an era of protectionism and colonial expansion.[6] Germany was now reinforcing her position by making a hard and fast alliance with Austria-Hungary and Italy; not much later Bismarck lost control of Reich policy. From then onward Great Britain was the leader of the peace interest in a Europe which still remained a group of independent sovereign states and thus subject to the balance of power. In the nineties *haute finance* was at its peak and peace seemed more secure than ever. British and French interests differed in Africa; the British and the Russians were competing with one another in Asia; the Concert, though limpingly, continued to function; in spite of the Triple Alliance, there were still more than two independent powers to watch one another jealously. Not for long. In 1904, Britain made a sweeping deal with France over Morocco and Egypt; a couple of years later she compromised with Russia over Persia, and the counter-alliance was formed. The Concert of Europe, that loose federation of independent powers, was finally replaced by two hostile power groupings; the balance of power as a system had now come to an end. With only two competing power groups left its mechanism ceased to function. There was no longer a third group which would unite with one of the other two to thwart whichever one sought to increase its power. About the same time the symptoms of the dissolution of the existing forms of world economy—colonial rivalry and competition for exotic markets—became acute. The ability of *haute finance* to avert the spread of wars was diminishing rapidly. For another seven years peace dragged on but it was only a question of time before the dissolution of nineteenth century economic organization would bring the Hundred Years' Peace to a close.

In the light of this recognition the true nature of the highly artificial economic organization on which peace rested becomes of utmost significance to the historian.

[6] Eulenburg, F., *Aussenhandel und Aussenhandelspolitik*. In "Grundriss der Sozialökonomik," Abt. VIII, 1929, p. 209.

2

CONSERVATIVE TWENTIES, REVOLUTIONARY
THIRTIES

THE BREAKDOWN of the international gold standard was the invisible link between the disintegration of world economy since the turn of the century and the transformation of a whole civilization in the thirties. Unless the vital importance of this factor is realized, it is not possible to see rightly either the mechanism which railroaded Europe to its doom, or the circumstances which accounted for the astounding fact that the forms and contents of a civilization should rest on so precarious foundations.

The true nature of the international system under which we were living was not realized until it failed. Hardly anyone understood the political function of the international monetary system; the awful suddenness of the transformation thus took the world completely by surprise. And yet the gold standard was the only remaining pillar of the traditional world economy; when it broke, the effect was bound to be instantaneous. To liberal economists the gold standard was a purely economic institution; they refused even to consider it as a part of a social mechanism. Thus it happened that the democratic countries were the last to realize the true nature of the catastrophe and the slowest to counter its effects. Not even when the cataclysm was already upon them did their leaders see that behind the collapse of the international system there stood a long development within the most advanced countries which made that system anachronistic; in other words, the failure of market economy itself still escaped them.

The transformation came on even more abruptly than is usually realized. World War I and the postwar revolutions still formed part of the nineteenth century. The conflict of 1914–18 merely precipitated and immeasurably aggravated a crisis that it did not create. But the roots of the dilemma could not be discerned at the time; and the horrors and devastations of the Great War seemed to the survivors the obvious source of the obstacles to international organization that had so unexpectedly emerged. For suddenly neither the economic nor the political system of the world would function, and the terrible injuries inflicted on the substance of the race by World War I appeared to offer an explanation. In reality, the postwar obstacles to peace and stability derived from the same sources from which the Great War itself had sprung. The dissolution of the system of world economy which had been in progress since 1900 was responsible for the political tension that exploded in 1914; the outcome of the War and the Treaties had eased that tension superficially by eliminating German competition while aggravating the causes of tension and thereby vastly increasing the political and economic impediments to peace.

Politically, the Treaties harbored a fatal contradiction. Through the unilateral disarmament of the defeated nations they forestalled any reconstruction of the balance-of-power system, since power is an indispensable requisite of such a system. In vain did Geneva look towards the restoration of such a system in an enlarged and improved Concert of Europe called the League of Nations; in vain were facilities for consultation and joint action provided in the Covenant of the League, for the essential precondition of independent power units was now lacking. The League could never be really established; neither Article 16 on the enforcement of Treaties, nor Article 19 on their peaceful revision was ever implemented. The only viable solution of the burning problem of peace—the restoration of the balance-of-power system—was thus completely out of reach; so much so that the true aim of the most constructive statesmen of the twenties was not even understood by the public, which continued to exist in an almost indescribable state of confusion. Faced by the appalling fact of the disarmament of one group of nations, while the other group remained armed—a situation which precluded any constructive step towards the organization of peace—the emotional attitude prevailed that the League was in some mysterious way the harbinger of an era of peace which needed only frequent verbal encouragement to become permanent. In America there was a widespread idea that if only America had joined the League, matters would have turned out quite differently. No better proof than this could be adduced for the lack of understanding of the organic weaknesses of the so-called postwar system—so-called, because, if words have a meaning, Europe was now without any political system whatever. A bare *status quo* such as this can last only as long as the physical exhaustion of the parties lasts; no wonder that a return to the nineteenth century system appeared as the only way out. In the meantime the League Council might have at least functioned as a kind of European directorium, very much as the Concert of Europe did at its zenith, but for the fatal unanimity rule which set up the obstreperous small state as the arbiter of world peace. The absurd device of the permanent disarmament of the defeated countries ruled out any constructive solution. The only alternative to this disastrous condition of affairs was the establishment of an international order endowed with an organized power which would transcend national sovereignty. Such a course, however, was entirely beyond the horizon of the time. No country in Europe, not to mention the United States, would have submitted to such a system.

Economically, the policy of Geneva was much more consistent in pressing for the restoration of world economy as a second line of defense for peace. For even a successfully re-established balance-of-power system would have worked for peace only if the international monetary system was restored. In the absence of stable exchanges and freedom of trade the governments of the various nations, as in the past, would regard peace as a minor interest, for which they would strive only as long as it did not interfere with any of their major interests. First among the statesmen of the time, Woodrow Wilson appears to have realized the interdependence of peace and trade, not only as a guarantee of trade, *but also of peace.* No wonder that the League persistently strove to reconstruct the international currency and credit organization as the only possible safeguard of peace among sovereign states, and that the world relied as never before on *haute finance.* J. P. Morgan had replaced N. M. Rothschild as the demiurge of a rejuvenated nineteenth century.

According to the standards of that century the first postwar decade appeared as a revolutionary era; in the light of our own recent experience it was precisely the contrary. The intent of that decade was deeply conservative and expressed the almost universal conviction that only the re-establishment of the pre-1914 system, "this time on solid foundations," could restore peace and prosperity. Indeed, it was out of the failure of this effort to return to the past that the transformation of the thirties sprang. Spectacular though the revolutions and counter-revolutions of the post-war decade were, they represented either mere mechanical reactions to military defeat or, at most, a re-enacting of the familiar liberal and constitutionalist drama of Western civilization on the Central and Eastern European scene; it was only in the thirties that entirely new elements entered the pattern of Western history.

The Central and Eastern European upheavals and counterup-
heavals of 1917–20 in spite of their scenario were merely roundabout
ways of recasting the regimes that had succumbed on the battlefields.
When the counterrevolutionary smoke dissolved, the political systems
in Budapest, Vienna, and Berlin were found to be not very far different
from what they had been before the War. This was true, roughly, of
Finland, the Baltic states, Poland, Austria, Hungary, Bulgaria, and
even Italy and Germany, up to the middle of the twenties. In some
countries a great advance was made in national freedom and land
reform—achievements which had been common to Western Europe
since 1789. Russia, in this respect, formed no exception. The tendency
of the times was simply to establish (or re-establish) the system commonly associated with the ideals of the English, the American, and the
French revolutions. Not only Hindenburg and Wilson, but also Lenin
and Trotzky were, in this broad sense, in the line of Western tradition.

In the early thirties, change set in with abruptness. Its landmarks
were the abandonment of the gold standard by Great Britain; the
Five-Year Plans in Russia; the launching of the New Deal; the
National Socialist Revolution in Germany; the collapse of the League
in favor of autarchist empires. While at the end of the Great War
nineteenth century ideals were paramount, and their influence dominated the following decade, by 1940 every vestige of the international
system had disappeared and, apart from a few enclaves, the nations
were living in an entirely new international setting.

The root cause of the crisis, we submit, was the threatening collapse
of the international economic system. It had only haltingly functioned
since the turn of the century, and the Great War and the Treaties
had wrecked it finally. This became apparent in the twenties when
there was hardly an internal crisis in Europe that did not reach its
climax on an issue of external economy. Students of politics now
grouped the various countries, not according to continents, but according to the degree of their adherence to a sound currency. Russia had
astonished the world by the destruction of the rouble, the value of
which was reduced to nothing by the simple means of inflation. Germany repeated this desperate feat in order to give the lie to the Treaty;
the expropriation of the rentier class, which followed in its wake, laid
the foundation for the Nazi revolution. The prestige of Geneva rested
on its success in helping Austria and Hungary to restore their currencies,
and Vienna became the Mecca of liberal economists on account of a
brilliantly successful operation on Austria's *krone* which the patient,

unfortunately, did not survive. In Bulgaria, Greece, Finland, Latvia, Lithuania, Esthonia, Poland, and Roumania the restoration of the currency provided counterrevolution with a claim to power. In Belgium, France, and England the Left was thrown out of office in the name of sound monetary standards. An almost unbroken sequence of currency crises linked the indigent Balkans with the affluent United States through the elastic band of an international credit system, which transmitted the strain of the imperfectly restored currencies, first, from Eastern Europe to Western Europe, then from Western Europe to the United States. Ultimately, the United States itself was engulfed by the effects of the premature stabilization of European currencies. The final breakdown had begun.

The first shock occurred within the national spheres. Some currencies, such as the Russian, the German, the Austrian, the Hungarian, were wiped out within a year. Apart from the unprecedented rate of change in the value of currencies there was the circumstance that this change happened in a completely monetarized economy. A cellular process was introduced into human society, the effects of which were outside the range of experience. Internally and externally alike, dwindling currencies spelled disruption. Nations found themselves separated from their neighbors, as by a chasm, while at the same time the various strata of the population were affected in entirely different and often opposite ways. The intellectual middle class was literally pauperized; financial sharks heaped up revolting fortunes. A factor of incalculable integrating and disintegrating force had entered the scene.

"Flight of capital" was a *novum*. Neither in 1848, nor in 1866, nor even in 1871 was such an event recorded. And yet, its vital role in the overthrow of the liberal governments of France in 1925, and again in 1938, as well as in the development of a fascist movement in Germany in 1930, was patent.

Currency had become the pivot of national politics. Under a modern money economy nobody could fail to experience daily the shrinking or expanding of the financial yardstick; populations became currency-conscious; the effect of inflation on real income was discounted in advance by the masses; men and women everywhere appeared to regard stable money as the supreme need of human society. But such awareness was inseparable from the recognition that the foundations of the currency might depend upon political factors outside the national boundaries. Thus the social *bouleversement* which shook confidence in the inherent stability of the monetary medium shattered also the naïve concept of financial sovereignty in an interdependent economy. Henceforth, internal crises associated with the currency would tend to raise grave external issues.

Belief in the gold standard was the faith of the age. With some it was a naïve, with some a critical, with others a satanistic creed implying acceptance in the flesh and rejection in the spirit. Yet the belief itself was the same, namely, that bank notes have value because they represent gold. Whether the gold itself has value for the reason that it embodies labor, as the socialists held, or for the reason that it is useful and scarce, as the orthodox doctrine ran, made for once no difference. The war between heaven and hell ignored the money issue, leaving capitalists and socialists miraculously united. Where Ricardo and Marx were at one, the nineteenth century knew not doubt. Bismarck and Lassalle, John Stuart Mill and Henry George, Philip Snowden and Calvin Coolidge, Mises and Trotzky equally accepted the faith. Karl Marx had gone to great pains to show up Proudhon's utopian labor notes (which were to replace currency) as based on self-delusion; and *Das Kapital* implied the commodity theory of money, in its Ricardian form. The Russian Bolshevik Sokolnikoff was the first postwar statesman to restore the value of his country's currency in terms of gold; the German Social Democrat Hilferding imperiled his party by his staunch advocacy of sound currency principles; the Austrian Social Democrat Otto Bauer supported the monetary principles underlying the restoration of the *krone* attempted by his bitter opponent Seipel; the English Socialist, Philip Snowden, turned against Labor when he believed the pound sterling not to be safe at their hands; and the Duce had the gold value of the lira at 90 carved in stone, and pledged himself to die in its defense. It would be hard to find any divergence between utterances of Hoover and Lenin, Churchill and Mussolini, on this point. Indeed, the essentiality of the gold standard to the functioning of the international economic system of the time was the one and only tenet common to men of all nations and all classes, religious denominations, and social philosophies. It was the invisible reality to which the will to live could cling, when mankind braced itself to the task of restoring its crumbling existence.

The effort, which failed, was the most comprehensive the world had ever seen. The stabilization of the all-but-destroyed currencies in Austria, Hungary, Bulgaria, Finland, Roumania, or Greece was not only an act of faith on the part of these small and weak countries, which literally starved themselves to reach the golden shores, but it also put their powerful and wealthy sponsors—the Western European victors—to a severe test. As long as the currencies of the victors fluctuated, the strain did not become apparent; they continued to lend abroad as before the War and thereby helped to maintain the economies of the defeated nations. But when Great Britain and France reverted to gold, the burden on their stabilized exchanges began to tell. Eventually, a silent concern for the safety of the pound entered into the position of the leading gold country, the United States. This preoccupation which spanned the Atlantic brought America unexpectedly into the danger zone. The point seems technical, but must be clearly understood. American support of the pound sterling in 1927 implied low rates of interest in New York in order to avert big movements of capital from London to New York. The Federal Reserve Board accordingly promised the Bank of England to keep its rate low; but presently America herself was in need of high rates as her own price system began to be perilously inflated (this fact was obscured by the existence of a stable price level, maintained in spite of tremendously diminished costs). When the usual swing of the pendulum after seven years of prosperity brought on the long overdue slump in 1929, matters were immeasurably aggravated by the existing state of cryptoinflation. Debtors, emaciated by deflation, lived to see the inflated creditor collapse. It was a portent. America, by an instinctive gesture of liberation, went off gold in 1933, and the last vestige of the traditional world economy vanished. Although hardly anybody discerned the deeper meaning of the event at the time, history almost at once reversed its trend.

For over a decade the restoration of the gold standard had been the symbol of world solidarity. Innumerable conferences from Brussels to Spa and Geneva, from London to Locarno and Lausanne met in order to achieve the political preconditions of stable currencies. The League of Nations itself had been supplemented by the International Labor Office partly in order to equalize conditions of competition amongst the nations so that trade might be liberated without danger to standards of living. Currency was at the heart of the campaigns launched by Wall Street to overcome the transfer problem and, first, to commercialize, then, to mobilize reparations; Geneva acted as the sponsor of a process of rehabilitation in which the combined pressure of the City of London and of the neo-classical monetary purists of Vienna was put into the service of the gold standard; every international endeavor was ultimately directed to this end, while national governments, as a rule, accommodated their policies to the need of safeguarding the currency, particularly those policies which were concerned with foreign trade, loans, banking, and exchange. Although everybody agreed that stable currencies ultimately depended upon the freeing of trade, all except dogmatic free traders knew that measures had to be taken immediately which would inevitably restrict foreign trade and foreign payments. Import quotas, moratoria and stand-still agreements, clearing systems and bilateral trade treaties, barter arrangements, embargoes on capital exports, foreign trade control, and exchange equalization funds developed in most countries to meet the same set of circumstances. Yet the incubus of self-sufficiency haunted the steps taken in protection of the currency. While the intent was the freeing of trade, the effect was its strangulation. Instead of gaining access to the markets of the world, the governments, by their own acts, were barring their countries from any international nexus, and ever-increasing sacrifices were needed to keep even a trickle of trade flowing. The frantic efforts to protect the external value of the currency as a medium of foreign trade drove the peoples, against their will, into an autarchized economy. The whole arsenal of restrictive measures, which formed a radical departure from traditional economics, was actually the outcome of conservative free trade purposes.

This trend was abruptly reversed with the final fall of the gold standard. The sacrifices that were made to restore it had now to be made once more in order that we might live without it. The same institutions which were designed to constrict life and trade in order to maintain a system of stable currencies were now used to adjust industrial life to the permanent absence of such a system. Perhaps that is why the mechanical and technological structure of modern industry survived the impact of the collapse of the gold standard. For in the struggle to retain it, the world had been unconsciously preparing for the kind of efforts and the type of organizations necessary to adapt itself to its loss. Yet the intent was now the opposite; in the countries that had suffered most during the long-drawn fight for the unattainable, titanic forces were released on the rebound. Neither the League of Nations nor international *haute finance* outlasted the gold standard; with its disappearance both the organized peace interest of the League and its chief instruments of enforcement—the Rothschilds and Morgans—vanished from politics. The snapping of the golden thread was the signal for a world revolution.

But the failure of the gold standard did hardly more than set the date of an event which was too big to have been caused by it. No less than a complete destruction of the national institutions of nineteenth century society accompanied the crisis in a great part of the world, and everywhere these institutions were changed and re-formed almost out of recognition. The liberal state was in many countries replaced by totalitarian dictatorships, and the central institution of the century—production based on free markets—was superseded by new forms of economy. While great nations recast the very mold of their thought and hurled themselves into wars to enslave the world in the name of unheard-of conceptions of the nature of the universe, even greater nations rushed to the defense of freedom which acquired an equally unheard-of meaning at their hands. The failure of the international system, though it triggered the transformation, could certainly not have accounted for its depth and content. Even though we may know why that which happened happened suddenly, we may still be in the dark about why it happened at all.

It was not by accident that the transformation was accompanied by wars on an unprecedented scale. History was geared to social change; the fate of nations was linked to their role in an institutional transformation. Such a symbiosis is no exception in history; though national groups and social institutions have origins of their own, they tend to hitch on to one another in their struggle for survival. A famous instance of such a symbiosis linked capitalism and the seaboard nations of the Atlantic. The Commercial Revolution, so closely connected with the rise of capitalism, became the vehicle to power for Portugal, Spain, Holland, France, England and the United States, each of them benefiting from the chances offered by that broad and deep-seated movement, while, on the other hand, capitalism itself was spreading over the planet through the instrumentality of these rising Powers.

The law applied also in the reverse. A nation may be handicapped in its struggle for survival by the fact that its institutions, or some of them, belong to a type that happens to be on the down grade—the gold standard in World War II was an instance of such an antiquated outfit. Countries, on the other hand, which, for reasons of their own, are opposed to the *status quo,* would be quick to discover the weaknesses of the existing institutional order and to anticipate the creation of institutions better adapted to their interests. Such groups are pushing that which is falling and holding on to that which, under its own steam, is moving their way. It may then seem as if they had originated the process of social change, while actually they were merely its beneficiaries, and may be even perverting the trend to make it serve their own aims.

Thus Germany, once defeated, was in the position to recognize the hidden shortcomings of the nineteenth century order, and to employ this knowledge to speed the destruction of that order. A kind of sinister intellectual superiority accrued to those of her statesmen in the thirties who turned their minds to this task of disruption, which often extended to the development of new methods of finance, trade, war, and social organization, in the course of their attempt to force matters into the trend of their policies. However, these problems themselves were emphatically not created by the governments which turned them to their advantage; they were real—objectively given—and will remain with us whatever be the fate of the individual countries. Again, the distinction between World Wars I and II is apparent: the former was still true to nineteenth century type—a simple conflict of powers, released by the lapse of the balance-of-power system; the latter already is part of the world upheaval.

This should allow us to detach the poignant national histories of the period from the social transformation that was in progress. It will then be easy to see in what manner Germany and Russia, Great Britain and the United States, as power units, were helped or hampered by their relation to the underlying social process. But the same is true of the social process itself: fascism and socialism found a vehicle in the rise of individual Powers which helped to spread their creed. Germany and Russia respectively became the representatives of fascism and socialism in the world at large. The true scope of these social movements can be gauged only if, for good or evil, their transcendant character is recognized and viewed as detached from the national interests enlisted in their service.

The roles which Germany or Russia, or for that matter, Italy or Japan, Great Britain or the United States, are playing in World War II, though forming part of universal history, are no direct concern of this book; fascism and socialism, however, were live forces in the institutional transformation which is its subject. The *élan vital* which produced the inscrutable urge in the German and Russian people to claim a greater share in the record of the race must be taken as factual data of the conditions under which our story unfolds, while the purport of Fascism and Socialism or New Deal is part of the story itself.

This leads up to our thesis which still remains to be proven: that the origins of the cataclysm lay in the utopian endeavor of economic liberalism to set up a self-regulating market system. Such a thesis seems to invest that system with almost mythical powers; it implies no less than that the balance of power, the gold standard, and the liberal state, those fundamentals of the civilization of the nineteenth century, were, in the last resort, all shaped by one common matrix, the self-regulating market.

The assertion appears extreme, if not shocking in its crass materialism. But the peculiarity of the civilization the collapse of which we have witnessed was precisely that it rested on economic foundations. Other societies and other civilizations, too, were limited by the material conditions of their existence—this is a common trait of all human life, indeed, of all life, whether religious or nonreligious, materialist or spiritualist. All types of societies are limited by economic factors. Nineteenth century civilization alone was economic in a different and distinctive sense, for it chose to base itself on a motive only rarely acknowledged as valid in the history of human societies, and certainly never before raised to the level of a justification of action and behavior in everyday life, namely, gain. The self-regulating market system was uniquely derived from this principle.

The mechanism which the motive of gain set in motion was comparable in effectiveness only to the most violent outburst of religious fervor in history. Within a generation the whole human world was subjected to its undiluted influence. As everybody knows, it grew to maturity in England, in the wake of the Industrial Revolution, during the first half of the nineteenth century. It reached the Continent and America about fifty years later. Eventually in England, on the Continent, and even in America, similar alternatives shaped daily issues into a pattern the main traits of which were identical in all countries of Western civilization. For the origins of the cataclysm we must turn to the rise and fall of market economy.

Market society was born in England—yet it was on the Continent that its weaknesses engendered the most tragic complications. In order to comprehend German fascism, we must revert to Ricardian England. The nineteenth century, as cannot be overemphasized, was England's century. The Industrial Revolution was an English event. Market economy, free trade, and the gold standard were English inventions. These institutions broke down in the twenties everywhere— in Germany, Italy, or Austria the event was merely more political and more dramatic. But whatever the scenery and the temperature of the final episodes, the long-run factors which wrecked that civilization should be studied in the birthplace of the Industrial Revolution, England.

PART TWO

Rise and Fall of Market Economy

I. SATANIC MILL

3

"HABITATION VERSUS IMPROVEMENT"

AT THE HEART of the Industrial Revolution of the eighteenth century there was an almost miraculous improvement in the tools of production, which was accompanied by a catastrophic dislocation of the lives of the common people.

We will attempt to disentangle the factors that determined the forms of this dislocation, as it appeared at its worst in England about a century ago. What "satanic mill" ground men into masses? How much was caused by the new physical conditions? How much by the economic dependencies, operating under the new conditions? And what was the mechanism through which the old social tissue was destroyed and a new integration of man and nature so unsuccessfully attempted?

Nowhere has liberal philosophy failed so conspicuously as in its understanding of the problem of change. Fired by an emotional faith in spontaneity, the common-sense attitude toward change was discarded in favor of a mystical readiness to accept the social consequences of economic improvement, whatever they might be. The elementary truths of political science and statecraft were first discredited, then forgotten. It should need no elaboration that a process of undirected change, the pace of which is deemed too fast, should be slowed down, if possible, so as to safeguard the welfare of the community. Such household truths of traditional statesmanship, often merely reflecting the teachings of a social philosophy inherited from the ancients, were in the nineteenth century erased from the thoughts of the educated by the corrosive of a crude utilitarianism combined with an uncritical reliance on the alleged self-healing virtues of unconscious growth.

Economic liberalism misread the history of the Industrial Revolution because it insisted on judging social events from the economic viewpoint. For an illustration of this we shall turn to what may at first seem a remote subject: to enclosures of open fields and conversions of arable land to pasture during the earlier Tudor period in England, when fields and commons were hedged by the lords, and whole counties were threatened by depopulation. Our purpose in thus evoking the plight of the people brought about by enclosures and conversions will be on the one hand to demonstrate the parallel between the devastations caused by the ultimately beneficial enclosures and those resulting from the Industrial Revolution, and on the other hand—and more broadly—to clarify the alternatives facing a community which is in the throes of unregulated economic improvement.

Enclosures were an obvious improvement *if* no conversion to pasture took place. Enclosed land was worth double and treble the unenclosed. Where tillage was maintained, employment did not fall off, and the food supply markedly increased. The yield of the land manifestly increased, especially where the land was let.

But even conversion of arable land to sheep runs was not altogether detrimental to the neighborhood in spite of the destruction of habitations and the restriction of employment it involved. Cottage industry was spreading by the second half of the fifteenth century, and a century later it began to be a feature of the countryside. The wool produced on the sheep farm gave employment to the small tenants and landless cottagers forced out of tillage, and the new centers of the woolen industry secured an income to a number of craftsmen.

But—this is the point—only in a market economy can such compensating effects be taken for granted. In the absence of such an economy the highly profitable occupation of raising sheep and selling their wool might ruin the country. The sheep which "turned sand into gold" could well have turned the gold into sand as happened ultimately to the wealth of seventeenth century Spain whose eroded soil never recovered from the overexpansion of sheep farming.

An official document of 1607, prepared for the use of the Lords of the Realm, set out the problem of change in one powerful phrase: "The poor man shall be satisfied in his end: Habitation; and the gentleman not hindered in his desire: Improvement." This formula appears to take for granted the essence of purely economic progress, which is to achieve improvement at the price of social dislocation. But it also hints at the tragic necessity by which the poor man clings to his hovel, doomed by the rich man's desire for a public improvement which profits him privately.

Enclosures have appropriately been called a revolution of the rich against the poor. The lords and nobles were upsetting the social order, breaking down ancient law and custom, sometimes by means of violence, often by pressure and intimidation. They were literally robbing the poor of their share in the common, tearing down the houses which, by the hitherto unbreakable force of custom, the poor had long regarded as theirs and their heirs'. The fabric of society was being disrupted; desolate villages and the ruins of human dwellings testified to the fierceness with which the revolution raged, endangering the defenses of the country, wasting its towns, decimating its population, turning its overburdened soil into dust, harassing its people and turning them from decent husbandmen into a mob of beggars and thieves. Though this happened only in patches, the black spots threatened to melt into a uniform catastrophe.[1] The King and his Council, the Chancellors, and the Bishops were defending the welfare of the community and, indeed, the human and natural substance of society against this scourge. With hardly any intermittence, for a century and a half—from the 1490's, at the latest, to the 1640's—they struggled against depopulation. Lord Protector Somerset lost his life at the hands of the counterrevolution which wiped the enclosure laws from the statute book and established the dictatorship of the grazier lords, after Kett's Rebellion was defeated with several thousand peasants slaughtered in the process. Somerset was accused, and nòt without truth, of having given encouragement to the rebellious peasants by his staunch denunciation of enclosures.

It was almost a hundred years later when a second trial of strength came between the same opponents, but by that time the enclosers were much more frequently wealthy country gentlemen and merchants rather than lords and nobles. High politics, lay and ecclesiastical, were now involved in the Crown's deliberate use of its prerogative to prevent enclosures and in its no less deliberate use of the enclosure issue to strengthen its position against the gentry in a constitutional struggle, which brought death to Strafford and Laud at the hands of Parliament. But their policy was not only industrially but politically reactionary; furthermore, enclosures were now much more often than before intended for tillage, and not for pasture. Presently the tide of the Civil War engulfed Tudor and early Stuart public policy forever.

Nineteenth century historians were unanimous in condemning Tudor and early Stuart policy as demagogic, if not as outright reactionary. Their sympathies lay, naturally, with Parliament and that body

[1] Tawney, R. H., *The Agrarian Problem in the 16th Century*, 1912.

had been on the side of the enclosers. H. de B. Gibbins, though an ardent friend of the common people, wrote: "Such protective enactments were, however, as protective enactments generally be, utterly vain." [2] Innes was even more definite: "The usual remedies of punishing vagabondage and attempting to force industry into unsuited fields and to drive capital into less lucrative investments in order to provide employment failed—as usual." [3] Gairdner had no hesitation in appealing to free trade notions as "economic law": "Economic laws were, of course, not understood," he wrote, "and attempts were made by legislation to prevent husbandmen's dwellings from being thrown down by landlords, who found it profitable to devote arable land to pasture to increase the growth of wool. The frequent repetition of these Acts only show how ineffective they were in practice." [4] Recently an economist like Heckscher emphasizes his conviction that mercantilism should, in the main, be explained by an insufficient understanding of the complexities of economic phenomena, a subject which the human mind obviously needed another few centuries to master.[5] In effect, anti-enclosure legislation never seemed to have stopped the course of the enclosure movement, nor even to have obstructed it seriously. John Hales, second to none in his fervor for the principles of the Commonwealth men, admitted that it proved impossible to collect evidence against the enclosers, who often had their servants sworn upon the juries, and such was the number "of their retainers and hangers-on that no jury could be made without them." Sometimes the simple expedient of driving a single furrow across the field would save the offending lord from a penalty.

Such an easy prevailing of private interests over justice is often regarded as a certain sign of the ineffectiveness of legislation, and the victory of the vainly obstructed trend is subsequently adduced as conclusive evidence of the alleged futility of "a reactionary interventionism." Yet such a view seems to miss the point altogether. Why should the ultimate victory of a trend be taken as a proof of the ineffectiveness of the efforts to slow down its progress? And why should the purpose of these measures not be seen precisely in that which they achieved, *i.e.,* in the slowing down of the rate of change? That which is ineffectual in stopping a line of development altogether is not, on that account, altogether ineffectual. The rate of change is often of no less importance

[2] Gibbins, H. de B., *The Industrial History of England*, 1895.
[3] Innes, A. D., *England under the Tudors*, 1932.
[4] Gairdner, J., "Henry VIII," *Cambridge Modern History*, Vol. II, 1918.
[5] Heckscher, E. F., *Mercantilism*, 1935, p. 104.

than the direction of the change itself; but while the latter frequently does not depend upon our volition, it is the rate at which we allow change to take place which well may depend upon us.

A belief in spontaneous progress must make us blind to the role of government in economic life. This role consists often in altering the rate of change, speeding it up or slowing it down as the case may be; if we believe that rate to be unalterable—or even worse, if we deem it a sacrilege to interfere with it—then, of course, no room is left for intervention. Enclosures offer an example. In retrospect nothing could be clearer than the Western European trend of economic progress which aimed at eliminating an artificially maintained uniformity of agricultural technique, intermixed strips, and the primitive institution of the common. As to England, it is certain that the development of the woolen industry was an asset to the country, leading, as it did, to the establishment of the cotton industry—that vehicle of the Industrial Revolution. Furthermore, it is clear that the increase of domestic weaving depended upon the increase of a home supply of wool. These facts suffice to identify the change from arable land to pasture and the accompanying enclosure movement as the trend of economic progress. Yet, but for the consistently maintained policy of the Tudor and early Stuart statesmen, the rate of that progress might have been ruinous, and have turned the process itself into a degenerative instead of a constructive event. For upon this rate, mainly, depended whether the dispossessed could adjust themselves to changed conditions without fatally damaging their substance, human and economic, physical and moral; whether they would find new employment in the fields of opportunity indirectly connected with the change; and whether the effects of increased imports induced by increased exports would enable those who lost their employment through the change to find new sources of sustenance.

The answer depended in every case on the relative rates of change and adjustment. The usual "long-run" considerations of economic theory are inadmissible; they would prejudge the issue by assuming that the event took place in a market economy. However natural it may appear to us to make that assumption, it is unjustified: market economy is an institutional structure which, as we all too easily forget, has been present at no time except our own, and even then it was only partially present. Yet apart from this assumption "long-run" considerations are meaningless. If the immediate effect of a change is deleterious, then, until proof to the contrary, the final effect is deleterious. If conversion of arable land to pasture involves the destruction of a definite number of houses, the scrapping of a definite amount of employment, and the diminution of the supplies of locally available food provisions, then these effects must be regarded as final, until evidence to the contrary is produced. This does not exclude the consideration of the possible effects of increased exports on the income of the landowners; of the possible chances of employment created by an eventual increase in the local wool supply; or of the uses to which the land-owners might put their increased incomes, whether in the way of further investments or of luxury expenditure. The time-rate of change compared with the time-rate of adjustment will decide what is to be regarded as the net effect of the change. But in no case can we assume the functioning of market laws unless a self-regulating market is shown to exist. Only in the institutional setting of market economy are market laws relevant; it was not the statesmen of Tudor England who strayed from the facts, but the modern economists, whose strictures upon them implied the prior existence of a market system.

England withstood without grave damage the calamity of the enclosures only because the Tudors and the early Stuarts used the power of the Crown to slow down the process of economic improvement until it became socially bearable—employing the power of the central government to relieve the victims of the transformation, and attempting to canalize the process of change so as to make its course less devastating. Their chancelleries and courts of prerogative were anything but conservative in outlook; they represented the scientific spirit of the new statecraft, favoring the immigration of foreign craftsmen, eagerly implanting new techniques, adopting statistical methods and precise habits of reporting, flouting custom and tradition, opposing prescriptive rights, curtailing ecclesiastical prerogatives, ignoring Common Law. If innovation makes the revolutionary, they were the revolutionaries of the age. Their commitment was to the welfare of the commonalty, glorified in the power and grandeur of the sovereign; yet the future belonged to constitutionalism and Parliament. The government of the Crown gave place to government by a class—the class which led in industrial and commercial progress. The great principle of constitutionalism became wedded to the political revolution that dispossessed the Crown, which by that time had shed almost all its creative faculties, while its protective function was no longer vital to a country that had weathered the storm of transition. The financial policy of the Crown now restricted the power of the country unduly, and began to constrain its trade; in order to maintain its prerogatives the Crown abused them more and more, and thereby harmed the resources of the nation. Its brilliant administration of labor and industry, its circumspect control of the enclosure movement, remained its last achievement. But it was the more easily forgotten as the capitalists and employers of the rising middle class were the chief victims of its protective activities. Not till another two centuries had passed did England enjoy again a social administration as effective and well ordered as that which the Commonwealth destroyed. Admittedly, an administration of this paternalistic kind was now less needed. But in one respect the break wrought infinite harm, for it helped to obliterate from the memory of the nation the horrors of the enclosure period and the achievements of government in overcoming the peril of depopulation. Perhaps this helps to explain why the real nature of the crisis was not realized when, some 150 years later, a similar catastrophe in the shape of the Industrial Revolution threatened the life and well-being of the country.

This time also the event was peculiar to England; this time also sea-borne trade was the source of a movement which affected the country as a whole; and this time again it was improvement on the grandest scale which wrought unprecedented havoc with the habitation of the common people. Before the process had advanced very far, the laboring people had been crowded together in new places of desolation, the so-called industrial towns of England; the country folk had been dehumanized into slum dwellers; the family was on the road to perdition; and large parts of the country were rapidly disappearing under the slack and scrap heaps vomited forth from the "satanic mills." Writers of all views and parties, conservatives and liberals, capitalists and socialists invariably referred to social conditions under the Industrial Revolution as a veritable abyss of human degradation.

No quite satisfactory explanation of the event has yet been put forward. Contemporaries imagined they had discovered the key to damnation in the iron regularities governing wealth and poverty, which they called the law of wages and the law of population; they have been disproved. Exploitation was put forth as another explanation both of wealth and of poverty; but this was unable to account for the fact that wages in the industrial slums were higher than those in any other areas and on the whole continued to rise for another century. More often a convolute of causes was adduced, which again was hardly satisfactory.

Our own solution is anything but simple; it actually fills the better part of this book. We submit that an avalanche of social dislocation, surpassing by far that of the enclosure period, came down upon England; that this catastrophe was the accompaniment of a vast movement of economic improvement; that an entirely new institutional mechanism was starting to act on Western society; that its dangers, which cut to the quick when they first appeared, were never really overcome; and that the history of nineteenth century civilization consisted largely in attempts to protect society against the ravages of such a mechanism. The Industrial Revolution was merely the beginning of a revolution as extreme and radical as ever inflamed the minds of sectarians, but the new creed was utterly materialistic and believed that all human problems could be resolved given an unlimited amount of material commodities.

The story has been told innumerable times: how the expansion of markets, the presence of coal and iron as well as a humid climate favorable to the cotton industry, the multitude of people dispossessed by the new eighteenth century enclosures, the existence of free institutions, the invention of the machines, and other causes interacted in such a manner as to bring about the Industrial Revolution. It has been shown conclusively that no one single cause deserves to be lifted out of the chain and set apart as *the* cause of that sudden and unexpected event.

But how shall this Revolution itself be defined? What was its basic characteristic? Was it the rise of the factory towns, the emergence of slums, the long working hours of children, the low wages of certain categories of workers, the rise in the rate of population increase, or the concentration of industries? We submit that all these were merely incidental to one basic change, the establishment of market economy, and that the nature of this institution cannot be fully grasped unless the impact of the machine on a commercial society is realized. We do not intend to assert that the machine caused that which happened, but we insist that once elaborate machines and plant were used for production in a commercial society, the idea of a self-regulating market was bound to take shape.

The use of specialized machines in an agrarian and commercial society must produce typical effects. Such a society consists of agriculturalists and of merchants who buy and sell the produce of the land. Production with the help of specialized, elaborate, expensive tools and plants can be fitted into such a society only by making it incidental to buying and selling. The merchant is the only person available for the undertaking of this, and he is fitted to do so as long as this activity will not involve him in a loss. He will sell the goods in the same manner in which he would otherwise sell goods to those who demand them; but he will procure them in a different way, namely, not by buying them ready-made, but by purchasing the necessary labor and raw material. The two put together according to the merchant's instructions, plus some waiting which he might have to undertake, amount to the new product. This is not a description of domestic industry or "putting out" only, but of any kind of industrial capitalism, including that of our own time. Important consequences for the social system follow.

Since elaborate machines are expensive, they do not pay unless large amounts of goods are produced.[6] They can be worked without a loss only if the vent of the goods is reasonably assured and if production need not be interrupted for want of the primary goods necessary to feed the machines. For the merchant this means that all factors involved must be on sale, that is, they must be available in the needed quantities to anybody who is prepared to pay for them. Unless this condition is fulfilled, production with the help of specialized machines is too risky to be undertaken both from the point of view of the merchant who stakes his money and of the community as a whole which comes to depend upon continuous production for incomes, employment, and provisions.

Now, in an agricultural society such conditions would not naturally be given; they would have to be created. That they would be created gradually in no way affects the startling nature of the changes involved. The transformation implies a change in the motive of action on the part of the members of society: for the motive of subsistence that of gain must be substituted. All transactions are turned into money transactions, and these in turn require that a medium of exchange be introduced into every articulation of industrial life. All incomes must derive from the sale of something or other, and whatever the actual source of a person's income, it must be regarded as resulting from sale. No less is implied in the simple term "market system," by which we designate the institutional pattern described. But the most startling peculiarity of the system lies in the fact that, once it is established, it must be allowed to function without outside interference. Profits are not any more guaranteed, and the merchant must make his profits on the market. Prices must be allowed to regulate themselves. Such a self-

6 Clapham, J. H., *Economic History of Modern Britain*, Vol. III.

regulating system of markets is what we mean by a market economy.

The transformation to this system from the earlier economy is so complete that it resembles more the metamorphosis of the caterpillar than any alteration that can be expressed in terms of continuous growth and development. Contrast, for example, the merchant-producer's selling activities with his buying activities; his sales concern only artifacts; whether he succeeds or not in finding purchasers, the fabric of society need not be affected. But what he *buys* is raw materials and labor— nature and man. Machine production in a commercial society involves, in effect, no less a transformation than that of the natural and human substance of society into commodities. The conclusion, though weird, is inevitable; nothing less will serve the purpose: obviously, the dislocation caused by such devices must disjoint man's relationships and threaten his natural habitat with annihilation.

Such a danger was, in fact, imminent. We shall perceive its true character if we examine the laws which govern the mechanism of a self-regulating market.

4

SOCIETIES AND ECONOMIC SYSTEMS

BEFORE WE CAN proceed to the discussion of the laws governing a market economy, such as the nineteenth century was trying to establish, we must first have a firm grip on the extraordinary assumptions underlying such a system.

Market economy implies a self-regulating system of markets; in slightly more technical terms, it is an economy directed by market prices and nothing but market prices. Such a system capable of organizing the whole of economic life without outside help or interference would certainly deserve to be called self-regulating. These rough indications should suffice to show the entirely unprecedented nature of such a venture in the history of the race.

Let us make our meaning more precise. No society could, naturally, live for any length of time unless it possessed an economy of some sort; but previously to our time no economy has ever existed that, even in principle, was controlled by markets. In spite of the chorus of academic incantations so persistent in the nineteenth century, gain and profit made on exchange never before played an important part in human economy. Though the institution of the market was fairly common since the later Stone Age, its role was no more than incidental to economic life.

We have good reason to insist on this point with all the emphasis at our command. No less a thinker than Adam Smith suggested that the division of labor in society was dependent upon the existence of markets, or, as he put it, upon man's "propensity to barter, truck and exchange one thing for another." This phrase was later to yield the concept of the Economic Man. In retrospect it can be said that no misreading of the past ever proved more prophetic of the future. For while up to Adam Smith's time that propensity had hardly shown up on a considerable scale in the life of any observed community, and had remained, at best, a subordinate feature of economic life, a hundred years later an industrial system was in full swing over the major part of the planet which, practically and theoretically, implied that the human race was swayed in all its economic activities, if not also in its political, intellectual, and spiritual pursuits, by that one particular propensity. Herbert Spencer, in the second half of the nineteenth century, could, without more than a cursory acquaintance with economics, equate the principle of the division of labor with barter and exchange, and another fifty years later, Ludwig von Mises and Walter Lippmann could repeat this same fallacy. By that time there was no need for argument. A host of writers on political economy, social history, political philosophy, and general sociology had followed in Smith's wake and established his paradigm of the bartering savage as an axiom of their respective sciences. In point of fact, Adam Smith's suggestions about the economic psychology of early man were as false as Rousseau's were on the political psychology of the savage. Division of labor, a phenomenon as old as society, springs from differences inherent in the facts of sex, geography, and individual endowment; and the alleged propensity of man to barter, truck, and exchange is almost entirely apocryphal. While history and ethnography know of various kinds of economies, most of them comprising the institution of markets, they know of no economy prior to our own, even approximately controlled and regulated by markets. This will become abundantly clear from a bird's-eye view of the history of economic systems and of markets, presented separately. The role played by markets in the internal economy of the various countries, it will appear, was insignificant up to recent times, and the change-over to an economy dominated by the market pattern will stand out all the more clearly.

To start with, we must discard some nineteenth century prejudices that underlay Adam Smith's hypothesis about primitive man's alleged predilection for gainful occupations. Since his axiom was much more relevant to the immediate future than to the dim past, it induced in his followers a strange attitude toward man's early history. On the face of it, the evidence seemed to indicate that primitive man, far from having a capitalistic psychology, had, in effect, a communistic one (later this also proved to be mistaken). Consequently, economic historians tended to confine their interest to that comparatively recent period of history in which truck and exchange were found on any considerable scale, and primitive economics was relegated to prehistory. Unconsciously, this led to a weighting of the scales in favor of a marketing psychology, for within the relatively short period of the last few centuries everything might be taken to tend towards the establishment of that which was eventually established, *i.e.*, a market system, irrespective of other tendencies which were temporarily submerged. The corrective of such a "short-run" perspective would obviously have been the linking up of economic history with social anthropology, a course which was consistently avoided.

We cannot continue today on these lines. The habit of looking at the last ten thousand years as well as at the array of early societies as a mere prelude to the true history of our civilization which started approximately with the publication of the *Wealth of Nations* in 1776, is, to say the least, out of date. It is this episode which has come to a close in our days, and in trying to gauge the alternatives of the future, we should subdue our natural proneness to follow the proclivities of our fathers. But the same bias which made Adam Smith's generation view primeval man as bent on barter and truck induced their successors to disavow all interest in early man, as he was now known *not* to have indulged in those laudable passions. The tradition of the classical economists, who attempted to base the law of the market on the alleged propensities of man in the state of nature, was replaced by an abandonment of all interest in the cultures of "uncivilized" man as irrelevant to an understanding of the problems of our age.

Such an attitude of subjectivism in regard to earlier civilizations should make no appeal to the scientific mind. The differences existing between civilized and "uncivilized" peoples have been vastly exaggerated, especially in the economic sphere. According to the historians, the forms of industrial life in agricultural Europe were, until recently, not much different from what they had been several thousand years earlier. Ever since the introduction of the plow—essentially a large hoe drawn by animals—the methods of agriculture remained substantially unaltered over the major part of Western and Central Europe until the beginning of the modern age. Indeed, the progress of civilization was, in these regions, mainly political, intellectual, and spiritual; in respect to material conditions, the Western Europe of 1100 A.D. had hardly caught up with the Roman world of a thousand years before. Even later, change flowed more easily in the channels of statecraft, literature, and the arts, but particularly in those of religion and learning, than in those of industry. In its economics, medieval Europe was largely on a level with ancient Persia, India, or China, and certainly could not rival in riches and culture the New Kingdom of Egypt, two thousand years before. Max Weber was the first among modern economic historians to protest against the brushing aside of primitive economics as irrelevant to the question of the motives and mechanisms of civilized societies. The subsequent work of social anthropology proved him emphatically right. For, if one conclusion stands out more clearly than another from the recent study of early societies it is the changelessness of man as a social being. His natural endowments reappear with a remarkable constancy in societies of all times and places; and the necessary preconditions of the survival of human society appear to be immutably the same.

The outstanding discovery of recent historical and anthropological research is that man's economy, as a rule, is submerged in his social relationships. He does not act so as to safeguard his individual interest in the possession of material goods; he acts so as to safeguard his social standing, his social claims, his social assets. He values material goods only in so far as they serve this end. Neither the process of production nor that of distribution is linked to specific economic interests attached to the possession of goods; but every single step in that process is geared to a number of social interests which eventually ensure that the required step be taken. These interests will be very different in a small hunting or fishing community from those in a vast despotic society, but in either case the economic system will be run on noneconomic motives.

The explanation, in terms of survival, is simple. Take the case of a tribal society. The individual's economic interest is rarely paramount, for the community keeps all its members from starving unless it is itself borne down by catastrophe, in which case interests are again threatened collectively, not individually. The maintenance of social ties, on the other hand, is crucial. First, because by disregarding the accepted code of honor, or generosity, the individual cuts himself off from the community and becomes an outcast; second, because, in the long run, all social obligations are reciprocal, and their fulfillment serves also the individual's give-and-take interests best. Such a situation must exert a continuous pressure on the individual to eliminate economic self-interest from his consciousness to the point of making him unable, in many cases (but by no means in all), even to comprehend the implications of his own actions in terms of such an interest. This attitude is reinforced by the frequency of communal activities such as partaking of food from the common catch or sharing in the results of some far-flung and dangerous tribal expedition. The premium set on generosity is so great when measured in terms of social prestige as to make any other behavior than that of utter self-forgetfulness simply not pay. Personal character has little to do with the matter. Man can be as good or evil, as social or asocial, jealous or generous, in respect to one set of values as in respect to another. Not to allow anybody reason for jealousy is, indeed, an accepted principle of ceremonial distribution, just as publicly bestowed praise is the due of the industrious, skillful, or otherwise successful gardener (unless he be *too* successful, in which case he may deservedly be allowed to wither away under the delusion of being the victim of black magic). The human passions, good or bad, are merely directed towards noneconomic ends. Ceremonial display serves to spur emulation to the utmost and the custom of communal labor tends to screw up both quantitative and qualitative standards to the highest pitch. The performance of all acts of exchange as free gifts that are expected to be reciprocated though not necessarily by the same individuals—a procedure minutely articulated and perfectly safeguarded by elaborate methods of publicity, by magic rites, and by the establishment of "dualities" in which groups are linked in mutual obligations—should in itself explain the absence of the notion of gain or even of wealth other than that consisting of objects traditionally enhancing social prestige.

In this sketch of the general traits characteristic of a Western Melanesian community we took no account of its sexual and territorial organization, in reference to which custom, law, magic, and religion exert their influence, as we only intended to show the manner in which so-called economic motives spring from the context of social life. For it is on this one negative point that modern ethnographers agree: the absence of the motive of gain; the absence of the principle of laboring for remuneration; the absence of the principle of least effort; and, especially, the absence of any separate and distinct institution based on economic motives. But how, then, is order in production and distribution ensured?

The answer is provided in the main by two principles of behavior not primarily associated with economics: *reciprocity* and *redistribution*.[1] With the Trobriand Islanders of Western Melanesia, who serve as an illustration of this type of economy, reciprocity works mainly in regard to the sexual organization of society, that is, family and kinship; redistribution is mainly effective in respect to all those who are under a common chief and is, therefore, of a territorial character. Let us take these principles separately.

The sustenance of the family—the female and the children—is the

---

[1] Cf. Notes on Sources, page 269. The works of Malinowski and Thurnwald have been extensively used in this chapter.

obligation of their matrilineal relatives. The male, who provides for his sister and her family by delivering the finest specimens of his crop, will mainly earn the credit due to his good behavior, but will reap little immediate material benefit in exchange; if he is slack, it is first and foremost his reputation that will suffer. It is for the benefit of his wife and her children that the principle of reciprocity will work, and thus compensate him economically for his acts of civic virtue. Ceremonial display of food both in his own garden and before the recipient's storehouse will ensure that the high quality of his gardening be known to all. It is apparent that the economy of garden and household here forms part of the social relations connected with good husbandry and fine citizenship. The broad principle of reciprocity helps to safeguard both production and family sustenance.

The principle of redistribution is no less effective. A substantial part of all the produce of the island is delivered by the village headmen to the chief who keeps it in storage. But as all communal activity centers around the feasts, dances, and other occasions when the islanders entertain one another as well as their neighbors from other islands (at which the results of long distance trading are handed out, gifts are given and reciprocated according to the rules of etiquette, and the chief distributes the customary presents to all), the overwhelming importance of the storage system becomes apparent. Economically, it is an essential part of the existing system of division of labor, of foreign trading, of taxation for public purposes, of defense provisions. But these functions of an economic system proper are completely absorbed by the intensely vivid experiences which offer superabundant noneconomic motivation for every act performed in the frame of the social system as a whole.

However, principles of behavior such as these cannot become effective unless existing institutional patterns lend themselves to their application. Reciprocity and redistribution are able to ensure the working of an economic system without the help of written records and elaborate administration only because the organization of the societies in question meets the requirements of such a solution with the help of patterns such as *symmetry* and *centricity*.

Reciprocity is enormously facilitated by the institutional pattern of symmetry, a frequent feature of social organization among nonliterate peoples. The striking "duality" which we find in tribal subdivisions lends itself to the pairing out of individual relations and thereby assists the give-and-take of goods and services in the absence of permanent records. The moieties of savage society which tend to create a "pendant" to each subdivision, turned out to result from, as well as help to perform, the acts of reciprocity on which the system rests. Little is known of the origin of "duality"; but each coastal village on the Trobriand Islands appears to have its counterpart in an inland village, so that the important exchange of breadfruits and fish, though disguised as a reciprocal distribution of gifts, and actually disjoint in time, can be organized smoothly. In the Kula trade, too, each individual has his partner on another isle, thus personalizing to a remarkable extent the relationship of reciprocity. But for the frequency of the symmetrical pattern in the subdivisions of the tribe, in the location of settlements, as well as in intertribal relations, a broad reciprocity relying on the long-run working of separated acts of give-and-take would be impracticable.

The institutional pattern of centricity, again, which is present to some extent in all human groups, provides a track for the collection, storage, and redistribution of goods and services. The members of a hunting tribe usually deliver the game to the headman for redistribution. It is in the nature of hunting that the output of game is irregular, besides being the result of a collective input. Under conditions such as these no other method of sharing is practicable if the group is not to break up after every hunt. Yet in all economies of kind a similar need exists, be the group ever so numerous. And the larger the territory and the more varied the produce, the more will redistribution result in an effective division of labor, since it must help to link up geographically differentiated groups of producers.

Symmetry and centricity will meet halfway the needs of reciprocity and redistribution; institutional patterns and principles of behavior are mutually adjusted. As long as social organization runs in its ruts, no individual economic motives need come into play; no shirking of personal effort need be feared; division of labor will automatically be ensured; economic obligations will be duly discharged; and, above all, the material means for an exuberant display of abundance at all public festivals will be provided. In such a community the idea of profit is barred; higgling and haggling is decried; giving freely is acclaimed as a virtue; the supposed propensity to barter, truck, and exchange does not appear. The economic system is, in effect, a mere function of social organization.

It should by no means be inferred that socioeconomic principles of this type are restricted to primitive procedures or small communities; that a gainless and marketless economy must necessarily be simple.

The Kula ring, in western Melanesia, based on the principle of reciprocity, is one of the most elaborate trading transactions known to man; and redistribution was present on a gigantic scale in the civilization of the pyramids.

The Trobriand Islands belong to an archipelago forming roughly a circle, and an important part of the population of this archipelago spends a considerable proportion of its time in activities of the Kula trade. We describe it as trade though no profit is involved, either in money or in kind; no goods are hoarded or even possessed permanently; the goods received are enjoyed by giving them away; no higgling and haggling, no truck, barter, or exchange enters; and the whole proceedings are entirely regulated by etiquette and magic. Still, it is trade, and large expeditions are undertaken periodically by natives of this approximately ring-shaped archipelago in order to carry one kind of valuable object to peoples living on distant islands situated clockwise, while other expeditions are arranged carrying another kind of valuable object to the islands of the archipelago lying counterclockwise. In the long run, both sets of objects—white-shell armbands and red-shell necklaces of traditional make—will move round the archipelago, a traject which may take them up to ten years to complete. Moreover, there are, as a rule, individual partners in Kula who reciprocate one another's Kula gift with equally valuable armbands and necklaces, preferably such that have previously belonged to distinguished persons. Now, a systematic and organized give-and-take of valuable objects transported over long distances is justly described as trade. Yet this complex whole is exclusively run on the lines of reciprocity. An intricate time-space-person system covering hundreds of miles and several decades, linking many hundreds of people in respect to thousands of strictly individual objects, is being handled here without any records or administration, but also without any motive of gain or truck. Not the propensity to barter, but reciprocity in social behavior dominates. Nevertheless, the result is a stupendous organizational achievement in the economic field. Indeed, it would be interesting to consider whether even the most advanced modern market organization, based on exact accountancy, would be able to cope with such a task, should it care to undertake it. It is to be feared that the unfortunate dealers, faced with innummerable monopolists buying and selling individual objects with extravagant restrictions attached to each transaction, would fail to make a standard profit and might prefer to go out of business.

Redistribution also has its long and variegated history which leads up almost to modern times. The Bergdama returning from his hunting excursion, the woman coming back from her search for roots, fruit, or leaves are expected to offer the greater part of their spoil for the benefit of the community. In practice, this means that the produce of their activity is shared with the other persons who happen to be living with them. Up to this point the idea of reciprocity prevails: today's giving will be recompensed by tomorrow's taking. Among some tribes, however, there is an intermediary in the person of the headman or other prominent member of the group; it is he who receives and distributes the supplies, especially if they need to be stored. This is redistribution proper. Obviously, the social consequences of such a method of distribution may be far reaching, since not all societies are as democratic as the primitive hunters. Whether the redistributing is performed by an influential family or an outstanding individual, a ruling aristocracy or a group of bureaucrats, they will often attempt to increase their political power by the manner in which they redistribute the goods. In the *potlatch* of the Kwakiutl it is a point of honor with the chief to display his wealth of hides and to distribute them; but he does this also in order to place the recipients under an obligation, to make them his debtors, and ultimately, his retainers.

All large-scale economies in kind were run with the help of the principle of redistribution. The kingdom of Hammurabi in Babylonia and, in particular, the New Kingdom of Egypt were centralized despotisms of a bureaucratic type founded on such an economy. The household of the patriarchal family was reproduced here on an enormously enlarged scale, while its "communistic" distribution was graded, involving sharply differentiated rations. A vast number of storehouses was ready to receive the produce of the peasant's activity, whether he was cattle breeder, hunter, baker, brewer, potter, weaver, or whatever else. The produce was minutely registered and, in so far as it was not consumed locally, transferred from smaller to larger storehouses until it reached the central administration situated at the court of the Pharaoh. There were separate treasure houses for cloth, works of art, ornamental objects, cosmetics, silverware, the royal wardrobe; there were huge grain stores, arsenals, and wine cellars.

But redistribution on the scale practiced by the pyramid builders was not restricted to economies which knew not money. Indeed, all archaic kingdoms made use of metal currencies for the payment of taxes and salaries, but relied for the rest on payments in kind from granaries and warehouses of every description, from which they dis-

tributed the most varied goods for use and consumption mainly to the
nonproducing part of the population, that is, to the officials, the military, and the leisure class. This was the system practiced in ancient
China, in the empire of the Incas, in the kingdoms of India, and also in
Babylonia. In these, and many other civilizations of vast economic
achievement, an elaborate division of labor was worked by the mechanism of redistribution.

Under feudal conditions also this principle held. In the ethnically
stratified societies of Africa it sometimes happens that the superior
strata consist of herdsmen settled among agriculturalists who are still
using the digging stick or the hoe. The gifts collected by the herdsmen
are mainly agricultural—such as cereals and beer—while the gifts distributed by them may be animals, especially sheep or goats. In these
cases there is division of labor, though usually an unequal one, between
the various strata of society: distribution may often cover up a measure
of exploitation, while at the same time the symbiosis benefits the standards of both strata owing to the advantages of an improved division of
labor. Politically, such societies live under a regime of feudalism,
whether cattle or land be the privileged value. There are "regular cattle
fiefs in East Africa." Thurnwald, whom we follow closely on the subject of redistribution, could therefore say that feudalism implied everywhere a system of redistribution. Only under very advanced conditions
and exceptional circumstances does this system become predominantly
political as happened in Western Europe, where the change arose out
of the vassal's need for protection, and gifts were converted into feudal
tributes.

These instances show that redistribution also tends to enmesh the
economic system proper in social relationships. We find, as a rule, the
process of redistribution forming part of the prevailing political regime,
whether it be that of tribe, city-state, despotism, or feudalism of cattle
or land. The production and distribution of goods is organized in the
main through collection, storage, and redistribution, the pattern being
focused on the chief, the temple, the despot, or the lord. Since the relations of the leading group to the led are different according to the
foundation on which political power rests, the principle of redistribution will involve individual motives as different as the voluntary sharing
of the game by hunters and the dread of punishment which urges the
fellaheen to deliver his taxes in kind.

We deliberately disregarded in this presentation the vital distinction
between homogeneous and stratified societies, *i.e.,* societies which are on

the whole socially unified, and such as are split into rulers and ruled. Though the relative status of slaves and masters may be worlds apart from that of the free and equal members of some hunting tribes, and, consequently, motives in the two societies will differ widely, the organization of the economic system may still be based on the same principles, though accompanied by very different culture traits, according to the very different human relations with which the economic system is intertwined.

The third principle, which was destined to play a big role in history and which we will call the principle of *householding*, consists in production for one's own use. The Greeks called it *oeconomia*, the etymon of the word "economy." As far as ethnographical records are concerned, we should not assume that production for a person's or group's own sake is more ancient than reciprocity or redistribution. On the contrary, orthodox tradition as well as some more recent theories on the subject have been emphatically disproved. The individualistic savage collecting food and hunting on his own or for his family has never existed. Indeed, the practice of catering for the needs of one's household becomes a feature of economic life only on a more advanced level of agriculture; however, even then it has nothing in common either with the motive of gain or with the institution of markets. Its pattern is the closed group. Whether the very different entities of the family or the settlement or the manor formed the self-sufficient unit, the principle was invariably the same, namely, that of producing and storing for the satisfaction of the wants of the members of the group. The principle is as broad in its application as either reciprocity or redistribution. The nature of the institutional nucleus is indifferent: it may be sex as with the patriarchal family, locality as with the village settlement, or political power as with the seigneurial manor. Nor does the internal organization of the group matter. It may be as despotic as the Roman *familia* or as democratic as the South Slav *zadruga;* as large as the great domains of the Carolingian magnates or as small as the average peasant holding of Western Europe. The need for trade or markets is no greater than in the case of reciprocity or redistribution.

It is such a condition of affairs which Aristotle tried to establish as a norm more than two thousand years ago. Looking back from the rapidly declining heights of a world-wide market economy we must concede that his famous distinction of householding proper and money-making, in the introductory chapter of his *Politics*, was probably the most prophetic pointer ever made in the realm of the social sciences; it is certainly still the best analysis of the subject we possess. Aristotle insists on production for use as against production for gain as the essence of householding proper; yet accessory production for the market need not, he argues, destroy the self-sufficiency of the household as long as the cash crop would also otherwise be raised on the farm for sustenance, as cattle or grain; the sale of the surpluses need not destroy the basis of householding. Only a genius of common sense could have maintained, as he did, that gain was a motive peculiar to production for the market, and that the money factor introduced a new element into the situation, yet nevertheless, as long as markets and money were mere accessories to an otherwise self-sufficient household, the principle of production for use could operate. Undoubtedly, in this he was right, though he failed to see how impracticable it was to ignore the existence of markets at a time when Greek economy had made itself dependent upon wholesale trading and loaned capital. For this was the century when Delos and Rhodes were developing into emporia of freight insurance, sea-loans, and giro-banking, compared with which the Western Europe of a thousand years later was the very picture of primitivity. Yet Jowett, Master of Balliol, was grievously mistaken when he took it for granted that his Victorian England had a fairer grasp than Aristotle of the nature of the difference between householding and money-making. He excused Aristotle by conceding that the "subjects of knowledge that are concerned with man run into one another; and in the age of Aristotle were not easily distinguished." Aristotle, it is true, did not recognize clearly the implications of the division of labor and its connection with markets and money; nor did he realize the uses of money as credit and capital. So far Jowett's strictures were justified. But it was the Master of Balliol, not Aristotle, who was impervious to the human implications of money-making. He failed to see that the distinction between the principle of use and that of gain was the key to the utterly different civilization the outlines of which Aristotle accurately forecast two thousand years before its advent out of the bare rudiments of a market economy available to him, while Jowett, with the full-blown specimen before him, overlooked its existence. In denouncing the principle of production for gain "as not natural to man," as boundless and limitless, Aristotle was, in effect, aiming at the crucial point, namely the divorcedness of a separate economic motive from the social relations in which these limitations inhered.

Broadly, the proposition holds that all economic systems known to us up to the end of feudalism in Western Europe were organized either on the principles of reciprocity or redistribution, or householding, or some combination of the three. These principles were institutionalized with the help of a social organization which, *inter alia*, made use of the patterns of symmetry, centricity, and autarchy. In this framework, the orderly production and distribution of goods was secured through a great variety of individual motives disciplined by general principles of behavior. Among these motives gain was not prominent. Custom and law, magic and religion co-operated in inducing the individual to comply with rules of behavior which, eventually, ensured his functioning in the economic system.

The Greco-Roman period, in spite of its highly developed trade, represented no break in this respect; it was characterized by the grand scale on which redistribution of grain was practiced by the Roman administration in an otherwise householding economy, and it formed no exception to the rule that up to the end of the Middle Ages, markets played no important part in the economic system; other institutional patterns prevailed.

From the sixteenth century onwards markets were both numerous and important. Under the mercantile system they became, in effect, a main concern of government; yet there was still no sign of the coming control of markets over human society. On the contrary. Regulation and regimentation were stricter than ever; the very idea of a self-regulating market was absent. To comprehend the sudden change-over to an utterly new type of economy in the nineteenth century, we must now turn to the history of the market, an institution we were able practically to neglect in our review of the economic systems of the past.

5

EVOLUTION OF THE MARKET PATTERN

THE DOMINATING part played by markets in capitalist economy together with the basic significance of the principle of barter or exchange in this economy calls for a careful inquiry into the nature and origin of markets, if the economic superstitions of the nineteenth century are to be discarded.[1]

Barter, truck, and exchange is a principle of economic behavior dependent for its effectiveness upon the market pattern. A market is a meeting place for the purpose of barter or buying and selling. Unless such a pattern is present, at least in patches, the propensity to barter will find but insufficient scope: it cannot produce prices.[2] For just as reciprocity is aided by a symmetrical pattern of organization, as redistribution is made easier by some measure of centralization, and householding must be based on autarchy, so also the principle of barter depends for its effectiveness on the market pattern. But in the same manner in which either reciprocity, redistribution, or householding may occur in a society without being prevalent in it, the principle of barter also may take a subordinate place in a society in which other principles are in the ascendant.

However, in some other respects the principle of barter is not on a strict parity with the three other principles. The market pattern, with which it is associated, is more specific than either symmetry, centricity, or autarchy—which, in contrast to the market pattern, are mere "traits," and do not create institutions designed for one function only. Symmetry is no more than a sociological arrangement, which gives rise to no separate institutions, but merely patterns out existing ones (whether a tribe or a village is symmetrically patterned or not involves no distinctive institution). Centricity, though frequently creating dis-

---

[1] Cf. Notes on Sources, page 274.

[2] Hawtrey, G. R., *The Economic Problem*, 1925, p. 13. "The practical application of the principle of individualism is entirely dependent on the practice of exchange." Hawtrey, however, was mistaken in assuming that the existence of markets simply followed from the practice of exchange.

tinctive institutions, implies no motive that would single out the resulting institution for a single specific function (the headman of a village or another central official might assume, for instance, a variety of political, military, religious, or economic functions, indiscriminately). Economic autarchy, finally, is only an accessory trait of an existing closed group.

The market pattern, on the other hand, being related to a peculiar motive of its own, the motive of truck or barter, is capable of creating a specific institution, namely, the market. Ultimately, that is why the control of the economic system by the market is of overwhelming consequence to the whole organization of society: it means no less than the running of society as an adjunct to the market. Instead of economy being embedded in social relations, social relations are embedded in the economic system. The vital importance of the economic factor to the existence of society precludes any other result. For once the economic system is organized in separate institutions, based on specific motives and conferring a special status, society must be shaped in such a manner as to allow that system to function according to its own laws. This is the meaning of the familiar assertion that a market economy can function only in a market society.

The step which makes isolated markets into a market economy, regulated markets into a self-regulating market, is indeed crucial. The nineteenth century—whether hailing the fact as the apex of civilization or deploring it as a cancerous growth—naïvely imagined that such a development was the natural outcome of the spreading of markets. It was not realized that the gearing of markets into a self-regulating system of tremendous power was not the result of any inherent tendency of markets towards excrescence, but rather the effect of highly artificial stimulants administered to the body social in order to meet a situation which was created by the no less artificial phenomenon of the machine. The limited and unexpansive nature of the market pattern, as such, was not recognized; and yet it is this fact which emerges with convincing clarity from modern research.

"Markets are not found everywhere; their absence, while indicating a certain isolation and a tendency to seclusion, is not associated with any particular development any more than can be inferred from their presence." This colorless sentence from Thurnwald's *Economics in Primitive Communities* sums up the significant results of modern research on the subject. Another author repeats in respect to money what Thurnwald says of markets: "The mere fact, that a tribe used money differentiated it very little economically from other tribes on the same cultural level, who did not." We need hardly do more than point to some of the more startling implications of these statements.

The presence or absence of markets or money does not necessarily affect the economic system of a primitive society—this refutes the nineteenth century myth that money was an invention the appearance of which inevitably transformed a society by creating markets, forcing the pace of the division of labor, and releasing man's natural propensity to barter, truck, and exchange. Orthodox economic history, in effect, was based on an immensely exaggerated view of the significance of markets as such. A "certain isolation," or, perhaps, a "tendency to seclusion" is the only economic trait that can be correctly inferred from their absence; in respect to the internal organization of an economy, their presence or absence need make no difference.

The reasons are simple. Markets are not institutions functioning mainly within an economy, but without. They are meeting places of long-distance trade. Local markets proper are of little consequence. Moreover, neither long-distance nor local markets are essentially competitive, and consequently there is, in either case, but little pressure to create territorial trade, a so-called internal or national market. Every one of these assertions strikes at some axiomatically held assumption of the classical economists, yet they follow closely from the facts as they appear in the light of modern research.

The logic of the case is, indeed, almost the opposite of that underlying the classical doctrine. The orthodox teaching started from the individual's propensity to barter; deduced from it the necessity of local markets, as well as of division of labor; and inferred, finally, the necessity of trade, eventually of foreign trade, including even long-distance trade. In the light of our present knowledge we should almost reverse the sequence of the argument: the true starting point is long-distance trade, a result of the geographical location of goods, and of the "division of labor" given by location. Long-distance trade often engenders markets, an institution which involves acts of barter, and, if money is used, of buying and selling, thus, eventually, but by no means necessarily, offering to some individuals an occasion to indulge in their alleged propensity for bargaining and haggling.

The dominating feature of this doctrine is the origin of trade in an external sphere unrelated to the internal organization of economy: "The application of the principles observed in hunting to the obtaining of goods found *outside the limits of the district*, led to certain forms of exchange which appear to us later as trade." [3] In looking for the origins of trade, our starting point should be the obtaining of goods from a distance, as in a hunt. "The Central Australian Dieri every year, in July or August, make an expedition to the south to obtain the red ochre used by them for painting their bodies. . . . Their neighbors, the Yantruwunta, organize similar enterprises for fetching red ochre and sandstone slabs, for crushing grass seed, from the Flinders Hills, 800 kilometers distant. In both cases it might be necessary to fight for the articles wanted, if the local people offer resistance to their removal." This kind of requisitioning or treasure hunting is clearly as much akin to robbery and piracy as to what we are used to regard as trade ; basically, it is a one-sided affair. It becomes two-sided, *i.e.,* "a certain form of exchange" often only through blackmail practiced by the powers on the site; or through reciprocity arrangements, as in the Kula ring, as with visiting parties of the Pengwe of West Africa, or with the Kpelle, where the chief monopolizes foreign trade by insisting on entertaining all the guests. True, such visits are not accidental, but —in our terms, not theirs—genuine trading journeys; the exchange of goods, however, is always conducted under the guise of reciprocal presents and usually by way of return visits.

We reach the conclusion that while human communities never seem to have foregone external trade entirely, such trade did not necessarily involve markets. External trade is, originally, more in the nature of adventure, exploration, hunting, piracy and war than of barter. It may as little imply peace as two-sidedness, and even when it implies both it is usually organized on the principle of reciprocity, not on that of barter.

The transition to peaceful barter can be traced in two directions, *viz.,* in that of barter and in that of peace. A tribal expedition may have to comply, as indicated above, with the conditions set by the powers on the spot, who may exact some kind of counterpart from the strangers; this type of relationship, though not entirely peaceful, may give rise to barter—one-sided carrying will be transformed into two-sided carrying. The other line of development is that of "silent trading" as in the African bush, where the risk of combat is avoided through an organized truce, and the element of peace, trust, and confidence is, with due circumspection, introduced into trade.

At a later stage, as we all know, markets become predominant in the organization of external trade. But from the economic point of

[3] Thurnwald, R. C., *Economics in Primitive Communities*, 1932, p. 147.

view external markets are an entirely different matter from either local markets or internal markets. They differ not only in size; they are institutions of different function and origin. External trade is carrying; the point is the absence of some types of goods in that region; the exchange of English woolens against Portuguese wine was an instance. Local trade is limited to the goods of that region, which do *not* bear carrying because they are too heavy, bulky, or perishable. Thus both external trade and local trade are relative to geographical distance, the one being confined to the goods which cannot overcome it, the other to such only as can. Trade of this type is rightly described as complementary. Local exchange between town and countryside, foreign trade between different climatic zones are based on this principle. Such trade need not imply competition, and if competition would tend to disorganize trade, there is no contradiction in eliminating it. In contrast to both external and local trade, internal trade, on the other hand is essentially competitive; apart from complementary exchanges it includes a very much larger number of exchanges in which similar goods from different sources are offered in competition with one another. Accordingly, only with the emergence of internal or national trade does competition tend to be accepted as a general principle of trading.

These three types of trade which differ sharply in their economic function are also distinct in their origin. We have dealt with the beginnings of external trade. Markets developed naturally out of it where the carriers had to halt as at fords, seaports, riverheads, or where the routes of two land expeditions met. "Ports" developed at the places of transshipment.[4] The short flowering of the famous fairs of Europe was another instance where long-distance trade produced a definite type of market; England's staples were another example. But while fairs and staples disappeared again with an abruptness disconcerting to the dogmatic evolutionist, the *portus* was destined to play an enormous role in the settling of Western Europe with towns. Yet even where the towns were founded on the sites of external markets, the local markets often remained separate in respect not only to function but also to organization. Neither the port, nor the fair, nor the staple was the parent of internal or national markets. Where, then, should we seek for their origin?

It might seem natural to assume that, given individual acts of barter, these would in the course of time lead to the development of local

[4] Pirenne, H., *Medieval Cities*, 1925, p. 148 (footnote 12).

markets, and that such markets, once in existence, would just as naturally lead to the establishment of internal or national markets. However, neither the one nor the other is the case. Individual acts of barter or exchange—this is the bare fact—do not, as a rule, lead to the establishment of markets in societies where other principles of economic behavior prevail. Such acts are common in almost all types of primitive society, but they are considered as incidental since they do not provide for the necessaries of life. In the vast ancient systems of redistribution, acts of barter as well as local markets were a usual, but no more than a subordinate trait. The same is true where reciprocity rules: acts of barter are here usually embedded in long-range relations implying trust and confidence, a situation which tends to obliterate the bilateral character of the transaction. The limiting factors arise from all points of the sociological compass: custom and law, religion and magic equally contribute to the result, which is to restrict acts of exchange in respect to persons and objects, time and occasion. As a rule, he who barters merely enters into a ready-made type of transaction in which both the objects and their equivalent amounts are given. *Utu* in the language of the Tikopia [5] denotes such a traditional equivalent as part of reciprocal exchange. That which appeared as the essential feature of exchange to eighteenth century thought, the voluntaristic element of bargain, and the higgling so expressive of the assumed motive of truck, finds but little scope in the actual transaction; in so far as this motive underlies the procedure, it is seldom allowed to rise to the surface.

The customary way to behave is, rather, to give vent to the opposite motivation. The giver may simply drop the object on the ground and the receiver will pretend to pick it up accidentally, or even leave it to one of his hangers-on to do so for him. Nothing could be more contrary to accepted behavior than to have a good look at the counterpart received. As we have every reason to believe that this sophisticated attitude is not the outcome of a genuine lack of interest in the material side of the transaction, we might describe the etiquette of barter as a counteracting development designed to limit the scope of the trait.

Indeed, on the evidence available it would be rash to assert that local markets ever developed from individual acts of barter. Obscure as the beginnings of local markets are, this much can be asserted: that from the start this institution was surrounded by a number of safeguards designed to protect the prevailing economic organization of

[5] Firth, R., *Primitive Polynesian Economics*, 1939, p. 347.

society from interference on the part of market practices. The peace of the market was secured at the price of rituals and ceremonies which restricted its scope while ensuring its ability to function within the given narrow limits. The most significant result of markets—the birth of towns and urban civilization—was, in effect, the outcome of a paradoxical development. Because the towns, the offspring of the markets, were not only their protectors, but also the means of preventing them from expanding into the countryside and thus encroaching on the prevailing economic organization of society. The two meanings of the word "contain" express perhaps best this double function of the towns, in respect to the markets which they both enveloped and prevented from developing.

If barter was surrounded by taboos devised to keep this type of human relationship from abusing the functions of the economic organization proper, the discipline of the market was even stricter. Here is an example from the Chaga country: "The market must be regularly visited on market days. If any occurrence should prevent the holding of the market on one or more days, business cannot be resumed until the market-place has been purified. . . . Every injury occurring on the market-place and involving the shedding of blood necessitated immediate expiation. From that moment no woman was allowed to leave the market-place and no goods might be touched; they had to be cleansed before they could be carried away and used for food. At the very least a goat had to be sacrificed at once. A more expensive and more serious expiation was necessary if a woman bore a child or had a miscarriage on the market-place. In that case a milch animal was necessary. In addition to this, the homestead of the chief had to be purified by means of sacrificial blood of a milch-cow. All the women in the country were thus sprinkled, district by district." [6] Rules such as these would not make the spreading of markets easier.

The typical local market at which housewives procure some of their daily needs, and growers of grain or vegetables as well as local craftsmen offer their wares for sale, shows an amazing indifference to time and place. Gatherings of this kind are not only fairly general in primitive societies, but remain almost unchanged right up to the middle of the eighteenth century in the most advanced countries of Western Europe. They are an adjunct of local existence and differ but little whether they form part of Central African tribal life, or a *cité* of Merovingian France, or a Scottish village of Adam Smith's time. But

[6] Thurnwald, R. C., *op. cit.*, p. 162–164.

what is true of the village is also true of the town. Local markets are, essentially, neighborhood markets, and, though important to the life of the community, they nowhere showed any sign of reducing the prevailing economic system to their pattern. They were not starting points of internal or national trade.

Internal trade in Western Europe was actually created by the intervention of the state. Right up to the time of the Commercial Revolution what may appear to us as national trade was not national, but municipal. The Hanse were not German merchants; they were a corporation of trading oligarchs, hailing from a number of North Sea and Baltic towns. Far from "nationalizing" German economic life, the Hanse deliberately cut off the hinterland from trade. The trade of Antwerp or Hamburg, Venice or Lyons, was in no way Dutch or German, Italian or French. London was no exception: it was as little "English" as Luebeck was "German." The trade map of Europe in this period should rightly show only towns, and leave blank the countryside—it might as well have not existed as far as organized trade was concerned. So-called nations were merely political units, and very loose ones at that, consisting economically of innumerable smaller and bigger self-sufficing households and insignificant local markets in the villages. Trade was limited to organized townships which carried it on either locally as neighborhood trade or as long-distance trade—the two were strictly separated, and neither was allowed to infiltrate the countryside indiscriminately.

Such a permanent severance of local trade and long-distance trade within the organization of the town must come as another shock to the evolutionist, with whom things always seem so easily to grow into one another. And yet this peculiar fact forms the key to the social history of urban life in Western Europe. It strongly tends to support our assertion in respect to the origin of markets which we inferred from conditions in primitive economies. The sharp distinction drawn between local and long-distance trade might have seemed too rigid, especially as it led us to the somewhat surprising conclusion that neither long-distance trade nor local trade was the parent of the internal trade of modern times—thus apparently leaving no alternative but to turn for an explanation to the *deus ex machina* of state intervention. We will see presently that in this respect also recent investigations bear out our conclusions. But let us first give a bare outline of the history of urban civilization as it was shaped by the peculiar severance of local and long-distance trade within the confines of the medieval town.

This severance was, indeed, at the heart of the institution of medieval urban centers.[7] The town was an organization of the burgesses. They alone had right of citizenship and on the distinction between the burgess and the non-burgess the system rested. Neither the peasants of the countryside nor the merchants from other towns were, naturally, burgesses. But while the military and political influence of the town made it possible to deal with the peasants of the surroundings, in respect to the foreign merchant such authority could not be exerted. Consequently, the burgesses found themselves in an entirely different position in respect to local trade and long-distance trade.

As to food supplies, regulation involved the application of such methods as enforced publicity of transactions and exclusion of middlemen, in order to control trade and provide against high prices. But such regulation was effective only in respect to trade carried on between the town and its immediate surroundings. In respect to long-distance trade the position was entirely different. Spices, salted fish, or wine had to be transported from a long distance and were thus the domain of the foreign merchant and his capitalistic wholesale trade methods. This type of trade escaped local regulation and all that could be done was to exclude it as far as possible from the local market. The complete prohibition of retail sale by foreign merchants was designed to achieve this end. The more the volume of capitalistic wholesale trade grew, the more strictly was its exclusion from the local markets enforced as far as imports were concerned.

In respect to industrial wares, the separation of local and long-distance trade cut even deeper, as in this case the whole organization of production for export was affected. The reason for this lay in the very nature of craft gilds, in which industrial production was organized. On the local market, production was regulated according to the needs of the producers, thus restricting production to a remunerative level. This principle would naturally not apply to exports, where the interests of the producers set no limits to production. Consequently, while local trade was strictly regulated, production for export was only formally controlled by corporations of crafts. The dominating export industry of the age, the cloth trade, was actually organized on the capitalistic basis of wage labor.

An increasingly strict separation of local trade from export trade was the reaction of urban life to the threat of mobile capital to disintegrate the institutions of the town. The typical medieval town did not

[7] Our presentation follows H. Pirenne's well-known works.

try to avoid the danger by bridging the gap between the controllable local market and the vagaries of an uncontrollable long-distance trade, but, on the contrary, met the peril squarely by enforcing with the utmost rigor that policy of exclusion and protection which was the *rationale* of its existence.

In practice this meant that the towns raised every possible obstacle to the formation of that national or internal market for which the capitalist wholesaler was pressing. By maintaining the principle of a noncompetitive local trade and an equally noncompetitive long-distance trade carried on from town to town, the burgesses hampered by all means at their disposal the inclusion of the countryside into the compass of trade and the opening up of indiscriminate trade between the towns of the country. It was this development which forced the territorial state to the fore as the instrument of the "nationalization" of the market and the creator of internal commerce.

Deliberate action of the state in the fifteenth and sixteenth centuries foisted the mercantile system on the fiercely protectionist towns and principalities. Mercantilism destroyed the outworn particularism of local and intermunicipal trading by breaking down the barriers separating these two types of noncompetitive commerce and thus clearing the way for a national market which increasingly ignored the distinction between town and countryside as well as that between the various towns and provinces.

The mercantile system was, in effect, a response to many challenges. Politically, the centralized state was a new creation called forth by the Commercial Revolution which had shifted the center of gravity of the Western world from the Mediterranean to the Atlantic seaboard and thus compelled the backward peoples of larger agrarian countries to organize for commerce and trade. In external politics, the setting up of sovereign power was the need of the day; accordingly, mercantilist statecraft involved the marshaling of the resources of the whole national territory to the purposes of power in foreign affairs. In internal politics, unification of the countries fragmented by feudal and municipal particularism was the necessary by-product of such an endeavor. Economically, the instrument of unification was capital, *i.e.*, private resources available in form of money hoards and thus peculiarly suitable for the development of commerce. Finally the administrative technique underlying the economic policy of the central government was supplied by the extension of the traditional municipal system to the larger territory of the state. In France, where the craft gilds tended to become

state organs, the gild system was simply extended over the whole territory of the country; in England, where the decay of the walled towns
had weakened that system fatally, the countryside was industrialized
without the supervision of the gilds, while in both countries trade and
commerce spread over the whole territory of the nation and became the
dominating form of economic activity. In this situation lie the origins
of the internal trade policy of mercantilism.

State intervention, which had freed trade from the confines of the
privileged town, was now called to deal with two closely connected
dangers which the town had successfully met, namely, monopoly and
competition. That competition must ultimately lead to monopoly was
a truth well understood at the time, while monopoly was feared even
more than later as it often concerned the necessaries of life and thus
easily waxed into a peril to the community. All-round regulation of
economic life, only this time on a national, no more on a merely municipal, scale was the given remedy. What to the modern mind may easily
appear as a shortsighted exclusion of competition was in reality the
means of safeguarding the functioning of markets under the given
conditions. For any temporary intrusion of buyers or sellers in the
market must destroy the balance and disappoint regular buyers or
sellers, with the result that the market will cease to function. The
former purveyors will cease to offer their goods as they cannot be sure
that their goods will fetch a price, and the market left without sufficient
supply will become a prey to the monopolist. To a lesser degree, the
same dangers were present on the demand side, where a rapid falling
off might be followed by a monopoly of demand. With every step that
the state took to rid the market of particularist restrictions, of tolls and
prohibitions, it imperiled the organized system of production and distribution which was now threatened by unregulated competition and
the intrusion of the interloper who "scooped" the market but offered
no guarantee of permanency. Thus it came that although the new
national markets were, inevitably, to some degree competitive, it was
the traditional feature of regulation, not the new element of competition, which prevailed.[8] The self-sufficing household of the peasant
laboring for his subsistence remained the broad basis of the economic
system, which was being integrated into large national units through the
formation of the internal market. This national market now took its
place alongside, and partly overlapping, the local and foreign markets.

[8] Montesquieu, *L'Esprit des lois*, 1748. "The English constrain the merchant,
but it is in favor of commerce."

Agriculture was now being supplemented by internal commerce—a system of relatively isolated markets, which was entirely compatible with the principle of householding still dominant in the countryside.

This concludes our synopsis of the history of the market up to the time of the Industrial Revolution. The next stage in mankind's history brought, as we know, an attempt to set up one big self-regulating market. There was nothing in mercantilism, this distinctive policy of the Western nation-state, to presage such a unique development. The "freeing" of trade performed by mercantilism merely liberated trade from particularism, but at the same time extended the scope of regulation. The economic system was submerged in general social relations; markets were merely an accessory feature of an institutional setting controlled and regulated more than ever by social authority.

6

THE SELF-REGULATING MARKET AND THE FICTITIOUS
COMMODITIES: LABOR, LAND, AND MONEY

THIS CURSORY OUTLINE of the economic system and markets, taken separately, shows that never before our own time were markets more than accessories of economic life. As a rule, the economic system was absorbed in the social system, and whatever principle of behavior predominated in the economy, the presence of the market pattern was found to be compatible with it. The principle of barter or exchange, which underlies this pattern, revealed no tendency to expand at the expense of the rest. Where markets were most highly developed, as under the mercantile system, they throve under the control of a centralized administration which fostered autarchy both in the households of the peasantry and in respect to national life. Regulation and markets, in effect, grew up together. The self-regulating market was unknown; indeed the emergence of the idea of self-regulation was a complete reversal of the trend of development. It is in the light of these facts that the extraordinary assumptions underlying a market economy can alone be fully comprehended.

A market economy is an economic system controlled, regulated, and directed by markets alone; order in the production and distribution of goods is entrusted to this self-regulating mechanism. An economy of this kind derives from the expectation that human beings behave in such a way as to achieve maximum money gains. It assumes markets in which the supply of goods (including services) available at a definite price will equal the demand at that price. It assumes the presence of money, which functions as purchasing power in the hands of its owners. Production will then be controlled by prices, for the profits of those who direct production will depend upon them; the distribution of the goods also will depend upon prices, for prices form incomes, and it is with the help of these incomes that the goods produced are distributed amongst the members of society. Under these assumptions order in the production and distribution of goods is ensured by prices alone.

Self-regulation implies that all production is for sale on the market and that all incomes derive from such sales. Accordingly, there are markets for all elements of industry, not only for goods (always including services) but also for labor, land, and money, their prices being called respectively commodity prices, wages, rent, and interest. The very terms indicate that prices form incomes: interest is the price for the use of money and forms the income of those who are in the position to provide it; rent is the price for the use of land and forms the income of those who supply it; wages are the price for the use of labor power, and form the income of those who sell it; commodity prices, finally, contribute to the incomes of those who sell their entrepreneurial services, the income called profit being actually the difference between two sets of prices, the price of the goods produced and their costs, *i.e.*, the price of the goods necessary to produce them. If these conditions are fulfilled, all incomes will derive from sales on the market, and incomes will be just sufficient to buy all the goods produced.

A further group of assumptions follows in respect to the state and its policy. Nothing must be allowed to inhibit the formation of markets, nor must incomes be permitted to be formed otherwise than through sales. Neither must there be any interference with the adjustment of prices to changed market conditions—whether the prices are those of goods, labor, land, or money. Hence there must not only be markets for all elements of industry,[1] but no measure or policy must be countenanced that would influence the action of these markets. Neither price, nor supply, nor demand must be fixed or regulated; only such policies and measures are in order which help to ensure the self-regulation of the market by creating conditions which make the market the only organizing power in the economic sphere.

To realize fully what this means, let us return for a moment to the mercantile system and the national markets which it did so much to develop. Under feudalism and the gild system land and labor formed part of the social organization itself (money had yet hardly developed into a major element of industry). Land, the pivotal element in the feudal order, was the basis of the military, judicial, administrative, and political system; its status and function were determined by legal and customary rules. Whether its possession was transferable or not, and if so, to whom and under what restrictions; what the rights of property

---

[1] Henderson, H. D., *Supply and Demand*, 1922. The practice of the market is twofold: the apportionment of factors between different uses, and the organizing of the forces influencing aggregate supplies of factors.

entailed; to what uses some types of land might be put—all these questions were removed from the organization of buying and selling, and subjected to an entirely different set of institutional regulations.

The same was true of the organization of labor. Under the gild system, as under every other economic system in previous history, the motives and circumstances of productive activities were embedded in the general organization of society. The relations of master, journeyman, and apprentice; the terms of the craft; the number of apprentices; the wages of the workers were all regulated by the custom and rule of the gild and the town. What the mercantile system did was merely to unify these conditions either through statute as in England, or through the "nationalization" of the gilds as in France. As to land, its feudal status was abolished only in so far as it was linked with provincial privileges; for the rest, land remained *extra commercium*, in England as in France. Up to the time of the Great Revolution of 1789, landed estate remained the source of social privilege in France, and even after that time in England Common Law on land was essentially medieval. Mercantilism, with all its tendency towards commercialization, never attacked the safeguards which protected these two basic elements of production—labor and land—from becoming the objects of commerce. In England the "nationalization" of labor legislation through the Statute of Artificers (1563) and the Poor Law (1601), removed labor from the danger zone, and the anti-enclosure policy of the Tudors and early Stuarts was one consistent protest against the principle of the gainful use of landed property.

That mercantilism, however emphatically it insisted on commercialization as a national policy, thought of markets in a way exactly contrary to market economy, is best shown by its vast extension of state intervention in industry. On this point there was no difference between mercantilists and feudalists, between crowned planners and vested interests, between centralizing bureaucrats and conservative particularists. They disagreed only on the methods of regulation: gilds, towns, and provinces appealed to the force of custom and tradition, while the new state authority favored statute and ordinance. But they were all equally averse to the idea of commercializing labor and land—the precondition of market economy. Craft gilds and feudal privileges were abolished in France only in 1790; in England the Statute of Artificers was repealed only in 1813–14, the Elizabethan Poor Law in 1834. Not before the last decade of the eighteenth century was, in either country, the establishment of a free labor market even discussed; and the idea of the self-regulation of economic life was utterly beyond the horizon of the age. The mercantilist was concerned with the development of the resources of the country, including full employment, through trade and commerce; the traditional organization of land and labor he took for granted. He was in this respect as far removed from modern concepts as he was in the realm of politics, where his belief in the absolute powers of an enlightened despot was tempered by no intimations of democracy. And just as the transition to a democratic system and representative politics involved a complete reversal of the trend of the age, the change from regulated to self-regulating markets at the end of the eighteenth century represented a complete transformation in the structure of society.

A self-regulating market demands nothing less than the institutional separation of society into an economic and political sphere. Such a dichotomy is, in effect, merely the restatement, from the point of view of society as a whole, of the existence of a self-regulating market. It might be argued that the separateness of the two spheres obtains in every type of society at all times. Such an inference, however, would be based on a fallacy. True, no society can exist without a system of some kind which ensures order in the production and distribution of goods. But that does not imply the existence of separate economic institutions; normally, the economic order is merely a function of the social, in which it is contained. Neither under tribal, nor feudal, nor mercantile conditions was there, as we have shown, a separate economic system in society. Nineteenth century society, in which economic activity was isolated and imputed to a distinctive economic motive, was, indeed, a singular departure.

Such an institutional pattern could not function unless society was somehow subordinated to its requirements. A market economy can exist only in a market society. We reached this conclusion on general grounds in our analysis of the market pattern. We can now specify the reasons for this assertion. A market economy must comprise all elements of industry, including labor, land, and money. (In a market economy the last also is an essential element of industrial life and its inclusion in the market mechanism has, as we will see, far-reaching institutional consequences.) But labor and land are no other than the human beings themselves of which every society consists and the natural surroundings in which it exists. To include them in the market mechanism means to subordinate the substance of society itself to the laws of the market.

We are now in the position to develop in a more concrete form the institutional nature of a market economy, and the perils to society which it involves. We will, first, describe the methods by which the market mechanism is enabled to control and direct the actual elements of industrial life; second, we will try to gauge the nature of the effects of such a mechanism on the society which is subjected to its action.

It is with the help of the commodity concept that the mechanism of the market is geared to the various elements of industrial life. Commodities are here empirically defined as objects produced for sale on the market; markets, again, are empirically defined as actual contacts between buyers and sellers. Accordingly, every element of industry is regarded as having been produced for sale, as then and then only will it be subject to the supply-and-demand mechanism interacting with price. In practice this means that there must be markets for every element of industry; that in these markets each of these elements is organized into a supply and a demand group; and that each element has a price which interacts with demand and supply. These markets—and they are numberless—are interconnected and form One Big Market.[2]

The crucial point is this: labor, land, and money are essential elements of industry; they also must be organized in markets; in fact, these markets form an absolutely vital part of the economic system. But labor, land, and money are obviously *not* commodities; the postulate that anything that is bought and sold must have been produced for sale is emphatically untrue in regard to them. In other words, according to the empirical definition of a commodity they are not commodities. Labor is only another name for a human activity which goes with life itself, which in its turn is not produced for sale but for entirely different reasons, nor can that activity be detached from the rest of life, be stored or mobilized; land is only another name for nature, which is not produced by man; actual money, finally, is merely a token of purchasing power which, as a rule, is not produced at all, but comes into being through the mechanism of banking or state finance. None of them is produced for sale. The commodity description of labor, land, and money is entirely fictitious.

Nevertheless, it is with the help of this fiction that the actual markets for labor, land, and money are organized; [3] they are being actually bought and sold on the market; their demand and supply

---

[2] Hawtrey, G. R., *op. cit.* Its function is seen by Hawtrey in making "the relative market values of all commodities mutually consistent."

[3] Marx's assertion of the fetish character of the value of commodities refers to the exchange value of genuine commodities and has nothing in common with the fictitious commodities mentioned in the text.

are real magnitudes; and any measures or policies that would inhibit the formation of such markets would *ipso facto* endanger the self-regulation of the system. The commodity fiction, therefore, supplies a vital organizing principle in regard to the whole of society affecting almost all its institutions in the most varied way, namely, the principle according to which no arrangement or behavior should be allowed to exist that might prevent the actual functioning of the market mechanism on the lines of the commodity fiction.

Now, in regard to labor, land, and money such a postulate cannot be upheld. To allow the market mechanism to be sole director of the fate of human beings and their natural environment, indeed, even of the amount and use of purchasing power, would result in the demolition of society. For the alleged commodity "labor power" cannot be shoved about, used indiscriminately, or even left unused, without affecting also the human individual who happens to be the bearer of this peculiar commodity. In disposing of a man's labor power the system would, incidentally, dispose of the physical, psychological, and moral entity "man" attached to that tag. Robbed of the protective covering of cultural institutions, human beings would perish from the effects of social exposure; they would die as the victims of acute social dislocation through vice, perversion, crime, and starvation. Nature would be reduced to its elements, neighborhoods and landscapes defiled, rivers polluted, military safety jeopardized, the power to produce food and raw materials destroyed. Finally, the market administration of purchasing power would periodically liquidate business enterprise, for shortages and surfeits of money would prove as disastrous to business as floods and droughts in primitive society. Undoubtedly, labor, land, and money markets *are* essential to a market economy. But no society could stand the effects of such a system of crude fictions even for the shortest stretch of time unless its human and natural substance as well as its business organization was protected against the ravages of this satanic mill.

The extreme artificiality of market economy is rooted in the fact that the process of production itself is here organized in the form of buying and selling.[4] No other way of organizing production for the market is possible in a commercial society. During the late Middle Ages industrial production for export was organized by wealthy burgesses, and carried on under their direct supervision in the home town. Later, in the mercantile society, production was organized by mer-

[4] Cunningham, W., "Economic Change," *Cambridge Modern History*, Vol. I.

chants and was not restricted any more to the towns; this was the age of "putting out" when domestic industry was provided with raw materials by the merchant capitalist, who controlled the process of production as a purely commercial enterprise. It was then that industrial production was definitely and on a large scale put under the organizing leadership of the merchant. He knew the market, the volume as well as the quality of the demand; and he could vouch also for the supplies which, incidentally, consisted merely of wool, woad, and, sometimes, the looms or the knitting frames used by the cottage industry. If supplies failed it was the cottager who was worst hit, for his employment was gone for the time; but no expensive plant was involved and the merchant incurred no serious risk in shouldering the responsibility for production. For centuries this system grew in power and scope until in a country like England the wool industry, the national staple, covered large sectors of the country where production was organized by the clothier. He who bought and sold, incidentally, provided for production—no separate motive was required. The creation of goods involved neither the reciprocating attitudes of mutual aid; nor the concern of the householder for those whose needs are left to his care; nor the craftsman's pride in the exercise of his trade; nor the satisfaction of public praise—nothing but the plain motive of gain so familiar to the man whose profession is buying and selling. Up to the end of the eighteenth century, industrial production in Western Europe was a mere accessory to commerce.

As long as the machine was an inexpensive and unspecific tool there was no change in this position. The mere fact that the cottager could produce larger amounts than before within the same time might induce him to use machines to increase earnings, but this fact in itself did not necessarily affect the organization of production. Whether the cheap machinery was owned by the worker or by the merchant made some difference in the social position of the parties and almost certainly made a difference in the earnings of the worker, who was better off as long as he owned his tools; but it did not force the merchant to become an industrial capitalist, or to restrict himself to lending his money to such persons as were. The vent of goods rarely gave out; the greater difficulty continued to be on the side of supply of raw materials, which was sometimes unavoidably interrupted. But, even in such cases, the loss to the merchant who owned the machines was not substantial. It was not the coming of the machine as such but the invention of elaborate and therefore specific machinery and plant

which completely changed the relationship of the merchant to production. Although the new productive organization was introduced
by the merchant—a fact which determined the whole course of the
transformation—the use of elaborate machinery and plant involved
the development of the factory system and therewith a decisive shift
in the relative importance of commerce and industry in favor of the
latter. Industrial production ceased to be an accessory of commerce
organized by the merchant as a buying and selling proposition; it now
involved long-term investment with corresponding risks. Unless the
continuance of production was reasonably assured, such a risk was not
bearable.

But the more complicated industrial production became, the more
numerous were the elements of industry the supply of which had to be
safeguarded. Three of these, of course, were of outstanding importance: labor, land, and money. In a commercial society their supply
could be organized in one way only: by being made available for
purchase. Hence, they would have to be organized for sale on the
market—in other words, as commodities. The extension of the market
mechanism to the elements of industry—labor, land, and money—
was the inevitable consequence of the introduction of the factory system in a commercial society. The elements of industry had to be on
sale.

This was synonymous with the demand for a market system. We
know that profits are ensured under such a system only if self-regulation
is safeguarded through interdependent competitive markets. As the
development of the factory system had been organized as part of a
process of buying and selling, therefore labor, land, and money had
to be transformed into commodities in order to keep production going.
They could, of course, not be really transformed into commodities, as
actually they were not produced for sale on the market. But the fiction
of their being so produced became the organizing principle of society.
Of the three, one stands out: labor is the technical term used for
human beings, in so far as they are not employers but employed; it
follows that henceforth the organization of labor would change concurrently with the organization of the market system. But as the
organization of labor is only another word for the forms of life of the
common people, this means that the development of the market system
would be accompanied by a change in the organization of society itself. All along the line, human society had become an accessory of the
economic system.

We recall our parallel between the ravages of the enclosures in English history and the social catastrophe which followed the Industrial Revolution. Improvements, we said, are, as a rule, bought at the price of social dislocation. If the rate of dislocation is too great, the community must succumb in the process. The Tudors and early Stuarts saved England from the fate of Spain by regulating the course of change so that it became bearable and its effects could be canalized into less destructive avenues. But nothing saved the common people of England from the impact of the Industrial Revolution. A blind faith in spontaneous progress had taken hold of people's minds, and with the fanaticism of sectarians the most enlightened pressed forward for boundless and unregulated change in society. The effects on the lives of the people were awful beyond description. Indeed, human society would have been annihilated but for protective countermoves which blunted the action of this self-destructive mechanism.

Social history in the nineteenth century was thus the result of a double movement: the extension of the market organization in respect to genuine commodities was accompanied by its restriction in respect to fictitious ones. While on the one hand markets spread all over the face of the globe and the amount of goods involved grew to unbelievable proportions, on the other hand a network of measures and policies was integrated into powerful institutions designed to check the action of the market relative to labor, land, and money. While the organization of world commodity markets, world capital markets, and world currency markets under the aegis of the gold standard gave an unparalleled momentum to the mechanism of markets, a deep-seated movement sprang into being to resist the pernicious effects of a market-controlled economy. Society protected itself against the perils inherent in a self-regulating market system—this was the one comprehensive feature in the history of the age.

7

SPEENHAMLAND, 1795

EIGHTEENTH CENTURY society unconsciously resisted any attempt at making it a mere appendage of the market. No market economy was conceivable that did not include a market for labor; but to establish such a market, especially in England's rural civilization, implied no less than the wholesale destruction of the traditional fabric of society. During the most active period of the Industrial Revolution, from 1795 to 1834, the creating of a labor market in England was prevented through the Speenhamland Law.

The market for labor was, in effect, the last of the markets to be organized under the new industrial system, and this final step was taken only when market economy was set to start, and when the absence of a market for labor was proving a greater evil even to the common people themselves than the calamities that were to accompany its introduction. In the end the free labor market, in spite of the inhuman methods employed in creating it, proved financially beneficial to all concerned.

Yet it was only now that the crucial problem appeared. The economic advantages of a free labor market could not make up for the social destruction wrought by it. Regulation of a new type had to be introduced under which labor was again protected, only this time from the working of the market mechanism itself. Though the new protective institutions, such as trade unions and factory laws, were adapted, as far as possible, to the requirements of the economic mechanism, they nevertheless interfered with its self-regulation and, ultimately, destroyed the system.

In the broad logic of this development the Speenhamland Law occupied a strategic position.

In England both land and money were mobilized before labor was. The latter was prevented from forming a national market by strict

legal restrictions on its physical mobility, since the laborer was practically bound to his parish. The Act of Settlement of 1662, which laid
down the rules of so-called parish serfdom, was loosened only in 1795.
This step would have made possible the setting up of a national labor
market had not in the very same year the Speenhamland Law or
"allowance system" been introduced. The tendency of this law was
to the opposite; namely, towards a powerful reinforcement of the
paternalistic system of labor organization as inherited from the Tudors
and Stuarts. The justices of Berkshire, meeting at the Pelikan Inn, in
Speenhamland, near Newbury, on May 6, 1795, in a time of great
distress, decided that subsidies in aid of wages should be granted in
accordance with a scale dependent upon the price of bread, so that
a minimum income should be assured to the poor *irrespective of their
earnings.* The magistrates' famous recommendation ran: When the
gallon loaf of bread of definite quality "shall cost 1 shilling, then every
poor and industrious person shall have for his support 3 shillings
weekly, either procured by his own or his family's labor, *or an allowance from the poor rates,* and for the support of his wife and every
other of his family, 1 shilling, 6 pence; when the gallon loaf shall cost
1/6, then 4 shillings weekly, plus 1/10; on every pence which the
bread price raises above 1 shilling he shall have 3 pence for himself
and 1 pence for the others." The figures varied somewhat in various
counties, but in most cases the Speenhamland *scale* was adopted.
This was meant as an emergency measure, and was informally introduced. Although commonly called a law, *the scale itself was never
enacted.* Yet very soon it became the law of the land over most of the
countryside, and later even in a number of manufacturing districts;
actually it introduced no less a social and economic innovation than
the "right to live," and until abolished in 1834, it effectively prevented the establishment of a competitive labor market. Two years
earlier, in 1832, the middle class had forced its way to power, partly
in order to remove this obstacle to the new capitalistic economy. Indeed, nothing could be more obvious than that the wage system
imperatively demanded the withdrawal of the "right to live" as proclaimed in Speenhamland—under the new regime of the economic
man, nobody would work for a wage if he could make a living by
doing nothing.

Another feature of the reversal of the Speenhamland method was
less obvious to most nineteenth century writers, namely, that the wage
system had to be made universal in the interest also of the wage

earners themselves, even though this meant depriving them of their legal claim to subsistence. The "right to live" had proved a death-trap.

The paradox was merely apparent. Allegedly, Speenhamland meant that the Poor Law was to be administered liberally—actually, it was turned into the opposite of its original intent. Under Elizabethan Law the poor were forced to work at whatever wages they could get and only those who could obtain no work were entitled to relief; relief in *aid of wages* was neither intended nor given. Under the Speenhamland Law a man was relieved even if he was in employment, as long as his wages amounted to less than the family income granted to him by the scale. Hence, no laborer had any material interest in satisfying his employer, his income being the same whatever wages he earned; this was different only in case standard wages, *i.e.*, the wages actually paid, exceeded the scale, an occurrence which was not the rule in the countryside since the employer could obtain labor at almost any wages; however little he paid, the subsidy from the rates brought the workers' income up to scale. Within a few years the productivity of labor began to sink to that of pauper labor, thus providing an added reason for employers not to raise wages above the scale. For, once the intensity of labor, the care and efficiency with which it was performed, dropped below a definite level, it became indistinguishable from "boondoggling" or the semblance of work maintained for the sake of appearances. Though in principle work was still enforced, in practice outdoor relief became general and even when relief was administered in the poor-house the enforced occupation of the inmates now hardly deserved the name of work. This amounted to the abandonment of Tudor legislation not for the sake of less but of more paternalism. The extension of outdoor relief, the introduction of aid-in-wages supplemented by separate allowances for wife and children, each item rising and falling with the bread price, meant a dramatic re-entry in regard to labor of that same regulative principle that was being rapidly eliminated in regard to industrial life as a whole.

No measure was ever more universally popular.[1] Parents were free of the care of their children, and children were no more dependent upon parents; employers could reduce wages at will and laborers were safe from hunger whether they were busy or slack; humanitarians applauded the measure as an act of mercy even though not of justice and the selfish gladly consoled themselves with the thought that though

[1] Meredith, H. O., *Outlines of the Economic History of England*, 1908.

it was merciful at least it was not liberal; and even ratepayers were slow to realize what would happen to the rates under a system which proclaimed the "right to live" whether a man earned a living wage or not.

In the long run the result was ghastly. Although it took some time till the self-respect of the common man sank to the low point where he preferred poor relief to wages, his wages which were subsidized from public funds were bound eventually to be bottomless, and to force him upon the rates. Little by little the people of the countryside were pauperized; the adage, "once on the rates, always on the rates" was a true saying. But for the protracted effects of the allowance system, it would be impossible to explain the human and social degradation of early capitalism.

The Speenhamland episode revealed to the people of the leading country of the century the true nature of the social adventure on which they were embarking. Neither the rulers nor the ruled ever forgot the lessons of that fool's paradise; if the Reform Bill of 1832 and the Poor Law Amendment of 1834 were commonly regarded as the starting point of modern capitalism, it was because they put an end to the rule of the benevolent landlord and his allowance system. The attempt to create a capitalistic order without a labor market had failed disastrously. The laws governing such an order had asserted themselves, and manifested their radical antagonism to the principle of paternalism. The rigor of these laws had become apparent and their violation had been cruelly visited upon those who had disobeyed them.

Under Speenhamland society was rent by two opposing influences, the one emanating from paternalism and protecting labor from the dangers of the market system; the other organizing the elements of production, including land, under a market system, and thus divesting the common people of their former status, compelling them to gain a living by offering their labor for sale, while at the same time depriving their labor of its market value. A new class of employers was being created, but no corresponding class of employees could constitute itself. A new gigantic wave of enclosures was mobilizing the land and producing a rural proletariat, while the "maladministration of the Poor Law" precluded them from gaining a living by their labor. No wonder that the contemporaries were appalled at the seeming contradiction of an almost miraculous increase in production accompanied by a near starvation of the masses. By 1834, there was a general conviction—with many thinking people a passionately held conviction—that anything was preferable to the continuance of Speenhamland. Either machines had to be demolished, as the Luddites had tried to do, or a regular labor market had to be created. Thus was mankind forced into the paths of a utopian experiment.

This is not the place to expatiate upon the economics of Speenhamland; there will be occasion for that later on. On the face of it the "right to live" should have stopped wage labor altogether. Standard wages should have gradually dropped to zero, thus putting the actual wage bill wholly on the parish, a procedure which would have made the absurdity of the arrangement manifest. But this was an essentially precapitalistic age, when the common people were still traditionally minded, and far from being directed in their behavior by monetary motives alone. The great majority of the countryfolk were occupier-owners or lifeholders, who preferred any kind of existence to the status of pauper, even if it was not deliberately burdened by irksome or ignominious disabilities, as subsequently happened. If laborers had been free to combine for the furtherance of their interests, the allowance system might, of course, have had a contrary effect on standard wages: for trade union action would have been greatly helped by the relief of the unemployed implied in so liberal an administration of the Poor Law. That was presumably one of the reasons for the unjust Anti-Combination Laws of 1799–1800, which would be otherwise hardly explicable since the Berkshire magistrates and members of Parliament were both, on the whole, concerned about the economic condition of the poor, and after 1797 political unrest had subsided. Indeed, it might be argued that the paternalistic intervention of Speenhamland called forth the Anti-Combination Laws, a further intervention, but for which Speenhamland might have had the effect of raising wages instead of depressing them as it actually did. In conjunction with the Anti-Combination Laws, which were not revoked for another quarter century, Speenhamland led to the ironical result that the financially implemented "right to live" eventually ruined the people whom it was ostensibly designed to succor.

To later generations nothing could have been more patent than the mutual incompatibility of institutions like the wage system and the "right to live," or, in other words, than the impossibility of a functioning capitalistic order as long as wages were subsidized from public funds. But the contemporaries did not comprehend the order for which they were preparing the way. Only when a grave deterioration of the productive capacity of the masses resulted—a veritable national calamity which was obstructing the progress of machine civilization— did the necessity of abolishing the unconditional right of the poor to relief impose itself upon the consciousness of the community. The complicated economics of Speenhamland transcended the comprehension of even the most expert observers of the time; but the conclusion appeared only the more compelling that aid-in-wages must be inherently vicious, since it miraculously injured even those who received it.

The pitfalls of the market system were not readily apparent. To realize this clearly we must distinguish between the various vicissitudes to which the laboring people were exposed in England since the coming of the machine: first, those of the Speenhamland period, 1795 to 1834; second, the hardships caused by the Poor Law Reform, in the decade following 1834; third, the deleterious effects of a competitive labor market after 1834, until in the 1870's the recognition of the trade unions offered sufficient protection. Chronologically, Speenhamland antedated market economy; the decade of the Poor Law Reform Act was a transition to that economy. The last period—overlapping the former—was that of market economy proper.

The three periods differed sharply. Speenhamland was designed to prevent the proletarianization of the common people, or at least to slow it down. The outcome was merely the pauperization of the masses, who almost lost their human shape in the process.

The Poor Law Reform of 1834 did away with this obstruction to the labor market: the "right to live" was abolished. The scientific cruelty of that Act was so shocking to public sentiment in the 1830's and 1840's that the vehement contemporary protests blurred the picture in the eyes of posterity. Many of the most needy poor, it was true, were left to their fate as outdoor relief was withdrawn, and among those who suffered most bitterly were the "deserving poor" who were too proud to enter the workhouse which had become an abode of shame. Never perhaps in all modern history has a more ruthless act of social reform been perpetrated; it crushed multitudes of lives while merely pretending to provide a criterion of genuine destitution in the workhouse test. Psychological torture was coolly advocated and smoothly put into practice by mild philanthropists as a means of oiling the wheels of the labor mill. Yet the bulk of the complaints were really due to the abruptness with which an institution of old standing was uprooted and a radical transformation rushed into effect. Disraeli denounced this "inconceivable revolution" in the lives of the people. However, if money incomes alone had counted, the condition of the people would have soon been deemed improved.

The problems of the third period went incomparably deeper. The bureaucratic atrocities committed against the poor during the decade following 1834 by the new centralized Poor Law authorities were merely sporadic and as nothing compared to the all-round effects of that most potent of all modern institutions, the labor market. It was similar in scope to the threat Speenhamland offered, with the significant difference that not the absence but the presence of a competitive labor market was now the source of danger. If Speenhamland had prevented the emergence of a working class, now the laboring poor were being formed into such a class by the pressure of an unfeeling mechanism. If under Speenhamland the people had been taken care of as none too precious beasts deserved to be, now they were expected to take care of themselves, with all the odds against them. If Speenhamland meant the snug misery of degradation, now the laboring man was homeless in society. If Speenhamland had overworked the values of neighborhood, family, and rural surroundings, now man was detached from home and kin, torn from his roots and all meaningful environment. In short, if Speenhamland meant the rot of immobility, now the peril was that of death through exposure.

Not until 1834 was a competitive labor market established in England; hence, industrial capitalism as a social system cannot be said to have existed before that date. Yet almost immediately the self-protection of society set in: factory laws and social legislation, and a political and industrial working class movement sprang into being. It was in this attempt to stave off the entirely new dangers of the market mechanism that protective action conflicted fatally with the self-regulation of the system. It is no exaggeration to say that the social history of the nineteenth century was determined by the logic of the market system proper after it was released by the Poor Law Reform Act of 1834. The starting point of this dynamic was the Speenhamland Law.

If we suggest that the study of Speenhamland is the study of the birth of nineteenth century civilization, it is not its economic and social effect that we have exclusively in mind, nor even the determining influence of these effects upon modern political history, but the fact that, mostly unknown to the present generation, our social consciousness was cast in its mold. The figure of the pauper, almost forgotten since, dominated a discussion the imprint of which was as powerful as that of the most spectacular events in history. If the French Revolution was indebted to the thought of Voltaire and Diderot, Quesnay and Rousseau, the Poor Law discussion formed the minds of Bentham and Burke, Godwin and Malthus, Ricardo and Marx, Robert Owen and John Stuart Mill, Darwin and Spencer, who shared with the French Revolution the spiritual parentage of nineteenth century civilization. It was in the decades following Speenhamland and the Poor Law Reform that the mind of man turned towards his own community with a new anguish of concern: the revolution which the justices of Berkshire had vainly attempted to stem and which the Poor Law Reform eventually freed shifted the vision of men towards their own collective being as if they had overlooked its presence before. A world was uncovered the very existence of which had not been suspected, that of the laws governing a complex society. Although the emergence of society in this new and distinctive sense happened in the economic field, its reference was universal.

The form in which the nascent reality came to our consciousness was political economy. Its amazing regularities and stunning contradictions had to be fitted into the scheme of philosophy and theology in order to be assimilated to human meanings. The stubborn facts and the inexorable brute laws that appeared to abolish our freedom had in one way or another to be reconciled to freedom. This was the mainspring of the metaphysical forces that secretly sustained the positivists and utilitarians. Unbounded hope and limitless despair looking towards unexplored regions of human possibilities were the mind's ambivalent response to these awful limitations. Hope—the vision of perfectibility—was distilled out of the nightmare of population and wage laws, and was embodied in a concept of progress so inspiring that it appeared to justify the vast and painful dislocations to come. Despair was to prove an even more powerful agent of transformation.

Man was forced to resign himself to secular perdition: he was doomed either to stop the procreation of his race or to condemn himself wittingly to liquidation through war and pestilence, hunger and vice. Poverty was nature surviving in society; that the limitedness of food and the unlimitedness of men had come to an issue just when the promise of a boundless increase of wealth burst in upon us made the irony only the more bitter.

Thus was the discovery of society integrated with man's spiritual universe; but how was this new reality, society, to be translated into terms of life? As guides to practice the moral principles of harmony and conflict were strained to the utmost, and forced into a pattern of all but complete contradiction. Harmony was inherent in economy, it was said, the interests of the individual and the community being ultimately identical—but such harmonious self-regulation required that the individual respect economic law even if it happened to destroy him. Conflict, also, seemed inherent in economy, whether as competition of individuals or as struggle of classes—but such conflict, again, might turn out to be only the vehicle of a deeper harmony immanent in present, or perhaps future, society.

Pauperism, political economy, and the discovery of society were closely interwoven. Pauperism fixed attention on the incomprehensible fact that poverty seemed to go with plenty. Yet this was only the first of the baffling paradoxes with which industrial society was to confront modern man. He had entered his new abode through the door of economics, and this adventitious circumstance invested the age with its materialist aura. To Ricardo and Malthus nothing seemed more real than material goods. The laws of the market meant for them the limit of human possibilities. Godwin believed in unlimited possibilities and hence had to deny the laws of the market. That human possibilities were limited, not by the laws of the market, but by those of society itself was a recognition reserved to Owen who alone discerned behind the veil of market economy the emergent reality: society. However, his vision was lost again for a century.

Meanwhile, it was in relation to the problem of poverty that people began to explore the meaning of life in a complex society. The induction of political economy into the realm of the universal happened in two opposite perspectives, that of progress and perfectibility on the one hand, determinism and damnation on the other; its translation into practice was also achieved in two opposite ways, through the principle of harmony and self-regulation on the one hand, competition and conflict on the other. Economic liberalism and the class concept were preformed in these contradictions. With the finality of an elemental event, a new set of ideas entered our consciousness.

8

ANTECEDENTS AND CONSEQUENCES

THE SPEENHAMLAND SYSTEM was originally no more than a makeshift. Yet few institutions have shaped the fate of a whole civilization more decisively than this, which had to be discarded before the new era could begin. It was the typical product of an age of transformation and deserves the attention of any student of human affairs today.

Under the mercantile system the labor organization of England rested on the Poor Law and the Statute of Artificers. Poor Law, as applied to the laws of 1536 to 1601, is admittedly a misnomer; actually these laws, and subsequent amendments, formed half of the labor code of England; the other half consisted of the Statute of Artificers of 1563. The latter dealt with the employed; the Poor Law, with what we would call the unemployed and unemployable (apart from the aged and children). To these measures were added later, as we saw, the Act of Settlement of 1662 concerning the legal abode of the people which restricted their mobility to the utmost. (The neat distinction between employed, unemployed, and unemployable is, of course, anachronistic since it implies the existence of a modern wage system which was absent for another 250 years or so; we use these terms for the sake of simplicity in this very broad presentation.)

Labor organization, according to the Statute of Artificers, rested on three pillars: enforcement of labor, seven years' apprenticeship, and yearly wage assessments by public officials. The law—this should be emphasized—applied to agricultural laborers as much as to artisans, and was enforced in rural districts as well as in towns. For about eighty years the Statute was strictly executed; later the apprenticeship clauses fell partly into desuetude, being restricted to the traditional crafts; to the new industries like cotton they simply did not apply; yearly wage assessments, based on the cost of living, also were in abeyance in a large part of the country after the Restoration (1660). Formally, : assessment clauses of the Statute were repealed only in 1813, the wage clauses in 1814. However, in many respects the apprenticeship rule survived the Statute; it is still the general practice in the skilled trades in England. The enforcement of labor in the countryside was discontinued little by little. Still it can be said that for the two and a half centuries in question the Statute of Artificers laid down the outlines of a national organization of labor based on the principles of regulation and paternalism.

The Statute of Artificers was thus supplemented by the Poor Laws, a most confusing term in modern ears, to which "poor" and "pauper" sound much alike. Actually, the gentlemen of England judged all persons poor who did not command an income sufficient to keep them in leisure. "Poor" was thus practically synonymous with "common people," and the common people comprised all but the landed classes (hardly any successful merchant failed to acquire landed property). Hence the term "poor" meant all people who were in need and all the people, if and when they were in need. This, of course, included paupers, but not them alone. The aged, the infirm, the orphans had to be taken care of in a society which claimed that within its confines there was a place for every Christian. But over and above, there were the able-bodied poor, whom we would call the unemployed, on the assumption that they could earn their living by manual work if only they could find employment. Beggary was severely punished; vagrancy, in case of repetition, was a capital offense. The Poor Law of 1601 decreed that the able-bodied poor should be put to work so as to earn their keep, which the parish was to supply; the burden of relief was put squarely on the parish, which was empowered to raise the necessary sums by local taxes or rates. These were to be levied upon all householders and tenants, rich and nonrich alike, according to the rental of the land or houses they occupied.

The Statute of Artificers and the Poor Law together provided what might be called a Code of Labor. However, the Poor Law was administered locally; every parish—a tiny unit—had its own provisions for setting the able-bodied to work; for maintaining a poorhouse; for apprenticing orphans and destitute children; for caring for the aged and the infirm; for the burial of paupers; and every parish had its own scale of rates. All this sounds grander than it often was; many parishes had no poorhouses; a great many more had no reasonable provisions for the useful occupation of the able-bodied; there was an endless variety of ways in which the sluggardliness of the local ratepayers, the indifference of the overseers of the poor, the callousness of the interests centering on pauperism vitiated the working of the law.

Still, by and large, the nearly sixteen thousand Poor Law authorities of the country managed to keep the social fabric of village life unbroken and undamaged.

Yet under a national system of labor, the local organization of unemployment and poor relief was a patent anomaly. The greater the variety of local provisions for the poor, the greater the danger to the well-kept parish that it would be swamped by the professional pauper. After the Restoration the Act of Settlement and Removal was passed to protect the "better" parishes from the influx of paupers. More than a century later, Adam Smith inveighed against this Act because it immobilized the people, and thus prevented them from finding useful employment as it prevented the capitalist from finding employees. Only with the good will of the local magistrate and the parish authorities could a man stay in any other but his home parish; everywhere else he was liable to expulsion even though in good standing and employed. The legal status of the people was therefore that of freedom and equality subject to incisive limitations. They were equal before the law, and free as to their persons. But they were not free to choose their occupations or those of their children; they were not free to settle where they pleased; and they were forced to labor. The two great Elizabethan Statutes and the Act of Settlement together were a charter of liberty to the common people as well as a seal of their disabilities.

The Industrial Revolution was well on the way, when in 1795, under the pressure of the needs of industry, the Act of 1662 was partially repealed, parish serfdom was abolished, and the physical mobility of the laborer was restored. A labor market could now be established on a national scale. But in the very same year, as we know, a practice of Poor Law administration was introduced which meant the reversal of the Elizabethan principle of enforced labor. Speenhamland ensured the "right to live"; grants in aid-of-wages were made general; family allowances were superadded; and all this was to be given in outdoor relief, *i.e.*, without committing the recipient to the workhouse. Although the scale of relief was exiguous, it was enough for bare subsistence. This was a return to regulationism and paternalism with a vengeance just when, it would seem, the steam engine was clamoring for freedom and the machines were crying out for human hands. Yet the Speenhamland Law coincided in time with the withdrawal of the Act of Settlement. The contradiction was patent: the Act of Settlement was being repealed because the Industrial Revolution demanded a national supply of laborers who would offer to work for wages, while Speenhamland proclaimed the principle that no man need fear to starve and that the parish would keep him and his family however little he earned. There was stark contradiction between the two industrial policies; what else but a social enormity could be expected from their simultaneous continued application?

But the generation of Speenhamland was unconscious of what was on its way. On the eve of the greatest industrial revolution in history, no signs and portents were forthcoming. Capitalism arrived unannounced. No one had forecast the development of a machine industry; it came as a complete surprise. For some time England had been actually expecting a permanent recession of foreign trade when the dam burst, and the old world was swept away in one indomitable surge towards a planetary economy.

However, not until the 1850's could anybody have said so with assurance. The key to the comprehension of the Speenhamland magistrates' recommendation lay in their ignorance of the wider implications of the development they were facing. In the retrospect it may seem as if they had not only attempted the impossible, but had done so by means the inner contradictions of which should have been apparent at the time. Actually, they were successful in achieving their aim of protecting the village against dislocation, while the effects of their policy were all the more disastrous in other, unforeseen directions. Speenhamland policy was the outcome of a definite phase in the development of a market for labor power and should be understood in the light of the views taken of that situation by those in the position to shape policy. From this angle the allowance system will appear as a device contrived by squirearchy to meet a situation in which physical mobility could no longer be denied to labor, while the squire wished to avoid such unsettlement of local conditions, including higher wages, as was involved in the acceptance of a free national labor market.

The dynamic of Speenhamland was thus rooted in the circumstances of its origin. The rise in rural pauperism was the first symptom of the impending upheaval. Yet nobody seemed to have thought so at the time. The connection between rural poverty and the impact of world trade was anything but obvious. Contemporaries had no reason to link the number of the village poor with the development of commerce in the Seven Seas. The inexplicable increase in the number of the poor was almost generally put down to the method of Poor Law administration, and not without some good cause. Actually, beneath the surface, the ominous growth of rural pauperism was directly linked with the trend of general economic history. But this connection was still hardly perceptible. Scores of writers probed into the channels by which the poor trickled into the village, and the number as well as the variety of reasons adduced for their appearance was amazing. And yet only a few contemporary writers pointed to those symptoms of the dislocations which we are used to connect with the Industrial Revolution. Up to 1785 the English public was unaware of any major change in economic life, except for a fitful increase of trade and the growth of pauperism.

Where do the poor come from? was the question raised by a bevy of pamphlets which grew thicker with the advancing century. The causes of pauperism and the means of combating it could hardly be expected to be kept apart in a literature which was inspired by the conviction that if only the most apparent evils of pauperism could be sufficiently alleviated it would cease to exist altogether. On one point there appears to have been general agreement, namely, on the great variety of causes that accounted for the fact of the increase. Amongst them were scarcity of grain; too high agricultural wages, causing high food prices; too low agricultural wages; too high urban wages; irregularity of urban employment; disappearance of the yeomanry; ineptitude of the urban worker for rural occupations; reluctance of the farmers to pay higher wages; the landlords' fear that rents would have to be reduced if higher wages were paid; failure of the workhouse to compete with machinery; want of domestic economy; incommodious habitations; bigoted diets; drug habits. Some writers blamed a new type of large sheep; others, horses which should be replaced by oxen; still others urged the keeping of fewer dogs. Some writers believed that the poor should eat less, or no, bread, while others thought that even feeding on the "best bread should not be charged against them." Tea impaired the health of many poor, it was thought, while "home-brewed beer" would restore it; those who felt most strongly on this score insisted that tea was no better than the cheapest dram. Forty years later Harriet Martineau still believed in preaching the advantages of dropping the tea habit for the sake of relieving pauperism.[1] True, many writers complained of the unsettling effects of enclosures; a number of others insisted on the damage done to rural employment by the ups and downs of manufacturers. Yet on the whole, the impression prevails that pauperism was regarded as a

[1] Martineau, H., *The Hamlet*, 1833.

phenomenon *sui generis*, a social disease which was caused by a variety of reasons, most of which became active only through the failure of the Poor Law to apply the right remedy.

The true answer almost certainly was that the aggravation of pauperism and the higher rates were due to an increase in what we would today call invisible unemployment. Such a fact would not be obvious at a time when even employment was, as a rule, invisible, as it necessarily was up to a point under cottage industry. Still there remain these questions: how to account for this increase in the number of the unemployed and underemployed? and why did the signs of imminent changes in industry escape the notice even of observant contemporaries?

The explanation lies primarily in the excessive fluctuations of trade in early times which tended to cover up the absolute increase in trade. While the latter accounted for the rise in employment, the fluctuations accounted for the much bigger rise in unemployment. But while the increase in the general level of employment was slow, the increase in unemployment and underemployment would tend to be fast. Thus the building up of what Friedrich Engels called the industrial reserve army outweighed by much the creation of the industrial army proper.

This had the important consequence that the connection between unemployment and the rise of total trade could be easily overlooked. While it was often remarked that the rise in unemployment was due to the great fluctuations in trade, it escaped notice that these fluctuations formed part of an underlying process of even greater amplitude, namely, a general growth of commerce increasingly based on manufactures. For the contemporaries, there seemed to be no connection between the mainly urban manufactories and the great increase of the poor in the countryside.

The increase in the aggregate of trade naturally swelled the volume of employment while territorial division of labor combined with sharp fluctuations of trade was responsible for the severe dislocation of both village and town occupations, which resulted in the rapid growth of unemployment. The distant rumor of large wages made the poor dissatisfied with those which agriculture could afford, and it created a dislike for that labor as poorly recompensed. The industrial regions of that age resembled a new country, like another America, attracting immigrants by the thousands. Migration is usually accompanied by a very considerable remigration. That such a reflux towards the village must have taken place seems to find support also in the fact that no absolute decrease of the rural population was noted. Thus a cumulative unsettling of the population was proceeding as different groups were drawn for varying periods into the sphere of commercial and manufactural employment, and then left to drift back to their original rural habitat.

Much of the social damage done to England's countryside sprang at first from the dislocating effects of trade directly upon the countryside itself. The Revolution in Agriculture definitely antedated the Industrial Revolution. Both enclosures of the common and consolidations into compact holdings, which accompanied the new great advance in agricultural methods, had a powerfully unsettling effect. The war on cottages, the absorption of cottage gardens and grounds, the confiscation of rights in the common deprived cottage industry of its two mainstays: family earnings and agricultural background. As long as domestic industry was supplemented by the facilities and amenities of a garden plot, a scrap of land, or grazing rights, the dependence of the laborer on money earnings was not absolute; the potato plot or "stubbing geese," a cow or even an ass in the commons made all the difference; and family earnings acted as a kind of unemployment insurance. The rationalization of agriculture inevitably uprooted the laborer and undermined his social security.

On the urban scene the effects of the new scourge of fluctuating employment were, of course, manifest. Industry was generally regarded as a blind alley occupation. "Workmen who are today fully employed may be tomorrow in the streets begging for bread . . . ," wrote David Davies and added: "Uncertainty of labor conditions is the most vicious result of these new innovations." "When a Town employed in a Manufactory is deprived of it, the inhabitants are as it were struck with a palsy, and become instantly a rent-charge upon the Parish; but the mischief does not die with that generation . . ." For in the meantime division of labor wreaks its vengeance: the unemployed artisan returns in vain to his village for "the weaver can turn his hand to nothing." The fatal irreversibility of urbanization hinged upon this simple fact which Adam Smith foresaw when he described the industrial worker as intellectually the inferior of the poorest tiller of the soil, for the latter can usually take himself to any job. Still, up to the time Adam Smith published his *Wealth of Nations* pauperism was not increasing alarmingly.

In the next two decades the picture suddenly changed. In his *Thoughts & Details on Scarcity*, which Burke submitted to Pitt in

1795, the author admitted that in spite of the general progress there had been a "last bad cycle of twenty years." Indeed, in the decade following upon the Seven Years' War (1763) unemployment increased noticeably, as the rise in outdoor relief showed. It happened for the first time that a boom in trade was remarked to have been accompanied by signs of growing distress of the poor. This apparent contradiction was destined to become to the next generation of Western humanity the most perplexing of all the recurrent phenomena in social life. The specter of overpopulation was beginning to haunt people's minds. William Townsend warned in his *Dissertation on the Poor Laws:* "Speculation apart, it is a fact, that in England, we have more than we can feed, and many more than we can profitably employ under the present system of law." Adam Smith, in 1776, had been reflecting the mood of quiet progress. Townsend, writing only ten years later, was already conscious of a groundswell.

However, many things had to happen before (only five years later) a man as removed from politics, as successful, and as matter-of-fact as the Scotch bridgebuilder, Telford, could burst forth with the bitter complaint that little change is to be expected from the ordinary course of government, and that revolution was the only hope. A single copy of Paine's *Rights of Man* mailed by Telford to his home village caused a riot to break out there. Paris was catalyzing the European fermentation.

In Canning's conviction the Poor Law saved England from a revolution. He was primarily thinking of the 1790's and the French Wars. The new outburst of enclosures further depressed the standards of the poor in the countryside. J. H. Clapham, an apologist of these enclosures, conceded that the "coincidence of the area in which wages were most systematically augmented from the rates with the area of maximum recent enclosures is striking." In other words, but for aid-in-wages the poor would have sunk below the starvation level in wide areas of rural England. Rick burning was rampant. The Popgun Plot found wide credence. Rioting was frequent; rumors of rioting very much more so. In Hampshire—and not there alone—the Courts threatened death for any attempt at "forcibly lowering the price of commodities, either at market or on the road"; yet simultaneously, the magistrates of that same county urgently pressed for the general granting of subsidies to wages. Clearly, the time for preventive action had come.

But why, of all courses of action, was that one chosen which appeared later as the most impracticable of all? Let us consider the situation and the interests involved. Squire and parson ruled the village. Townsend summed up the situation by saying that the landed gentleman keeps manufactures "at a convenient distance" because "he considers that manufactures fluctuate; that the benefit which he is to derive from them will not bear proportion with the burthen which it must entail upon his property. . . ." The burden consisted mainly in two seemingly contradictory effects of manufactures, namely, the increase in pauperism and the rise in wages. But the two were contradictory only if the existence of a competitive labor market was assumed, which would, of course, have tended to diminish unemployment by reducing the wages of the employed. In the absence of such a market—and the Act of Settlement was still in force—pauperism and wages might rise simultaneously. Under such conditions the "social cost" of urban unemployment was mainly borne by the home village to which the out-of-work would often repair. High wages in the towns were a still greater burden on rural economy. Agricultural wages were more than the farmer could carry, though less than the laborer could subsist on. It seems clear that agriculture could not compete with town wages. On the other hand, there was general agreement that the Act of Settlement should be repealed, or at least loosened, so as to help labor to find employment and the employers to find laborers. This, it was felt, would increase the productivity of labor all around and, incidentally, diminish the real burden of wages. But the immediate question of the wage differential between town and village would obviously become even more pressing for the village by allowing wages to "find their own level." The flux and reflux of industrial employment alternating with spasms of unemployment would dislocate rural communities more than ever. A dam had to be erected to protect the village from the flood of rising wages. Methods had to be found which would protect the rural setting against social dislocation, reinforce traditional authority, prevent the draining off of rural labor, and raise agricultural wages without overburdening the farmer. Such a device was the Speenhamland Law. Shoved into the turbulent waters of the Industrial Revolution, it was bound to create an economic vortex. However, its social implications met squarely the situation, as it was judged by the ruling village interest—the squire's.

From the point of view of Poor Law administration Speenhamland was a grievously retrogressive step. The experience of 250 years had shown that the parish was too small a unit for Poor Law administration, since no treatment of this matter was adequate which failed to distinguish between the able-bodied unemployed on the one hand, the aged, infirm, and children on the other. It was as if a township today attempted to deal singlehanded with unemployment insurance, or as if such an insurance were mixed up with the care for the aged. Accordingly, only in those short periods, when the administration of the Poor Law was both *national* and *differentiated* could it be more or less satisfactory. Such a period was that from 1590 to 1640, under Burleigh and Laud, when the Crown handled the Poor Law through the justices of peace, and an ambitious scheme of erecting poorhouses, together with the enforcement of labor, was initiated. But the Commonwealth (1642–60) destroyed again what was now denounced as the personal rule of the Crown, and the Restoration, ironically enough, completed the work of the Commonwealth. The Act of Settlement of 1662 restricted the Poor Law to the parish basis, and legislation paid but scant attention to pauperism up to the third decade of the eighteenth century. In 1722, at last, efforts at differentiation set in; workhouses were to be built by unions of parishes, as distinct from local poorhouses; and occasional outdoor relief was permitted, as the workhouse would now provide a test of need. In 1782, with Gilbert's Act, a long step was taken to expand the units of administration by encouraging the setting up of parish unions; at that time it was urged that parishes find employment for the able-bodied in the neighborhood. Such a policy was to be supplemented by the granting of outdoor relief and even of aid-in-wages, in order to diminish the cost of relief to the able-bodied. Although the setting up of unions of parishes was permissive, not mandatory, it meant an advance toward the larger unit of administration and the differentiation of the various categories of the relieved poor. Thus in spite of the deficiencies of the system, Gilbert's Act represented an attempt in the right direction, and as long as outdoor relief and aid-in-wages were merely subsidiary to positive social legislation, they need not have been fatal to a rational solution. Speenhamland put a stop to reform. By making outdoor relief and aid-in-wages *general,* it did not (as has been falsely asserted) follow up the line of Gilbert's Act, but completely reversed its tendency and actually demolished the whole system of the Elizabethan Poor Law. The laboriously established distinction between workhouse and poorhouse became meaningless; the various categories of paupers and able-bodied unemployed now tended to fuse into one indiscriminate mass of dependent poverty. The opposite of a process of differentiation set in: the workhouse merged into the poorhouse, the poorhouse itself tended more and more to disappear; and the parish was again made the sole and final unit in this veritable masterpiece of institutional degeneration.

The supremacy of squire and parson was even enhanced in consequence of Speenhamland, if such a thing was at all possible. The "undistinguishing benevolence of power," of which the overseers of the poor complained, was at its best in that role of "Tory socialism" in which the justices of peace swayed the benevolent power, while the brunt of the rates was borne by the rural middle class. The bulk of yeomanry had long vanished in the vicissitudes of the Agricultural Revolution, and the remaining lifeholders and occupying-proprietors tended to merge with the cottagers and scrap-holders into one social stratum in the eyes of the potentate of the countryside. He did not too well distinguish between needy people, and people who happened to be in need; from the lofty heights from which he was watching the struggling life of the village there seemed to be no hard and fast line separating the poor from the destitute, and he may have been not unduly surprised to learn in a bad year that a small farmer was going "on the rates," after having been ruined by their disastrous level. Surely such cases were not frequent, but their very possibility emphasized the fact that many ratepayers were themselves poor. On the whole, the relationship of the ratepayer and the pauper was somewhat similar to that of the employed and the unemployed of our times under various schemes of insurance which make the employed bear the burden of keeping the temporarily unemployed. Still, the typical ratepayer was usually not eligible for poor relief, and the typical agricultural laborer paid no rates. Politically, the squire's pull with the village poor was strengthened by Speenhamland while that of the rural middle class was weakened.

The craziest aspect of the system was its economics proper. The question "Who paid for Speenhamland?" was practically unanswerable. Directly, the main burden fell, of course, on the ratepayers. But the farmers were partly compensated by the low wages they had to pay their laborers—a direct result of the Speenhamland system. Moreover, the farmer was frequently remitted a part of his rates, if he was willing to employ a villager who would otherwise fall on the rates. The consequent overcrowding of the farmer's kitchen and yard with unnecessary hands, some of them not too keen performers, had to be set down on the debit side. The labor of those who were actually on the rates was to be had even more cheaply. They had often to work as "roundsmen" at alternating places, being paid only their food, or being put up for auction in the village "pound," for a few pence a day. How much this kind of indented labor was worth is another question. To top it all, aids-in-rent were sometimes allowed to the poor, while the unscrupulous proprietor of the cottages made money by rack-renting the unsanitary habitations; the village authorities were likely to close an eye as long as the rates for the hovels continued to be turned in. That such a tangle of interests would undermine any sense of financial responsibility and encourage every kind of petty corruption is evident.

Still, in a broader sense, Speenhamland paid. It was started as aid-in-wages, ostensibly benefiting the employees, but actually using public means to subsidize the employers. For the main effect of the allowance system was to depress wages below the subsistence level. In the thoroughly pauperized areas, farmers did not care to employ agricultural laborers who still owned a scrap of land, "because none with property was eligible for parish relief and the standard wage was so low that, without relief of some sort, it was insufficient for a married man." Consequently, in some areas only those people who were on the rates had a chance of employment; those who tried to keep off the rates and earn a living by their own exertions were hardly able to secure a job. Yet in the country at large the great majority must have been of the latter sort and on each of them employers as a class made an extra profit since they benefited from the lowness of wages, without having to make up for it from the rates. In the long run, a system as uneconomical as that was bound to affect the productivity of labor and to depress standard wages, and ultimately even the "scale" set by the magistrates for the benefit of the poor. By the 1820's the scale of bread was actually being whittled down in various counties, and the wretched incomes of the poor were reduced even further. Between 1815 and 1830 the Speenhamland scale, which was fairly equal all over the country, was reduced by almost one-third (this fall also was practically universal). Clapham doubts whether the total burden of the rates was as severe as the rather sudden outburst of complaints would have made one believe. Rightly. For although the rise in the rates was spectacular and in some regions must have been felt as a calamity, it seems most probable that it was not so much the burden itself as rather the economic effect of aid-in-wages on the productivity of labor that was at the root of the trouble. Southern England, which was most sorely hit, paid out in poor rates not quite 3.3 per cent of its income— a very tolerable charge, Clapham thought, in view of the fact that a considerable part of this sum "ought to have gone to the poor in wages." Actually, total rates were falling steadily in the 1830's, and their relative burden must have even more quickly decreased in view of the growing national welfare. In 1818 the sums actually spent on the relief of the poor totaled near eight million pounds; they fell almost continuously until they were less than six million in 1826, while national income was rising rapidly. And yet the criticism of Speenhamland became more and more violent owing to the fact, so it appears, that the dehumanization of the masses began to paralyze national life, and notably to constrain the energies of industry itself.

Speenhamland precipitated a social catastrophe. We have become accustomed to discount the lurid presentations of early capitalism as "sob-stuff." For this there is no justification. The picture drawn by Harriet Martineau, the perfervid apostle of Poor Law Reform, coincides with that of the Chartist propagandists who were leading the outcry against the Poor Law Reform. The facts set out in the famous Report of the Commission on the Poor Law (1834), advocating the immediate repeal of the Speenhamland Law, could have served as the material for Dickens' campaign against the Commission's policy. Neither Charles Kingsley nor Friedrich Engels, neither Blake nor Carlyle, was mistaken in believing that the very image of man had been defiled by some terrible catastrophe. And more impressive even than the outbursts of pain and anger that came from poets and philanthropists was the icy silence with which Malthus and Ricardo passed over the scenes out of which their philosophy of secular perdition was born.

Undoubtedly, the social dislocation caused by the machine and the circumstances under which man was now condemned to serve it had many results that were unavoidable. England's rural civilization was lacking in those urban surroundings out of which the later industrial towns of the Continent grew.[2] There was in the new towns no settled urban middle class, no such nucleus of artisans and craftsmen, of respectable petty bourgeois and townspeople as could have served as an assimilating medium for the crude laborer who—attracted by high

---

[2] Professor Usher puts the date of the beginning of general urbanization about 1795.

wages or chased from the land by tricky enclosers—was drudging in the early mills. The industrial town of the Midlands and the North West was a cultural wasteland; its slums merely reflected its lack of tradition and civic self-respect. Dumped into this bleak slough of misery, the immigrant peasant, or even the former yeoman or copyholder was soon transformed into a nondescript animal of the mire. It was not that he was paid too little, or even that he labored too long—though either happened often to excess—but that he was now existing under physical conditions which denied the human shape of life. Negroes of the African forest who found themselves caged, panting for air in the hull of a slave trader might have felt as these people felt. And yet all this was not irremediable. As long as a man had a status to hold on to, a pattern set by his kin or fellows, he could fight for it, and regain his soul. But in the case of the laborer this could happen only in one way: by his constituting himself the member of a new class. Unless he was able to make a living by his own labor, he was not a worker but a pauper. To reduce him artificially to such a condition was the supreme abomination of Speenhamland. This act of an ambiguous humanitarianism prevented laborers from constituting themselves an economic class and thus deprived them of the only means of staving off the fate to which they were doomed in the economic mill.

Speenhamland was an unfailing instrument of popular demoralization. If a human society is a self-acting machine for maintaining the standards on which it is built, Speenhamland was an automaton for demolishing the standards on which any kind of society could be based. Not only did it put a premium on the shirking of work and the pretense of inadequacy, but it increased the attraction of pauperism precisely at the juncture when a man was straining to escape the fate of the destitute. Once a man was in the poorhouse (he would usually land there if he and his family had been for some time on the rates) he was trapped, and could rarely leave it. The decencies and self-respect of centuries of settled life wore off quickly in the promiscuity of the poorhouse, where a man had to be cautious not to be thought better off than his neighbor, lest he be forced to start out on the hunt for work, instead of "boon-doggling" in the familiar fold. "The poor-rate had become public spoil. . . . To obtain their share the brutal bullied the administrators, the profligate exhibited their bastards which must be fed, the idle folded their arms and waited till they got it; ignorant boys and girls married upon it; poachers, thieves and prostitutes extorted it by intimidation; country justices lavished it for popularity, and Guardians for convenience. This was the way the fund went. . . ." "Instead of the proper number of laborers to till his land—laborers paid by himself—the farmer was compelled to take double the number, whose wages were paid partly out of the rates; and these men, being employed by compulsion on him, were beyond his control—worked or not as they chose—let down the quality of his land, and disabled him from employing the better men who would have toiled hard for independence. These better men sank down amongst the worst; the rate paying cottager, after a vain struggle, went to the pay table to seek relief. . . ." Thus Harriet Martineau.[3] Bashful later-day liberals ungratefully neglected the memory of this outspoken apostle of their creed. Yet even her exaggerations, which they now feared, put the highlights in the right place. She herself belonged to that struggling middle class, whose genteel poverty made them only the more sensitive to the moral intricacies of the Poor Law. She understood and clearly expressed the need of society for a new class, a class of "independent laborers." They were the heroes of her dreams, and she makes one of them—a chronically unemployed laborer who refuses to go on relief—say proudly to a colleague who decides to go on the rates: "Here I stand, and defy anybody to despise me. I could set my children into the middle of the church aisle and dare anyone to taunt at them about the place they hold in society. There may be some wiser; there may be many richer; but there are none more honorable." The big men of the ruling class were still far from comprehending the need for this new class. Miss Martineau pointed to "the vulgar error of the aristocracy, of supposing only one class of society to exist below that wealthy one with which they are compelled by their affairs to have business." Lord Eldon, she complained, like others who must know better, "included under one head ['the lower classes'] everybody below the wealthiest bankers—manufacturers, tradesmen, artisans, laborers and paupers. . . ."[4] But it was the distinction between these last two, she passionately insisted, that the future of society depended upon. "Except the distinction between sovereign and subject, there is no social difference in England so wide as that between the independent laborer and the pauper; and it is equally ignorant, immoral, and impolitic to confound the two," she

[3] Martineau, H., *History of England During the Thirty Years' Peace* (1816–1846), 1849.

[4] Martineau, H., *The Parish*, 1833.

wrote. This, of course, was hardly a statement of fact; the difference between the two strata had become nonexistent under Speenhamland. Rather it was a statement of policy based upon a prophetic anticipation. The policy was that of the Poor Law Reform Commissioners; the prophecy looked to a free competitive labor market, and the consequent emergence of an industrial proletariat. The abolishment of Speenhamland was the true birthday of the modern working class, whose immediate self-interest destined them to become the protectors of society against the intrinsic dangers of a machine civilization. But whatever the future had in store for them, working class and market economy appeared in history together. The hatred of public relief, the distrust of state action, the insistence on respectability and self-reliance, remained for generations characteristics of the British worker.

The repeal of Speenhamland was the work of a new class entering on the historical scene, the middle classes of England. Squirearchy could not do the job these classes were destined to perform: the transformation of society into a market economy. Dozens of laws were repealed and others enacted before that transformation was on the way. The Parliamentary Reform Bill of 1832 disfranchised the rotten boroughs and gave power in the Commons once and for all to commoners. Their first great act of reform was the abolishing of Speenhamland. Now that we realize the degree to which its paternalist methods were merged with the life of the country, we will understand why even the most radical supporters of reform hesitated to suggest a shorter period than ten or fifteen years for the transition. Actually, it took place with an abruptness which makes nonsense of the legend of English gradualism fostered at a later time when arguments against radical reform were sought. The brutal shock of that event haunted for generations the daydreams of the British working class. And yet the success of this lacerating operation was due to the deep-seated convictions of the broad strata of the population, including the laborers themselves, that the system which to all appearances supported them was in truth despoiling them, and that the "right to live" was the sickness unto death.

The new law provided that in the future no outdoor relief should be given. Its administration was national and differentiated. In this respect also it was a thoroughgoing reform. Aid-in-wages was, of course, discontinued. The workhouse test was reintroduced, but in a new sense. It was now left to the applicant to decide whether he was so utterly destitute of all means that he would voluntarily repair to a shelter which was deliberately made into a place of horror. The workhouse was invested with a stigma; and staying in it was made a psychological and moral torture, while complying with the requirements of hygiene and decency—indeed, ingeniously using them as a pretense for further deprivations. Not the justices of peace, nor local overseers, but wider authorities—the guardians—were to administer the law under dictatorial central supervision. The very burial of a pauper was made an act by which his fellow men renounced solidarity with him even in death.

In 1834 industrial capitalism was ready to be started, and Poor Law Reform was ushered in. The Speenhamland Law which had sheltered rural England, and thereby the laboring population in general, from the full force of the market mechanism was eating into the marrow of society. By the time of its repeal huge masses of the laboring population resembled more the specters that might haunt a nightmare than human beings. But if the workers were physically dehumanized, the owning classes were morally degraded. The traditional unity of a Christian society was giving place to a denial of responsibility on the part of the well-to-do for the conditions of their fellows. The Two Nations were taking shape. To the bewilderment of thinking minds, unheard-of wealth turned out to be inseparable from unheard-of poverty. Scholars proclaimed in unison that a science had been discovered which put the laws governing man's world beyond any doubt. It was at the behest of these laws that compassion was removed from the hearts, and a stoic determination to renounce human solidarity in the name of the greatest happiness of the greatest number gained the dignity of secular religion.

The mechanism of the market was asserting itself and clamoring for its completion: human labor had to be made a commodity. Reactionary paternalism had in vain tried to resist this necessity. Out of the horrors of Speenhamland men rushed blindly for the shelter of a utopian market economy.

9

PAUPERISM AND UTOPIA

THE PROBLEM of poverty centered around two closely related subjects: pauperism and political economy. Though we will deal with their impact on modern consciousness separately, they formed part of one indivisible whole: the discovery of society.

Up to the time of Speenhamland no satisfactory answer could be found to the question of where the poor come from. It was, however, generally agreed among eighteenth century thinkers that pauperism and progress were inseparable. The greatest number of poor is not to be found in barren countries or amidst barbarous nations, but in those which are the most fertile and the most civilized, wrote John M'Farlane, in 1782. Giammaria Ortes, the Italian economist, pronounced it an axiom that the wealth of a nation corresponds with its population; and its misery corresponds with its wealth (1774). And even Adam Smith in his cautious manner declared that it is not in the richest countries that the wages of labor are highest. M'Farlane was not, therefore, venturing an unusual view when he expressed his belief that as England had now approached the meridian of her greatness, the "number of poor will continue to increase." [1]

Again, for an Englishman to forecast commercial stagnation was merely to echo a widely held opinion. If the rise in exports during the half century preceding 1782 was striking, the ups and downs of trade were even more so. Trade was just starting to recover from a slump which had reduced export figures to the level of almost half a century before. To contemporaries the great expansion of trade and apparent growth of national prosperity which followed upon the Seven Years' War merely signified that England too had had her chance after Portugal, Spain, Holland, and France. Her steep rise was now a matter of the past, and there was no reason to believe in the con-

[1] M'Farlane, J., *Enquiries Concerning the Poor*, 1782. Cf. also Postlethwayt's editorial remark in the Universal Dictionary of 1757 on the Dutch Poor Law of 7th October, 1531.

tinuance of her progress, which seemed merely the result of a lucky war. Almost unanimously, as we saw, a falling off of trade was expected.

In actual fact, prosperity was just round the corner, a prosperity of gigantic proportions which was destined to become a new form of life not for one nation alone but for the whole of mankind. But neither statesmen nor economists had the slightest intimation of its oncoming. As for the statesmen, this may have been a matter of indifference, as for another two generations the rocketing trade figures only dented the edge of popular misery. But in the case of the economists it was singularly unfortunate as their whole theoretical system was erected during this spate of "abnormalcy," when a tremendous rise in trade and production happened to be accompanied by an enormous increase in human misery—in effect, the apparent facts on which the principles of Malthus, Ricardo, and James Mill were grounded reflected merely paradoxical tendencies prevailing during a sharply defined period of transition.

The situation was indeed puzzling. It was in the first half of the sixteenth century that the poor first appeared in England; they became conspicuous as individuals unattached to the manor, "or to any feudal superior" and their gradual transformation into a class of free laborers was the combined result of the fierce persecution of vagrancy and the fostering of domestic industry which was powerfully helped by a continuous expansion of foreign trade. During the course of the seventeenth century there was less mention of pauperism, even the incisive measure of the Act of Settlement was passed without public discussion. When by the end of the century discussion revived, Thomas More's *Utopia* and the early Poor Laws were more than 150 years old, the dissolution of the monasteries and Kett's Rebellion were long forgotten. Some enclosing and "engrossing" had been going on all the time, for example, during the reign of Charles I, but the new classes as a whole had become settled. Also while the poor in the middle of the sixteenth century were a danger to society, on which they descended like hostile armies, at the end of the seventeenth century the poor were merely a burden on the rates. On the other hand, this was no more a semifeudal society but a semicommercial one, the representative members of which were favoring work for its own sake, and could accept neither the medieval view that poverty was no problem, nor that of the successful encloser that the unemployed were merely able-bodied idlers. From this time onward, opinions about pauperism began to reflect philosophical outlook, very much as theological questions had before. Views on the poor mirrored more and more views on existence as a whole. Hence, the variety and seeming confusion in these views, but also their paramount interest to the history of our civilization.

The Quakers, these pioneers in the exploration of the possibilities of modern existence, were the first to recognize that involuntary unemployment must be the outcome of some defect in the organization of labor. With their strong faith in businesslike methods they applied to the poor amongst themselves that principle of collective self-help which they occasionally practiced as conscientious objectors when wishing to avoid supporting the authorities by paying for their keep in prison. Lawson, a zealous Quaker, published an *Appeal to the Parliament concerning the Poor that there be no beggar in England* as a "Platforme," in which he suggested the establishment of Labor Exchanges in the modern sense of the public employment agency. This was in 1660; an "Office of Addresses and Encounters" had been proposed ten years before by Henry Robinson. But the Restoration government favored more pedestrian methods; the tendency of the Act of Settlement in 1662 was directly contrary to any rational system of labor exchanges, which would have created a wider market for labor; settlement—a term used for the first time in the Act—bound labor to the parish.

After the Glorious Revolution (1688), Quaker philosophy produced in John Bellers a veritable prognosticator of the trend of social ideas of the distant future. It was out of the atmosphere of the Meetings of Sufferings, in which statistics were now often used to give scientific precision to religious policies of relief, that, in 1696, his suggestion for the establishment of "Colleges of Industry" was born, in which the involuntary leisure of the poor could be turned to good account. Not the principles of a Labor Exchange, but the very different ones of exchange of labor underlay this scheme. The former was associated with the conventional idea of finding an employer for the unemployed; the latter implied no less than that laborers need no employer as long as they can exchange their products directly. "The labor of the poor being the mines of the rich," as Bellers said, why should they not be able to support themselves by exploiting those riches for their own benefit, leaving even something over? All that was needed was to organize them in a "College" or corporation, where they could pool their efforts. This was at the heart of all later socialist thought on the subject of poverty, whether it took the form of Owen's

Villages of Union, Fourier's *Phalanstères,* Proudhon's Banks of Exchange, Louis Blanc's *Ateliers Nationaux,* Lassalle's *Nationale Werkstätten,* or for that matter, Stalin's Five-Year Plans. Bellers' book contained *in nuce* most of the proposals that have been connected with the solution of this problem ever since the first appearance of those great dislocations that the machine produced in modern society. "This college-fellowship will make labor and not money, the standard to value all necessaries by. . . ." It was planned as "a College of all sorts of useful trades that shall work for one another without relief. . . ." The linking of labor-notes, self-help, and cooperation is significant. The laborers, to the number of three hundred, were to be self-supporting, and work in common for their bare existence, "what any doth more, to be paid for it." Thus subsistence rations and payment according to results were to be combined. In the case of some minor experiments of self-help the financial surplus had gone to the Meeting of Sufferings and was spent for the benefit of other members of the religious community. This surplus was destined to have a great future; the novel idea of profits was the panacea of the age. Bellers' national scheme for the relief of unemployment was actually to be run for profit by capitalists! In the same year, 1696, John Cary promoted the Bristol Corporation for the Poor, which, after some initial success failed to yield profits as did, ultimately, all other ventures of the kind. Yet Bellers' proposal was built on the same assumption as John Locke's labor-rate system, put forward also in 1696, according to which the village poor should be allocated to the local ratepayers for work, in the proportion in which these latter were contributing to the rates. This was the origin of the ill-starred system of roundsmen practiced under Gilbert's Act. The idea that pauperism could be made to pay had firmly gripped people's minds.

It was exactly a century later that Jeremy Bentham, the most prolific of all social projectors, formed the plan of using paupers on a large scale to run machinery devised by his even more inventive brother, Samuel, for the working of wood and metal. "Bentham," says Sir Leslie Stephen, "had joined his brother and they were looking out for a steam engine. It had now occurred to them to employ convicts instead of steam." This was in 1794; Jeremy Bentham's Panopticon plan with the help of which gaols could be designed so as to be cheaply and effectively supervised had been in existence for a couple of years, and he now decided to apply it to his convict-run factory; the place of the convicts was to be taken by the poor. Presently the

Bentham brothers' private business venture merged into a general scheme of solving the social problem as a whole. The decision of the Speenhamland magistrates, Whitbread's minimum wage proposal, and, above all, Pitt's privately circulated draft of a comprehensive Bill for the reform of the Poor Law made pauperism a topic among statesmen. Bentham, whose criticism of Pitt's Bill was supposed to have brought about its withdrawal, now came forward in Arthur Young's *Annals* with elaborate proposals of his own (1797). His Industry-Houses, on the Panopticon plan—five storeys in twelve sectors—for the exploitation of the labor of the assisted poor were to be ruled by a central board set up in the capital and modeled on the Bank of England's Board, all members with shares worth five or ten pounds having a vote. A text published a few years later ran: "(1) The management of the concerns of the poor throughout South Britain to be vested in *one* authority, and the expense to be charged upon *one* fund. (2) This Authority, that of a *Joint-Stock Company* under some such name as that of the *National Charity Company*."[2] No less than 250 Industry-Houses were to be erected, with approximately 500,000 inmates. The plan was accompanied by a detailed analysis of the various categories of unemployed, in which Bentham anticipated by more than a century the results of other investigators in this field. His classifying mind showed its capacity for realism at its best. "Out of place hands" who had been recently dismissed from jobs were distinguished from such as could not find employment on account of "casual-stagnation"; "periodical stagnation" of seasonal workers was distinguished from "superseded hands," such as had been "rendered superfluous by the introduction of machinery" or, in even more modern terms, from the technologically unemployed; a last group consisted of "disbanded hands," another modern category brought into prominence, in Bentham's time, by the French war. The most significant category, however, was that of "casual-stagnation," mentioned above, which included not only craftsmen and artists exercising occupations "dependent upon fashion" but also the much more important group of those unemployed "in the event of a general stagnation of manufactures." Bentham's plan amounted to no less than the leveling out of the business cycle through the commercialization of unemployment on a gigantic scale.

Robert Owen, in 1819, republished Bellers' more than 120-year-old plans for the setting up of Colleges of Industry. Sporadic destitution

[2] Bentham, J., *Pauper Management*. First published 1797.

had now grown into a torrent of misery. His own Villages of Union differed from Bellers' mainly by being much larger, comprising 1,200 persons on as many acres of land. The committee calling for subscriptions to this highly experimental plan to solve the problem of unemployment included no less an authority than David Ricardo. But no subscribers appeared. Somewhat later, the Frenchman Charles Fourier was ridiculed for expecting day by day the sleeping-partner to turn up who would invest in his *Phalanstère* plan, which was based on ideas very similar to those sponsored by one of the greatest contemporary experts on finance. And had not Robert Owen's firm in New Lanark—with Jeremy Bentham as a sleeping-partner—become world-famous through the financial success of its philanthropic schemes? There was yet no standard view of poverty nor any accepted way of making profits out of the poor.

Owen took over from Bellers the labor-notes idea and applied it in his National Equitable Labor Exchange in 1832; it failed. The closely related principle of the economic self-sufficiency of the laboring class—also an idea of Bellers—was at the back of the famous Trades-Union movement in the next two years. The Trades-Union was a general association of all trades, crafts, and arts, not excluding small masters, with the vague purpose of constituting them the body of society, in one peaceful manifestation. Who would have thought that this was the embryo of all violent One Big Union attempts for a hundred years to come? Syndicalism, capitalism, socialism, and anarchism were indeed almost indistinguishable in their plans for the poor. Proudhon's Bank of Exchange, the first practical exploit of philosophical anarchism, in 1848, was, essentially, an outgrowth of Owen's experiment. Marx, the state-socialist, sharply assailed Proudhon's ideas and henceforth it was the state that would be called upon to supply the capital for collectivist schemes of this type, of which Louis Blanc's and Lassalle's went down to history.

The economic reason why no money could be made out of the paupers should have been no mystery. It was given almost 150 years before by Daniel Defoe whose pamphlet, published in 1704, stalled the discussion started by Bellers and Locke. Defoe insisted that if the poor were relieved, they would not work for wages; and that if they were put to manufacturing goods in public institutions, they would merely create more unemployment in private manufactures. His pamphlet bore the satanistic title: *Giving Alms no Charity and employing the Poor a Grievance to the Nation,* and was followed by

Doctor Mandeville's more famous doggerels about the sophisticated bees whose community was prosperous only because it encouraged vanity and envy, vice and waste. But while the whimsical doctor indulged in a shallow moral paradox, the pamphleteer had hit upon basic elements of the new political economy. His essay was soon forgotten outside the circles of "inferior politics," as problems of policing were called in the eighteenth century, while Mandeville's cheap paradox exercised minds of the quality of a Berkeley, Hume, and Smith. Evidently, in the first half of the eighteenth century mobile wealth was still a moral issue, while poverty was not yet one. The Puritan classes were shocked by the feudal forms of conspicuous waste which their conscience condemned as luxury and vice, while they had reluctantly to agree with Mandeville's bees that but for those evils commerce and trade would quickly decay. Later these wealthy merchants were to be reassured about the morality of business: the new cotton mills did not cater any more to idle ostentation but to drab daily needs, and subtle forms of waste developed which pretended to be less conspicuous while managing to be even more wasteful than the old. Defoe's jibe at the perils of relieving the poor was not topical enough to penetrate consciences preoccupied with the moral dangers of wealth; the Industrial Revolution was still to come. And yet, as far as it went, Defoe's paradox was a forecast of the perplexities to come: "Giving alms no charity"—for in taking away the edge of hunger one hindered production and merely created famine; "employing the poor, a grievance to the nation"—for by creating public employment one merely increased the glut of the goods on the market and hastened the ruin of private traders. Between John Bellers, the Quaker, and Daniel Defoe, the time-serving journalist, between saint and cynic, somewhere around the turn of the seventeenth century, the issues were raised to which more than two centuries of work and thought, hope and suffering, were to provide the laborious solutions.

But at the time of Speenhamland the true nature of pauperism was still hidden from the minds of men. There was complete agreement on the desirability of a large population, as large as possible, since the power of the state consisted in men. There was also ready agreement on the advantages of cheap labor, since only if labor were cheap could manufactures flourish. Moreover, but for the poor, who would man the ships and go to the wars? Yet, there was doubt whether pauperism was not an evil after all. And in any case, why should not paupers be as profitably employed for public profit as they obviously were for private profit? No convincing answer to these questions could be given. Defoe had chanced upon the truth which seventy years later Adam Smith may or may not have comprehended; the undeveloped condition of the market system concealed its inherent weaknesses. Neither the new wealth nor the new poverty was yet quite comprehensible.

That the question was in its chrysalid stage was shown by the amazing congruence of the projects reflecting minds as different as those of the Quaker Bellers, the atheist Owen, and the utilitarian Bentham. Owen, a socialist, was an ardent believer in the equality of man and his inborn rights; while Bentham despised equalitarianism, ridiculed the rights of man and bent heavily towards *laissez-faire*. Yet Owen's "parallelograms" resembled Bentham's Industry-Houses so closely that one might imagine he was solely inspired by them until his indebtedness to Bellers is remembered. All three men were convinced that an appropriate organization of the labor of the unemployed must produce a surplus, which Bellers, the humanitarian, hoped to use primarily for the relief of other sufferers; Bentham, the utilitarian liberal, wanted to turn over to the shareholders; Owen, the socialist, wished to return to the unemployed themselves. But while their differences merely revealed the almost imperceptible signs of future rifts, their common illusions disclosed the same radical misunderstanding of the nature of pauperism in the nascent market economy. More important than all other differences between them, there had been meanwhile a continuous growth in the number of the poor: in 1696, when Bellers wrote, total rates approximated 400,000 pounds; in 1796, when Bentham struck out against Pitt's bill, they must have passed the 2 million mark; by 1818, Robert Owen's beginnings, they were nearing 8 million. In the 120 years that elapsed between Bellers and Owen the population may have trebled, but rates increased twentyfold. Pauperism had become a portent. But its meaning was still anybody's guess.

10

POLITICAL ECONOMY AND THE DISCOVERY OF SOCIETY

WHEN THE SIGNIFICANCE of poverty was realized, the stage was set for the nineteenth century. The watershed lay somewhere around 1780. In Adam Smith's great work poor relief was no problem as yet; only a decade later it was raised as a broad issue in Townsend's *Dissertation on the Poor Laws* and never ceased to occupy men's minds for another century and a half.

The change of atmosphere from Adam Smith to Townsend was, indeed, striking. The former marked the close of an age which opened with the inventors of the state, Thomas More and Machiavelli, Luther and Calvin; the latter belonged to that nineteenth century in which Ricardo and Hegel discovered from opposite angles the existence of a society that was not subject to the laws of the state, but, on the contrary, subjected the state to its own laws. Adam Smith, it was true, treated material wealth as a separate field of study; to have done so with a great sense of realism made him the founder of a new science, economics. For all that, wealth was to him merely an aspect of the life of the community, to the purposes of which it remained subordinate; it was an appurtenance of the nations struggling for survival in history and could not be dissociated from them. In his view, one set of conditions which governed the wealth of nations derived from the improving, stationary, or declining state of the country as a whole; another set derived from the paramountcy of safety and security as well as the needs of the balance of power; still another was given by the policy of the government as it favored town or countryside, industry or agriculture; hence, it was only within a given political framework that he deemed it possible to formulate the question of wealth, by which he for one meant the material welfare of "the great body of the people." There is no intimation in his work that the economic interests of the capitalists laid down the law to society; no intimation that they were the secular spokesmen of the divine providence which governed the economic world as a separate entity. The economic sphere, with him, is not yet subject to laws of its own that provide us with a standard of good and evil.

Smith wished to regard the wealth of the nations as a function of their national life, physical and moral; that is why his naval policy fitted in so well with Cromwell's Navigation Laws and his notions of human society harmonized with John Locke's system of natural rights. In his view nothing indicates the presence of an economic sphere in society that might become the source of moral law and political obligation. Self-interest merely prompts us to do what, intrinsically, will also benefit others, as the butcher's self-interest will ultimately supply us with a dinner. A broad optimism pervades Smith's thinking since the laws governing the economic part of the universe are consonant with man's destiny as are those that govern the rest. No hidden hand tries to impose upon us the rites of cannibalism in the name of self-interest. The dignity of man is that of a moral being, who is, as such, a member of the civic order of family, state, and "the great Society of mankind." Reason and humanity set a limit to piecework; emulation and gain must give way to them. Natural is that which is in accordance with the principles embodied in the mind of man; and the natural order is that which is in accordance with those principles. Nature in the physical sense was consciously excluded by Smith from the problem of wealth. "Whatever be the soil, climate or extent of territory of any particular nation, the abundance or scantiness of its annual supply, must, *in that particular situation,* depend upon two circumstances," namely, the skill of labor and the proportion between the useful and the idle members in society. Not the natural, but only the human factors enter. This exclusion of the biological and geographical factor in the very beginning of his book was deliberate. The fallacies of the Physiocrats served him as a warning; their predilection for agriculture tempted them to confuse physical nature with man's nature, and induced them to argue that the soil alone was truly creative. Nothing was further from the mind of Smith than such a glorification of Physis. Political economy should be a human science; it should deal with that which was natural to man, not to Nature.

Townsend's *Dissertation,* ten years afterwards, centered on the theorem of the goats and the dogs. The scene is Robinson Crusoe's island in the Pacific Ocean, off the coast of Chile. On this island Juan Fernandez landed a few goats to provide meat in case of future visits. The goats had multiplied at a Biblical rate and became a convenient store of food for the privateers, mostly English, who were molesting Spanish trade. In order to destroy them, the Spanish authorities landed a dog and a bitch, which also, in the course of time, greatly multiplied, and diminished the number of goats on which they fed. "Then a new kind of balance was restored," wrote Townsend. "The weakest of both species were among the first to pay the debt of nature; the most active and vigorous preserved their lives." To which he added: "It is the quantity of food which regulates the number of the human species."

We note that a search [1] in the sources failed to authenticate the story. Juan Fernandez duly landed the goats; but the legendary dogs were described by William Funnell as beautiful cats, and neither dogs nor cats are known to have multiplied; also the goats were inhabiting inaccessible rocks, while the beaches—on this all reports agree—were teeming with fat seals which would have been a much more engaging prey for the wild dogs. However, the paradigm is not dependent upon empirical support. Lack of antiquarian authenticity can detract nothing from the fact that Malthus and Darwin owed their inspiration to this source—Malthus learnt of it from Condorcet, Darwin from Malthus. Yet neither Darwin's theory of natural selection, nor Malthus' population laws might have exerted any appreciable influence on modern society but for the following maxims which Townsend deduced from his goats and dogs and wished to have applied to the reform of the Poor Law: "Hunger will tame the fiercest animals, it will teach decency and civility, obedience and subjection, to the most perverse. In general it is only hunger which can spur and goad them [the poor] on to labor; yet our laws have said they shall never hunger. The laws, it must be confessed, have likewise said, they shall be compelled to work. But then legal constraint is attended with much trouble, violence and noise; creates ill will, and never can be productive of good and acceptable service: whereas hunger is not only peaceable, silent, unremitting pressure, but, as the most natural motive to industry and labor, it calls forth the most powerful exertions; and, when satisfied by the free bounty of another, lays lasting and sure foundations for good will and gratitude. The slave must be compelled to work but the free man should be left to his own judgment, and discretion; should be

[1] Cf. Antonio de Ulloa, Wafer, William Funnell, as well as Isaac James (which also contains Captain Wood Rogers' account on Alexander Selkirk) and the observations of Edward Cooke.

protected in the full enjoyment of his own, be it much or little; and punished when he invades his neighbor's property."

Here was a new starting point for political science. By approaching human community from the animal side, Townsend by-passed the supposedly unavoidable question as to the foundations of government; and in doing so introduced a new concept of law into human affairs, that of the laws of Nature. Hobbes' geometrical bias, as well as Hume's and Hartley's, Quesnay's and Helvetius' hankering after Newtonian laws in society had been merely metaphorical: they were burning to discover a law as universal in society as gravitation was in Nature, but they thought of it as a human law—for instance, a mental force such as fear with Hobbes, association in Hartley's psychology, self-interest with Quesnay, or the quest for utility with Helvetius. There was no squeamishness about it: Quesnay like Plato occasionally took the breeder's view of man and Adam Smith did certainly not ignore the connection between real wages and long-run supply of labor. However, Aristotle had taught that only gods or beasts could live outside society, and man was neither. To Christian thought also the chasm between man and beast was constitutive; no excursions into the realm of physiological facts could confuse theology about the spiritual roots of the human commonwealth. If, to Hobbes, man was as wolf to man, it was because outside of society men behaved like wolves, not because there was any biological factor which men and wolves had in common. Ultimately, this was so because no human community had yet been conceived of which was not identical with law and government. But on the island of Juan Fernandez there was neither government nor law; and yet there was balance between goats and dogs. That balance was maintained by the difficulty the dogs found in devouring the goats which fled into the rocky part of the island, and the inconveniences the goats had to face when moving to safety from the dogs. No government was needed to maintain this balance; it was restored by the pangs of hunger on the one hand, the scarcity of food on the other. Hobbes had argued the need for a despot because men were *like* beasts; Townsend insisted that they were *actually* beasts and that, precisely for that reason, only a minimum of government was required. From this novel point of view, a free society could be regarded as consisting of two races: property owners and laborers. The number of the latter was limited by the amount of food; and as long as property was safe, hunger would drive them to work. No magistrates were necessary, for hunger was a better disciplinarian than the magistrate. To appeal to him, Townsend pungently remarked, would be "an appeal from the stronger to the weaker authority."

The new foundations closely fitted the society that was emerging. Since the middle of the eighteenth century national markets had been developing; the price of grain was no longer local, but regional; this presupposed the almost general use of money and a wide marketability of goods. Market prices and incomes, including rents and wages, showed considerable stability. The Physiocrats were the first to note these regularities, which they could not even theoretically fit into a whole as feudal incomes were still prevalent in France, and labor was often semiservile, so that neither rents nor wages were, as a rule, determined in the market. But the English countryside in Adam Smith's time had become part and parcel of a commercial society; the rent due to the landlord as well as the wages of the agricultural laborer showed a marked dependence on prices. Only exceptionally were wages or prices fixed by the authorities. And yet in this curious new order the old classes of society continued to exist more or less in their former hierarchy, notwithstanding the disappearance of their legal privileges and disabilities. Though no law constrained the laborer to serve the farmer, nor the farmer to keep the landlord in plenty, laborers and farmers acted as if such compulsion existed. By what law was the laborer ordained to obey a master, to whom he was bound by no legal bond? What force kept the classes of society apart as if they were different kinds of human beings? And what maintained balance and order in this human collective which neither invoked nor even tolerated the intervention of political government?

The paradigm of the goats and the dogs seemed to offer an answer. The biological nature of man appeared as the given foundation of a society that was not of a political order. Thus it came to pass that economists presently relinquished Adam Smith's humanistic foundations, and incorporated those of Townsend. Malthus' population law and the law of diminishing returns as handled by Ricardo made the fertility of man and soil constitutive elements of the new realm the existence of which had been uncovered. Economic society had emerged as distinct from the political state.

The circumstances under which the existence of this human aggregate—a complex society—became apparent were of the utmost importance for the history of nineteenth century thought. Since the emerging society was no other than the market system, human society was now in danger of being shifted to foundations utterly foreign to the moral world of which the body politic hitherto had formed part. The apparently insoluble problem of pauperism was forcing Malthus and Ricardo to endorse Townsend's lapse into naturalism.

Burke approached the issue of pauperism squarely from the angle of public security. Conditions in the West Indies convinced him of the danger of nurturing a large slave population without any adequate provision for the safety of the white masters, especially as the Negroes were often allowed to go armed. Similar considerations, he thought, applied to the increase of the number of the unemployed at home, seeing that the government had no police force at its disposal. Although an out-and-out defender of patriarchal traditions, he was a passionate adherent of economic liberalism, in which he saw the answer to the burning administrative problem of pauperism. Local authorities were gladly taking advantage of the unexpected demand of the cotton mills for destitute children whose apprenticing was left to the care of the parish. Many hundreds were indented with manufacturers, often in distant parts of the country. Altogether the new towns developed a healthy appetite for paupers; factories were even prepared to pay for the use of the poor. Adults were assigned to any employer who would take them for their keep; just as they would be billeted out in turn amongst the farmers of the parish, in one or another form of the roundsman system. Farming out was cheaper than the running of "gaols without guilt," as workhouses were sometimes called. From the administrative angle this meant that the "more persistent and more minutely detailed authority of the employer" [2] took the place of the government's and the parish's enforcement of work.

Clearly, a question of statesmanship was involved. Why should the poor be made a public charge and their maintenance put on the parish, if ultimately the parish discharged its obligation by farming out the able-bodied to the capitalist entrepreneurs, who were so eager to fill their mills with them that they would even spend money to obtain their services? Did this not clearly indicate that there was also a less expensive way of compelling the poor to earn their keep than the parish way? The solution lay in the abolishment of the Elizabethan legislation without replacing it by any other. No assessment of wages,

[2] Webb, S. and B., *English Local Government,* Vols. VII–IX, "Poor Law History."

no relief for the able-bodied unemployed, but no minimum wages either, nor a safeguarding of the right to live. Labor should be dealt with as that which it was, a commodity which must find its price in the market. The laws of commerce were the laws of nature and consequently the laws of God. What else was this than an appeal from the weaker magistrate to the stronger, from the justice of the peace to the all-powerful pangs of hunger? To the politician and administrator *laissez-faire* was simply a principle of the ensurance of law and order, with the minimum cost and effort. Let the market be given charge of the poor, and things will look after themselves. It was on this point that Bentham, the rationalist, agreed with Burke, the traditionalist. The calculus of pain and pleasure required that no avoidable pain should be inflicted. If hunger would do the job, no other penalty was needed. To the question, "What can the law do relative to subsistence?" Bentham answered, "Nothing, directly." [3] Poverty was Nature surviving in society; its physical sanction was hunger. "The force of the physical sanction being sufficient, the employment of the political sanction would be superfluous." [4] All that was needed was the "scientific and economical" treatment of the poor.[5] Bentham was strongly opposed to Pitt's Poor Law Bill which would have amounted to an enactment of Speenhamland, as it permitted both outdoor relief and aid-in-wages. Yet Bentham, unlike his pupils, was at this time no rigid economic liberal, nor was he a democrat. His Industry-Houses were a nightmare of minute utilitarian administration enforced by all the chicanery of scientific management. He maintained that there always would be a need for them as the community could not quite disinterest itself in the fate of the indigent. Bentham believed that poverty was part of plenty. "In the highest stage of social prosperity," he said, "the great mass of the citizens will most probably possess few other resources than their daily labor, and consequently will always be near to indigence. . . ." Hence he recommended that "a regular contribution should be established for the wants of indigence," though thereby "in *theory* WANT is decreased and thus industry hit," as he regretfully added, since from the utilitarian point of view the task of the government was to increase want in order to make the physical sanction of hunger effective.[6]

[3] Bentham, J., *Principles of Civil Code,* Ch. 4. (Bowring, Vol. I, p. 333.)
[4] Bentham, J., *ibid.*
[5] Bentham, J., *Observation on the Poor Bill,* 1797.
[6] Bentham, J., *Principles of Civil Code,* p. 314.

The acceptance of near-indigency of the mass of the citizens as the price to be paid for the highest stage of prosperity was accompanied by very different human attitudes. Townsend righted his emotional balance by indulging in prejudice and sentimentalism. The improvidence of the poor was a law of nature, for servile, sordid, and ignoble work would otherwise not be done. Also what would become of the fatherland unless we could rely on the poor? "For what is it but distress and poverty which can prevail upon the lower classes of the people to encounter all the horrors which await them on the tempestuous ocean or on the field of battle?" But this display of a rugged patriotism still left room for more tender sentiments. Poor relief should, of course, be abolished outright. The Poor Laws "proceed from principles which border on absurdity, as professing to accomplish that which, in the very nature and constitution of the world, is impracticable." But once the indigent were left to the mercy of the well-to-do, who can doubt that "the only difficulty" is to restrain the impetuosity of the latter's benevolence? And are the sentiments of charity not far nobler than those that flow from hard and fast legal obligations? "Can in nature anything be more beautiful than the mild complacency of benevolence?" he cried out, contrasting it with the cold heartlessness of "a parish pay-table," which knew not those scenes of an "artless expression of unfeigned gratitude for unexpected favors. . . ." "When the poor are obliged to cultivate the friendship of the rich, the rich will never want inclination to relieve the distress of the poor. . . ." No one who has read this touching portrayal of the intimate life of the Two Nations can doubt that, unconsciously, it was from the island of the goats and dogs that Victorian England drew its sentimental education.

Edmund Burke was a man of different stature. Where men like Townsend failed in a small way, he failed in a great way. His genius exalted brutal fact into tragedy, and invested sentimentality with the halo of mysticism. "When we affect to pity as poor those who must labor or the world cannot exist, we are trifling with the condition of mankind." This was undoubtedly better than coarse indifference, empty lamentations, or the cant of sympathetic uplift. But the virility of this realistic attitude was impaired by the subtle complacency with which he spotlighted the scenes of aristocratic pageantry. The result was to out-Herod Herod, but to underestimate the chances of timely reform. It is a fair guess that had Burke lived, the Parliamentary Reform Bill of 1832, which put an end to the *ancien régime*, would have been passed only at the cost of an avoidable bloody revolution. And yet, Burke might have countered, once the masses were fated by the laws of political economy to toil in misery, what else was the idea of equality but a cruel bait to goad mankind into self-destruction?

Bentham possessed neither the sleek complacency of a Townsend nor the all too precipitate historicism of a Burke. Rather, to this believer in reason and reform the newly discovered realm of social law appeared as the coveted no man's land of utilitarian experimentation. Like Burke, he refused to defer to zoological determinism, and he too rejected the ascendency of economics over politics proper. Though author of the *Essay on Usury,* and of a *Manual of Political Economy,* he was an amateur at that science and even failed to provide the one great contribution which utilitarianism might have been expected to make to economics, namely, the discovery that value derived from utility. Instead, he was induced by associationist psychology to give rein to his boundless imaginative faculties as a social engineer. *Laissez-faire* meant to Bentham only another device in social mechanics. Social not technical invention was the intellectual mainspring of the Industrial Revolution. The decisive contribution of the natural sciences to engineering was not made until a full century later, when the Industrial Revolution was long over. To the practical bridge or canal builder, the designer of machines or engines, knowledge of the general laws of nature was utterly useless before the new applied sciences in mechanics and chemistry were developed. Telford, founder and life-long President of the Society of Civil Engineers, refused membership in that body to applicants who had studied physics and, according to Sir David Brewster, never made himself acquainted with the elements of geometry. The triumphs of natural science had been theoretical in the true sense, and could not compare in practical importance with those of the social sciences of the day. It was to these latter that the prestige of science as against routine and tradition was due, and, unbelievable though it may seem to our generation, the standing of natural science greatly gained by its connection with the human sciences. The discovery of economics was an astounding revelation which hastened greatly the transformation of society and the establishment of a market system, while the decisive machines had been the inventions of uneducated artisans some of whom could hardly read or write. It was thus both just and appopriate that not the natural but the social sciences should rank as the intellectual parents of the mechanical revolution which subjected the powers of nature to man.

Bentham himself was convinced that he had discovered a new social science, that of morals and legislation. It was to be founded on the principle of utility, which allowed of exact calculation with the help of associationist psychology. Science, precisely because it became effective within the circumference of human affairs, meant in eighteenth century England invariably a practical art based on empirical knowledge. The need for such a pragmatic attitude was indeed overwhelming. As statistics were not available it was often not possible to say whether population was on the increase or decrease, what the trend of the balance of foreign trade was, or which class of the population was gaining on the other. It was frequently a mere matter of guesswork whether the wealth of the country was waxing or waning, where the poor came from, what the situation of credit, of banking, or profits was. An empirical instead of a purely speculative or antiquarian approach to matters such as these was what was in the first place meant by "science"; and as practical interests were naturally paramount, it fell to science to suggest how to regulate and organize the vast realm of new phenomena. We have seen how puzzled the Saints were by the nature of poverty, and how ingeniously they experimented with the forms of self-help; how the notion of profits was hailed as a cure-all for the most diverse ills; how none could say whether pauperism was a good or a bad sign; how bewildered scientific workhouse managements were to find themselves unable to make money out of the poor; how Owen made his fortune by running his factories on the lines of a conscious philanthropy; and how a number of other experiments which seemed to involve the same technique of enlightened self-help failed pitifully, thus causing dire perplexity to their philanthropic authors. Had we extended our purview from pauperism to credit, specie, monopolies, savings, insurance, investing, public finance or, for that matter, prisons, education, and lotteries we might have easily adduced as many new types of ventures in respect to each of them.

With Bentham's death, approximately, this period comes to an end;[7] since the 1840's projectors in business were simply promoters of definite ventures, not any more the alleged discoverers of new applications of the universal principles of mutuality, trust, risks, and other elements of human enterprise. Henceforth businessmen imagined they knew what forms their activities should take; they rarely inquired into the nature of money before founding a bank. Social engineers were now usually found only amongst cranks or frauds, and then often con-

[7] 1832.

fined behind iron bars. The spate of industrial and banking systems which from Paterson and John Law to the Pereires had flooded stock exchanges with the projects of religious, social, and academic sectarians had now become a mere trickle. With those engaged in the routine of business, analytical ideas were at a discount. The exploration of society, at least so it was thought, was concluded; no white spots were left on the human map. A man of Bentham's stamp had become impossible for a century. Once the market organization of industrial life had become dominant, all other institutional fields were subordinated to this pattern; the genius for social artifacts was homeless.

Bentham's Panopticon was not only a "mill to grind rogues honest, and idle men industrious";[8] it would also pay dividends like those of the Bank of England. He sponsored proposals as different as an improved system for patents; limited liability companies; a decennial census of population; the establishment of a Ministry of Health; interest-bearing notes to make savings general; a frigidarium for vegetables and fruit; armament factories on new technical principles, eventually run by convict labor, or alternatively, by the assisted poor; a Chrestomathic Day School to teach utilitarianism to the upper middle classes; a general register of real property; a system of public account keeping; reforms of public instruction; uniform registration; freedom from usury; the relinquishment of colonies; the use of contraceptives to keep the poor rate down; the junction of the Atlantic and the Pacific by means of a joint stock company; and others. Some of these projects harbored literally shoals of minor improvements as, for instance, that on Industry-Houses which was a congeries of innovations for the betterment and the exploitation of man based on the achievements of associationist psychology. While Townsend and Burke linked *laissez-faire* with legislative quietism, Bentham saw in it no obstacle to broadsides of reform.

Before we proceed to the answer which Malthus, in 1798, gave to Godwin and with which classical economics properly begins, let us remember the times. Godwin's *Political Justice* was written to counter Burke's *Reflections on the French Revolution* (1790). It appeared just before the wave of repression started with the suspension of habeas corpus (1794), and the persecution of the democratic Correspondence Societies. By this time England was at war with France and the *terreur* made the word "democracy" synonymous with social revolution. Yet the democratic movement in England which was in-

[8] Stephen, Sir L., *The English Utilitarians*, 1900.

augurated with Dr. Price's "Old Jewry" sermon (1789) and reached its literary height in Paine's *The Rights of Man* (1791) was restricted to the political field; the discontent of the laboring poor found no echo in it; the question of the Poor Law was barely mentioned in the pamphlets which raised the cry for universal suffrage and annual parliaments. Yet actually, it was in the sphere of the Poor Law that the squires' decisive countermove came, in the form of Speenhamland. The parish retired behind an artificial morass under the cover of which it outlived Waterloo by twenty years. But while the evil consequences of the panicky acts of political repression of the 1790's might have been soon overcome, had they stood alone, the degenerative process started by Speenhamland left its indelible mark on the country. The forty years' prolongation of squirearchy which it produced was bought at the price of the sacrifice of the virility of the common people. "When the owning classes complained of the poor rate becoming heavier and heavier," says Mantoux, "they overlooked the fact that it really amounted to an insurance against revolution, while the working class, when they accepted the scanty allowance doled out to them, did not realize that it was partly obtained by a reduction of their own legitimate earnings. For the inevitable result of 'allowances' was to keep wages down to the lowest level, and even to force them below the limit corresponding to the irreducible needs of the wage-earners. The farmer or the manufacturer relied on the parish to make up the difference between the sum he paid the men and the sum on which the men could live. For why should they incur an expense which could so easily be foisted on to the body of the rate payers? On the other hand, those in receipt of the parish relief were willing to work for a lower wage, and thus made competition quite impossible to those who received no parish help. The paradoxical result arrived at was that the so-called 'poor-rate' meant an economy for the employers, and a loss for the industrious workman who expected nothing from public charity. Thus the pitiless interplay of interests had turned a charitable law into a bond of iron." [9]

It was this bond, we submit, on which the new law of wages and of population rested. Malthus himself, like Burke and Bentham, was violently opposed to Speenhamland and advocated complete repeal of the Poor Law. Neither of them had foreseen that Speenhamland would force the wages of the laborer down to subsistence level and below; on the contrary, they expected that it would force wages up, or at least

[9] Mantoux, P. L., *The Industrial Revolution in the Eighteenth Century* 1928.

maintain them artificially, which, but for the Anti-Combination Laws, might well have been the case. This false anticipation helps to explain why the low level of rural wages was not traced by them to Speenhamland, which was its actual cause, but was regarded as incontrovertible proof of the working of the so-called iron law of wages. To this foundation of the new economic science we must now turn.

Townsend's naturalism was doubtless not the only possible basis for the new science of political economy. The existence of an economic society was manifest in the regularities of prices, and the stability of the incomes dependent upon those prices; consequently, economic law may well have been based directly on prices. What induced orthodox economics to seek its foundations in naturalism was the otherwise inexplicable misery of the great mass of the producers which, as we know today, could never have been deduced from the laws of the old market. But the facts as they appeared to contemporaries were roughly these: in times past the laboring people had habitually lived on the brink of indigence (at least, if one accounted for changing levels of customary standards); since the coming of the machine they had certainly never risen above subsistence level; and now that the economic society was finally taking shape, it was an indubitable fact that decade after decade the material level of existence of the laboring poor was not improving a jot, if, indeed, it was not becoming worse.

If ever the overwhelming evidence of the facts seemed to point in one direction, it was, therefore, in the case of the iron law of wages, which asserted that the bare subsistence level on which laborers actually lived was the result of a law which tended to keep their wages so low that no other standard was possible for them. This semblance was, of course, not only misleading but indeed implied an absurdity from the point of view of any consistent theory of prices and incomes under capitalism. Yet, in the last analysis, it was on account of this false appearance that the law of wages could not be based on any rational rule of human behavior, but had to be deduced from the naturalistic facts of the fertility of man and soil, as they were presented to the world by Malthus' law of population combined with the law of diminishing returns. The naturalistic element in the foundations of orthodox economics was the outcome of the conditions primarily created by Speenhamland.

It follows that neither Ricardo nor Malthus understood the working of the capitalist system. Not until a century after the publication of the *Wealth of Nations* was it clearly realized that under a market system the factors of production shared in the product, and as produce increased, their absolute share was bound to rise.[10] Although Adam Smith had followed Locke's false start on the labor origins of value, his sense of realism saved him from being consistent. Hence he had confused views on the elements of price, while justly insisting that no society can flourish, the members of which, in their great majority, are poor and miserable. However, what appears as a truism to us was a paradox in his time. Smith's own view was that universal plenty could not help percolate down to the people; it was impossible that society should get wealthier and wealthier and the people poorer and poorer. Unfortunately, the facts did not seem to bear him out for a long time to come; and as theorists had to account for the facts, Ricardo proceeded to argue that the more society advanced the greater would be the difficulty of procuring food and the richer would landlords grow, exploiting both capitalists and workers; that the capitalists' and the workers' interests were in fatal opposition to one another, but that this opposition was ultimately ineffective as the workers' wages could never rise above the subsistence level and profits were bound to shrivel up in any case. In some remote sense all these assertions contained an element of truth, but as an explanation of capitalism nothing more unreal and abstruse could have been produced. However, the facts themselves were formed on contradictory patterns and even today we find it difficult to unravel them. No wonder that the *deus ex machina* of animal and plant propagation had to be invoked in a scientific system the authors of which claimed to deduce the laws of production and distribution from the behavior not of plants or of animals but of men.

Let us briefly survey the consequences of the fact that the foundations of economic theory were laid down during the Speenhamland period, which made appear as a competitive market economy what actually was capitalism without a labor market.

First, the economic theory of the classical economists was essentially confused. The parallelism between wealth and value introduced the most perplexing pseudo problems into nearly every department of Ricardian economics. The wage-fund theory, a legacy of Adam Smith, was a rich source of misunderstandings. Apart from some special theories like that of rent, taxation, and foreign trade, where deep insights were gained, the theory consisted of the hopeless attempt to arrive at categorical conclusions about loosely defined terms purporting to explain the behavior of prices, the formation of incomes, the process

[10] Cannan, E., *A Review of Economic Theory*, 1930.

of production, the influence of costs on prices, the level of profits, wages, and interest, most of which remained as obscure as before.

Second, given the conditions under which the problem represented itself, no other result was possible. No unitary system could have explained the facts, as they did not form part of any one system, but were actually the result of the simultaneous action on the body social of two mutually exclusive systems, namely, a nascent market economy and a paternalistic regulationism in the sphere of the most important factor of production, labor.

Third, the solution hit upon by the classical economists had the most far-reaching consequences for the understanding of the nature of economic society. As gradually the laws governing a market economy were apprehended, these laws were put under the authority of Nature herself. The law of diminishing returns was a law of plant physiology. The Malthusian law of population reflected the relationship between the fertility of man and that of the soil. In both cases the forces in play were the forces of Nature, the animal instinct of sex and the growth of vegetation in a given soil. The principle involved was the same as that in the case of Townsend's goats and dogs: there was a natural limit beyond which human beings could not multiply and that limit was set by the available food supply. Like Townsend, Malthus concluded that the superfluous specimens would be killed off; while the goats are killed off by the dogs, the dogs must starve for lack of food. With Malthus the repressive check consisted in the destruction of the supernumerary specimens by the brute forces of Nature. As human beings are destroyed also by other causes than starvation—such as war, pestilence, and vice—these were equated with the destructive forces of Nature. This involved, strictly, an inconsistency as it made social forces responsible for achieving the balance required by Nature, a criticism, however, to which Malthus might have answered that in absence of wars and vice—that is, in a virtuous community—as many more people would have to starve as were spared by their peaceful virtues. Essentially, economic society was founded on the grim realities of Nature; if man disobeyed the laws which ruled that society, the fell executioner would strangle the offspring of the improvident. The laws of a competitive society were put under the sanction of the jungle.

The true significance of the tormenting problem of poverty now stood revealed: economic society was subjected to laws which were *not* human laws. The rift between Adam Smith and Townsend had broadened into a chasm; a dichotomy appeared which marked the birth of nineteenth century consciousness. From this time onward naturalism haunted the science of man, and the reintegration of society into the human world became the persistently sought aim of the evolution of social thought. Marxian economics—in this line of argument—was an essentially unsuccessful attempt to achieve that aim, a failure due to Marx's too close adherence to Ricardo and the traditions of liberal economics.

The classical economists themselves were far from unconscious of such a need. Malthus and Ricardo were in no way indifferent to the fate of the poor but their humane concern merely forced a false theory into even more tortuous paths. The iron law of wages carried a well-known saving clause according to which the higher the customary needs of the laboring class, the higher the subsistence level below which not even the iron law could depress wages. It was this "standard of wretchedness" on which Malthus set his hopes,[11] and which he wished to have raised by every means, for thus alone, he thought, could those be saved from the lowest forms of wretchedness, who, by virtue of his law were doomed to be wretched. Ricardo, too, for the same reason, wished that in all countries the laboring classes should have a taste for comforts and enjoyments, "and that they should be stimulated by all legal means in their exertions to procure them." Ironically, in order to evade the law of nature, men were here enjoined to raise their own starvation level. And yet, these were undoubtedly sincere attempts on the part of the classic economists to rescue the poor from the fate which their very theories helped to prepare for them.

In the case of Ricardo, theory itself included an element which counterbalanced rigid naturalism. This element, pervading his whole system, and firmly grounded in his theory of value, was the principle of labor. He completed what Locke and Smith had begun, the humanization of economic value; what the Physiocrats had credited to Nature, Ricardo reclaimed for man. In a mistaken theorem of tremendous scope he invested labor with the sole capacity of constituting value, thereby reducing all conceivable transactions in economic society to the principle of equal exchange in a society of free men.

Within Ricardo's system itself the naturalistic and the humanistic factors coexisted which were contending for supremacy in economic society. The dynamics of this situation was of overwhelming power. As its result the drive for a competitive market acquired the irresistible

[11] Hazlitt, W., *A Reply to the Essay on Population by the Rev. T. A. Malthus in a Series of Letters.* 1807.

impetus of a process of Nature. For the self-regulating market was now believed to follow from the inexorable laws of Nature, and the unshackling of the market to be an ineluctable necessity. The creation of a labor market was an act of vivisection performed on the body of society by such as were steeled to their task by an assurance which only science can provide. That the Poor Law must disappear was part of this certainty. "The principle of gravitation is not more certain than the tendency of such laws to change wealth and vigor into misery and weakness . . . until at last all classes should be infected with the plague of universal poverty," wrote Ricardo.[12] He would have been, indeed, a moral coward who, knowing this, failed to find the strength to save mankind from itself by the cruel operation of the abolishment of poor relief. It was on this point that Townsend, Malthus and Ricardo, Bentham and Burke were at one. Fiercely as they differed in method and outlook, they agreed on opposition to the principles of political economy and to Speenhamland. What made economic liberalism an irresistible force was this congruence of opinion between diametrically opposed outlooks; for what the ultrareformer Bentham and the ultratraditionalist Burke equally approved of automatically took on the character of self-evidence.

One man alone perceived the meaning of the ordeal, perhaps because amongst the leading spirits of the age he alone possessed intimate practical knowledge of industry and was also open to inner vision. No thinker ever advanced farther than Robert Owen did into the realm of industrial society. He was deeply aware of the distinction between society and state; while harboring no prejudice against the latter, as Godwin did, he looked to the state merely for that which it could perform; for helpful intervention designed to avert harm from the community, emphatically not for the organizing of society. In the same way, he nourished no animosity against the machine the neutral character of which he recognized. Neither the political mechanism of the state, nor the technological apparatus of the machine hid from him *the* phenomenon: society. He rejected the animalistic approach to society, refuting its Malthusian and Ricardian limitations. But the fulcrum of his thought was his turning away from Christianity, which he accused of "individualization," or of fixing the responsibility for character on the individual himself, thus denying, to Owen's mind, the reality of society and its all-powerful formative influence upon char-

[12] Ricardo, D., *Principles of Political Economy and Taxation* (ed. Gonner, 1929, p. 86).

acter. The true meaning of the attack on "individualization" lay in his insistence on the social origin of human motives: "Individualized man, and all that is truly valuable in Christianity, are so separated as to be utterly incapable of union through all eternity." It was Owen's discovery of society which made him transcend Christianity and reach a position beyond it. He grasped the truth that because society is real, man must ultimately submit to it. His socialism, one might say, was based on a reform of human consciousness to be reached through the recognition of the reality of society. "Should any of the causes of evil be irremovable by the new powers which men are about to acquire," he wrote, "they will know that they are necessary and unavoidable evils; and childish unavailing complaints will cease to be made."

Owen may have nourished an exaggerated notion of those powers; otherwise he hardly could have suggested to the magistrates of the County of Lanark that society should be forthwith newly started from the "nucleus of society" which he had discovered in his village communities. Such flux of the imagination is the privilege of the genius, but for whom mankind could not exist for lack of understanding of itself. All the more significant was the irremovable frontier of freedom to which he pointed, that was given by the necessary limits set to the absence of evil in society. But not until man had transformed society with the help of the new powers he acquired would this frontier become apparent, Owen felt; then man would have to accept this frontier in the spirit of maturity which knows not childish complaint.

Robert Owen, in 1817, described the course on which Western man had entered and his words summed up the problem of the coming century. He pointed to the mighty consequences which proceed from manufactures, *"when left to their natural progress."* "The general diffusion of manufactures throughout a country generates a new character in its inhabitants; and as this character is formed upon a principle quite unfavorable to individual or general happiness, it will produce the most lamentable and permanent evils, unless its tendency be counteracted by legislative interference and direction." The organization of the whole of society on the principle of gain and profit must have far-reaching results. He formulated these results in terms of human character. For the most obvious effect of the new institutional system was the destruction of the traditional character of settled populations and their transmutation into a new type of people, migratory, nomadic, lacking in self-respect and discipline—crude, callous beings of whom both laborer and capitalist were an example. He proceeded to the generalization that the principle involved was unfavorable to individual and social happiness. Grave evils would be produced in this fashion unless the tendencies inherent in market institutions were checked by conscious social direction made effective through legislation. True, the condition of the laborers which he deplored was partly the effect of the "allowance system." But essentially, what he observed was true of town and village laborers alike, namely, that "they are at present in a situation infinitely more degraded and miserable than they were before the introduction of those manufactories, upon the success of which their bare subsistence now depends." Here again, he hit rock bottom, emphasizing not incomes but degradation and misery. And as the prime cause of this degradation he, rightly again, pointed to the dependence for bare subsistence on the factory. He grasped the fact that what appeared primarily as an economic problem was essentially a social one. In economic terms the worker was certainly exploited: he did not get in exchange that which was his due. But important though this was, it was far from all. In spite of exploitation, he might have been financially better off than before. But a principle quite unfavorable to individual and general happiness was working havoc with his social environment, his neighborhood, his standing in the community, his craft; in a word, with those relationships to nature and man in which his economic existence was formerly embedded. The Industrial Revolution was causing a social dislocation of stupendous proportions, and the problem of poverty was merely the economic aspect of this event. Owen justly pronounced that unless legislative interference and direction counteracted these devastating forces, great and permanent evils would follow.

He did not, at this time, foresee that the self-protection of society for which he was calling would prove incompatible with the functioning of the economic system itself.

II. SELF-PROTECTION OF SOCIETY

11

MAN, NATURE, AND PRODUCTIVE ORGANIZATION

FOR A CENTURY the dynamics of modern society was governed by a double movement: the market expanded continuously but this movement was met by a countermovement checking the expansion in definite directions. Vital though such a countermovement was for the protection of society, in the last analysis it was incompatible with the self-regulation of the market, and thus with the market system itself.

That system developed in leaps and bounds; it engulfed space and time, and by creating bank money it produced a dynamic hitherto unknown. By the time it reached its maximum extent, around 1914, every part of the globe, all its inhabitants and yet unborn generations, physical persons as well as huge fictitious bodies called corporations, were comprised in it. A new way of life spread over the planet with a claim to universality unparalleled since the age when Christianity started out on its career, only this time the movement was on a purely material level.

Yet simultaneously a countermovement was on foot. This was more than the usual defensive behavior of a society faced with change; it was a reaction against a dislocation which attacked the fabric of society, and which would have destroyed the very organization of production that the market had called into being.

Robert Owen's was a true insight: market economy if left to evolve according to its own laws would create great and permanent evils.

Production is interaction of man and nature; if this process is to be organized through a self-regulating mechanism of barter and exchange, then man and nature must be brought into its orbit; they must be subject to supply and demand, that is, be dealt with as commodities, as goods produced for sale.

Such precisely was the arrangement under a market system. Man under the name of labor, nature under the name of land, were made available for sale; the use of labor power could be universally bought and sold at a price called wages, and the use of land could be negotiated for a price called rent. There was a market in labor as well as in land, and supply and demand in either was regulated by the height of wages and rents, respectively; the fiction that labor and land were produced for sale was consistently upheld. Capital invested in the various combinations of labor and land could thus flow from one branch of production to another, as was required for an automatic leveling of earnings in the various branches.

But, while production could theoretically be organized in this way, the commodity fiction disregarded the fact that leaving the fate of soil and people to the market would be tantamount to annihilating them. Accordingly, the countermove consisted in checking the action of the market in respect to the factors of production, labor, and land. This was the main function of interventionism.

Productive organization also was threatened from the same quarter. The danger was to the single enterprise—industrial, agricultural, or commercial—in so far as it was affected by changes in the price level. For under a market system, if prices fell, business was impaired; unless all elements of cost fell proportionately, "going concerns" were forced to liquidate, while the fall in prices might have been due not to a general fall in costs, but merely to the manner in which the monetary system was organized. Actually, as we shall see, such was the case under a self-regulating market.

Purchasing power is, in principle, here supplied and regulated by the action of the market itself; this is meant when we say that money is a commodity the amount of which is controlled by the supply and demand of the goods which happen to function as money—the well-known classical theory of money. According to this doctrine money is only another name for a commodity used in exchange more often than another, and which is therefore acquired mainly in order to facilitate exchange. Whether hides, oxen, shells, or gold are used to this end is immaterial; the value of the objects functioning as money is determined as if they were sought only for their usefulness in regard to nutrition, clothing, ornaments, or other purposes. If gold happens to be used as money, its value, amount, and movements are governed by exactly the same laws that apply to other commodities. Any other means of exchange would involve the creating of currency outside the market, the act of its creation—whether by banks or government—

constituting an interference with the self-regulation of the market. The crucial point is that goods used as money are not different from other commodities; that their supply and demand is regulated by the market like that of other commodities; and that consequently all notions investing money with any other character than that of a commodity being used as a means of indirect exchange are inherently false. It follows also that if gold is used as money, bank notes, if such exist, must represent gold. It was in accordance with this doctrine that the Ricardian school wished to organize the supply of currency by the Bank of England. Indeed, no other method was conceivable which would keep the monetary system from being "interfered" with by the state, and thus safeguard the self-regulation of the market.

Therefore, in respect to business a very similar situation existed as in respect to the natural and human substance of society. The self-regulating market was a threat to them all, and for essentially similar reasons. And if factory legislation and social laws were required to protect industrial man from the implications of the commodity fiction in regard to labor power, if land laws and agrarian tariffs were called into being by the necessity of protecting natural resources and the culture of the countryside against the implications of the commodity fiction in respect to them, it was equally true that central banking and the management of the monetary system were needed to keep manufactures and other productive enterprises safe from the harm involved in the commodity fiction as applied to money. Paradoxically enough, not human beings and natural resources only but also the organization of capitalistic production itself had to be sheltered from the devastating effects of a self-regulating market.

Let us return to what we have called the double movement. It can be personified as the action of two organizing principles in society, each of them setting itself specific institutional aims, having the support of definite social forces and using its own distinctive methods. The one was the principle of economic liberalism, aiming at the establishment of a self-regulating market, relying on the support of the trading classes, and using largely *laissez-faire* and free trade as its methods; the other was the principle of social protection aiming at the conservation of man and nature as well as productive organization, relying on the varying support of those most immediately affected by the deleterious action of the market—primarily, but not exclusively, the working and the landed classes—and using protective legislation, restrictive associations, and other instruments of intervention as its methods.

The emphasis on class is important. The services to society performed by the landed, the middle, and the working classes shaped the whole social history of the nineteenth century. Their part was cut out for them by their being available for the discharge of various functions that derived from the total situation of society. The middle classes were the bearers of the nascent market economy; their business interests ran, on the whole, parallel to the general interest in regard to production and employment; if business was flourishing, there was a chance of jobs for all and of rents for the owners; if markets were expanding, investments could be freely and readily made; if the trading community competed successfully with the foreigner, the currency was safe. On the other hand, the trading classes had no organ to sense the dangers involved in the exploitation of the physical strength of the worker, the destruction of family life, the devastation of neighborhoods, the denudation of forests, the pollution of rivers, the deterioration of craft standards, the disruption of folkways, and the general degradation of existence including housing and arts, as well as the innumerable forms of private and public life that do not affect profits. The middle classes fulfilled their function by developing an all but sacramental belief in the universal beneficence of profits, although this disqualified them as the keepers of other interests as vital to a good life as the furtherance of production. Here lay the chance of those classes which were not engaged in applying expensive, complicated, or specific machines to production. Roughly, to the landed aristocracy and the peasantry fell the task of safeguarding the martial qualities of the nation which continued to depend largely on men and soil, while the laboring people, to a smaller or greater extent, became representatives of the common human interests that had become homeless. But at one time or another, each social class stood, even if unconsciously, for interests wider than its own.

By the turn of the nineteenth century—universal suffrage was now fairly general—the working class was an influential factor in the state; the trading classes, on the other hand, whose sway over the legislature was no longer unchallenged, became conscious of the political power involved in their leadership in industry. This peculiar localization of influence and power caused no trouble as long as the market system continued to function without great stress and strain; but when, for inherent reasons, this was no longer the case, and when tensions between the social classes developed, society itself was endangered by the fact that the contending parties were making government and business, state and industry, respectively, their strongholds. Two vital functions of society, the political and the economic, were being used and abused as weapons in a struggle for sectional interests. It was out of such a perilous deadlock that in the twentieth century the fascist crisis sprang.

From these two angles, then, do we intend to outline the movement which shaped the social history of the nineteenth century. The one was given by the clash of the organizing principles of economic liberalism and social protection which led to a deep-seated institutional strain; the other by the conflict of classes which, interacting with the first, turned the crisis into a catastrophe.

12

BIRTH OF THE LIBERAL CREED

ECONOMIC LIBERALISM was the organizing principle of a society engaged in creating a market system. Born as a mere penchant for non-bureaucratic methods, it evolved into a veritable faith in man's secular salvation through a self-regulating market. Such fanaticism was the result of the sudden aggravation of the task it found itself committed to : the magnitude of the sufferings that were to be inflicted on innocent persons as well as the vast scope of the interlocking changes involved in the establishment of the new order. The liberal creed assumed its evangelical fervor only in response to the needs of a fully deployed market economy.

To antedate the policy of *laissez-faire*, as is often done, to the time when this catchword was first used in France in the middle of the eighteenth century would be entirely unhistorical; it can be safely said that not until two generations later was economic liberalism more than a spasmodic tendency. Only by the 1820's did it stand for the three classical tenets: that labor should find its price on the market; that the creation of money should be subject to an automatic mechanism; that goods should be free to flow from country to country without hindrance or preference; in short, for a labor market, the gold standard, and free trade.

To credit François Quesnay with having envisaged such a state of affairs would be little short of fantastic. All that the Physiocrats demanded in a mercantilistic world was the free export of grain in order to ensure a better income to farmers, tenants, and landlords. For the rest their *ordre naturel* was no more than a directive principle for the regulation of industry and agriculture by a supposedly all-powerful and omniscient government. Quesnay's *Maximes* were intended to provide such a government with the viewpoints needed to translate into practical policy the principles of the *Tableau* on the basis of statistical data which he offered to have furnished periodically. The idea of a self-regulating system of markets had never as much as entered his mind.

In England, too, *laissez-faire* was interpreted narrowly; it meant freedom from regulations in production; trade was not comprised. Cotton manufactures, the marvel of the time, had grown from insignificance into the leading export industry of the country—yet the import of printed cottons remained forbidden by positive statute. Notwithstanding the traditional monopoly of the home market an export bounty for calico or muslin was granted. Protectionism was so ingrained that Manchester cotton manufacturers demanded, in 1800, the prohibition of the export of yarn, though they were conscious of the fact that this meant loss of business to them. An Act passed in 1791 extended the penalties for the export of tools used in manufacturing cotton goods to the export of models or specifications. The free trade origins of the cotton industry are a myth. Freedom from regulation in the sphere of production was all the industry wanted; freedom in the sphere of exchange was still deemed a danger.

One might suppose that freedom of production would naturally spread from the purely technological field to that of the employment of labor. However, only comparatively late did Manchester raise the demand for free labor. The cotton industry had never been subject to the Statute of Artificers and was consequently not hampered either by yearly wage assessments or by rules of apprenticeship. The Old Poor Law, on the other hand, to which latter-day liberals so fiercely objected, was a help to the manufacturers; it not only supplied them with parish apprentices, but also permitted them to divest themselves of responsibility towards their dismissed employees, thus throwing much of the burden of unemployment on public funds. Not even the Speenhamland system was at first unpopular with the cotton manufacturers; as long as the moral effect of allowances did not reduce the productive capacity of the laborer, the industry might have well regarded family endowment as a help in sustaining that reserve army of labor which was urgently required to meet the tremendous fluctuations of trade. At a time when employment in agriculture was still on a year's term, it was of great importance that such a fund of mobile labor should be available to industry in periods of expansion. Hence the attacks of the manufacturers on the Act of Settlement which hampered the physical mobility of labor. Yet not before 1795 was the repeal of that Act carried—only to be replaced by more, not less, paternalism in regard to the Poor Law. Pauperism still remained the concern of squire and countryside; and even harsh critics of Speenhamland like Burke, Bentham, and Malthus regarded themselves less as representatives of industrial progress than as propounders of sound principles of rural administration.

Not until the 1830's did economic liberalism burst forth as a crusading passion, and *laissez-faire* become a militant creed. The manufacturing class was pressing for the amendment of the Poor Law, since it prevented the rise of an industrial working class which depended for its income on achievement. The magnitude of the venture implied in the creation of a free labor market now became apparent, as well as the extent of the misery to be inflicted on the victims of improvement. Accordingly, by the early 1830's a sharp change of mood was manifest. An 1817 reprint of Townsend's *Dissertation* contained a preface in praise of the foresight with which the author had borne down on the Poor Laws and demanded their complete abandonment; but the editors warned of his "rash and precipitate" suggestion that outdoor relief to the poor should be abolished within so short a term as *ten* years. Ricardo's *Principles*, which appeared in the same year, insisted on the necessity of abolishing the allowance system, but urged strongly that this should be done only very gradually. Pitt, a disciple of Adam Smith, had rejected such a course on account of the innocent suffering it would entail. And as late as 1829, Peel "doubted whether the allowance system could be safely removed otherwise than gradually." [1] Yet after the political victory of the middle class, in 1832, the Poor Law Amendment Bill was carried in its most extreme form and rushed into effect without any period of grace. *Laissez-faire* had been catalyzed into a drive of uncompromising ferocity.

A similar keying up of economic liberalism from academic interest to boundless activism occurred in the two other fields of industrial organization: currency and trade. In respect to both of these *laissez-faire* waxed into a fervently held creed when the uselessness of any other but extreme solutions became apparent.

The currency issue was first brought home to the English community in the form of a general rise in the cost of living. Between 1790 and 1815 prices doubled. Real wages fell and business was hit by a slump in foreign exchanges. Yet not until the 1825 panic did sound currency become a tenet of economic liberalism, *i.e.*, only when Ricardian principles were already so deeply impressed on the minds of politicians and businessmen alike that the "standard" was maintained in spite of the enormous number of financial casualties. This was the beginning of that unshakable belief in the automatic steering mecha-

[1] Webb, S. and B., *op. cit.*

nism of the gold standard without which the market system could never have got under way.

International free trade involved no less an act of faith. Its implications v. ere entirely extravagant. It meant that England would depend for her food supply upon overseas sources; would sacrifice her agriculture, if necessary, and enter on a new form of life under which she would be part and parcel of some vaguely conceived world unity of the future; that this planetary community would have to be a peaceful one, or, if not, would have to be made safe for Great Britain by the power of the Navy; and that the English nation would face the prospects of continuous industrial dislocations in the firm belief in its superior inventive and productive ability. However, it was believed that if only the grain of all the world could flow freely to Britain, then her factories would be able to undersell all the world. Again, the measure of the determination needed was set by the magnitude of the proposition and the vastness of the risks involved in complete acceptance. Yet less than complete acceptance would have spelt certain ruin.

The utopian springs of the dogma of *laissez-faire* are but incompletely understood as long as they are viewed separately. The three tenets —competitive labor market, automatic gold standard, and international free trade—formed one whole. The sacrifices involved in achieving any one of them were useless, if not worse, unless the other two were equally secured. It was everything or nothing.

Anybody could see that the gold standard, for instance, meant danger of deadly deflation and, maybe, of fatal monetary stringency in a panic. The manufacturer could, therefore, hope to hold his own only if he was assured of an increasing scale of production at remunerative prices (in other words, only if wages fell at least in proportion to the general fall in prices, so as to allow the exploitation of an ever-expanding world market). Thus the Anti-Corn Law Bill of 1846 was the corollary of Peel's Bank Act of 1844, and both assumed a laboring class which, since the Poor Law Amendment Act of 1834, was forced to give their best under the threat of hunger, so that wages were regulated by the price of grain. The three great measures formed a coherent whole.

The global sweep of economic liberalism can now be taken in at a glance. Nothing less than a self-regulating market on a world scale could ensure the functioning of this stupendous mechanism. Unless the price of labor was dependent upon the cheapest grain available, there was no guarantee that the unprotected industries would not succumb in the grip of the voluntarily accepted task-master, gold. The expansion of the market system in the nineteenth century was synonymous with the simultaneous spreading of international free trade, competitive labor market, and gold standard; they belonged together. No wonder that economic liberalism turned into a secular religion once the great perils of this venture were evident.

There was nothing natural about *laissez-faire*; free markets could never have come into being merely by allowing things to take their course. Just as cotton manufactures—the leading free trade industry— were created by the help of protective tariffs, export bounties, and indirect wage subsidies, *laissez-faire* itself was enforced by the state. The thirties and forties saw not only an outburst of legislation repealing restrictive regulations, but also an enormous increase in the administrative functions of the state, which was now being endowed with a central bureaucracy able to fulfill the tasks set by the adherents of liberalism. To the typical utilitarian, economic liberalism was a social project which should be put into effect for the greatest happiness of the greatest number; *laissez-faire* was not a method to achieve a thing, it was the thing to be achieved. True, legislation could do nothing directly, except by repealing harmful restrictions. But that did not mean that *government* could no nothing, especially indirectly. On the contrary, the utilitarian liberal saw in government the great agency for achieving happiness. In respect to material welfare, Bentham believed, the influence of legislation "is as nothing" in comparison with the unconscious contribution of the "minister of the police." Of the three things needed for economic success—inclination, knowledge, and power— the private person possessed only inclination. Knowledge and power, Bentham taught, can be administered much cheaper by government than by private persons. It was the task of the executive to collect statistics and information, to foster science and experiment, as well as to supply the innumerable instruments of final realization in the field of government. Benthamite liberalism meant the replacing of Parliamentary action by action through administrative organs.

For this there was ample scope. Reaction in England had not governed—as it did in France—through administrative methods but used exclusively Parliamentary legislation to put political repression into effect. "The revolutionary movements of 1785 and of 1815–1820 were combated, not by departmental action, but by Parliamentary legislation. The suspension of the Habeas Corpus Act, the passing of the Libel Act, and of the 'Six Acts' of 1819, were severely coercive measures; but they contain no evidence of any attempt to give a Continental character to administration. Insofar as individual liberty was destroyed, it was destroyed by and in pursuance of Acts of Parliament." [2] Economic liberals had hardly gained influence on government, in 1832, when the position changed completely in favor of administrative methods. "The net result of the legislative activity which has characterized, though with different degrees of intensity, the period since 1832, has been the building up piecemeal of an administrative machine of great complexity which stands in as constant need of repair, renewal, reconstruction, and adaptation to new requirements as the plant of a modern manufactury." [3] This growth of administration reflected the spirit of utilitarianism. Bentham's fabulous Panopticon, his most personal utopia, was a star-shaped building from the center of which prison wardens could keep the greatest number of jailbirds under the most effective supervision at the smallest cost to the public. Similarly, in the utilitarian state his favorite principle of "inspectability" ensured that the Minister at the top should keep effective control over all local administration.

The road to the free market was opened and kept open by an enormous increase in continuous, centrally organized and controlled interventionism. To make Adam Smith's "simple and natural liberty" compatible with the needs of a human society was a most complicated affair. Witness the complexity of the provisions in the innumerable enclosure laws; the amount of bureaucratic control involved in the administration of the New Poor Laws which for the first time since Queen Elizabeth's reign were effectively supervised by central authority; or the increase in governmental administration entailed in the meritorious task of municipal reform. And yet all these strongholds of governmental interference were erected with a view to the organizing of some simple freedom—such as that of land, labor, or municipal administration. Just as, contrary to expectation, the invention of labor-saving machinery had not diminished but actually increased the uses of human labor, the introduction of free markets, far from doing away with the need for control, regulation, and intervention, enormously increased their range. Administrators had to be constantly on the watch to ensure the free working of the system. Thus even those who wished most

---

[2] Redlich and Hirst, J., *Local Government in England*, Vol. II, p. 240, quoted Dicey, A. V., *Law and Opinion in England*, p. 305.

[3] Ilbert, *Legislative Methods*, pp. 212–3, quoted Dicey, A. V., *op. cit.*

ardently to free the state from all unnecessary duties, and whose whole philosophy demanded the restriction of state activities, could not but entrust the self-same state with the new powers, organs, and instruments required for the establishment of *laissez-faire*.

This paradox was topped by another. While *laissez-faire* economy was the product of deliberate state action, subsequent restrictions on *laissez-faire* started in a spontaneous way. *Laissez-faire* was planned; planning was not. The first half of this assertion was shown above to be true. If ever there was conscious use of the executive in the service of a deliberate government-controlled policy, it was on the part of the Benthamites in the heroic period of *laissez-faire*. The other half was first mooted by that eminent liberal, Dicey, who made it his task to inquire into the origins of the "anti-*laissez-faire*" or, as he called it, the "collectivist" trend in English public opinion, the existence of which was manifest since the late 1860's. He was surprised to find that no evidence of the existence of such a trend could be traced *save the acts of legislation themselves*. More exactly, no evidence of a "collectivist trend" in public opinion *prior* to the laws which appeared to represent such a trend could be found. As to later "collectivist" opinion, Dicey inferred that the "collectivist" legislation itself might have been its prime source. The upshot of his penetrating inquiry was that there had been complete absence of any deliberate intention to extend the functions of the state, or to restrict the freedom of the individual, on the part of those who were directly responsible for the restrictive enactments of the 1870's and 1880's. The legislative spearhead of the countermovement against a self-regulating market as it developed in the half century following 1860 turned out to be spontaneous, undirected by opinion, and actuated by a purely pragmatic spirit.

Economic liberals must strongly take exception to this view. Their whole social philosophy hinges on the idea that *laissez-faire* was a natural development, while subsequent anti-*laissez-faire* legislation was the result of a purposeful action on the part of the opponents of liberal principles. In these two mutually exclusive interpretations of the double movement, it is not too much to say, the truth or untruth of the liberal position is involved today.

Liberal writers like Spencer and Sumner, Mises and Lippmann offer an account of the double movement substantially similar to our own, but they put an entirely different interpretation on it. While in our view the concept of a self-regulating market was utopian, and its progress was stopped by the realistic self-protection of society, in their view all protectionism was a mistake due to impatience, greed, and shortsightedness, but for which the market would have resolved its difficulties. The question as to which of these two views is correct is perhaps the most important problem of recent social history, involving as it does no less than a decision on the claim of economic liberalism to be the basic organizing principle in society. Before we turn to the testimony of the facts, a more precise formulation of the issue is needed.

In retrospect our age will be credited with having seen the end of the self-regulating market. The 1920's saw the prestige of economic liberalism at its height. Hundreds of millions of people had been afflicted by the scourge of inflation; whole social classes, whole nations had been expropriated. Stabilization of currencies became the focal point in the political thought of peoples and governments; the restoration of the gold standard became the supreme aim of all organized effort in the economic field. The repayment of foreign loans and the return to stable currencies were recognized as the touchstones of rationality in politics; and no private suffering, no infringement of sovereignty, was deemed too great a sacrifice for the recovery of monetary integrity. The privations of the unemployed made jobless by deflation; the destitution of public servants dismissed without a pittance; even the relinquishment of national rights and the loss of constitutional liberties were judged a fair price to pay for the fulfillment of the requirement of sound budgets and sound currencies, these *a priori* of economic liberalism.

The thirties lived to see the absolutes of the twenties called in question. After several years during which currencies were practically restored and budgets balanced, the two most powerful countries, Great Britain and the United States, found themselves in difficulties, dismissed the gold standard, and started out on the management of their currencies. International debts were repudiated wholesale and the tenets of economic liberalism were disregarded by the wealthiest and most respectable. By the middle of the thirties France and some other states still adhering to gold were actually forced off the standard by the Treasuries of Great Britain and the United States, formerly jealous guardians of the liberal creed.

In the forties economic liberalism suffered an even worse defeat. Although Great Britain and the United States departed from monetary orthodoxy, they retained the principles and methods of liberalism in industry and commerce, the general organization of their economic life. This was to prove a factor in precipitating the war and a handicap in fighting it, since economic liberalism had created and fostered the illusion that dictatorships were bound for economic catastrophe. By virtue of this creed democratic governments were the last to understand the implications of managed currencies and directed trade, even when they happened by force of circumstances to be practicing these methods themselves; also, the legacy of economic liberalism barred the way to timely rearmament in the name of balanced budgets and free enterprise, which were supposed to provide the only secure foundations of economic strength in war. In Great Britain budgetary and monetary orthodoxy induced adherence to the traditional strategic principle of limited commitments upon a country actually faced with total war; in the United States vested interests—such as oil and aluminum—entrenched themselves behind the taboos of liberal business and successfully resisted preparations for an industrial emergency. But for the stubborn and impassioned insistence of economic liberals on their fallacies, the leaders of the race as well as the masses of free men would have been better equipped for the ordeal of the age and might perhaps even have been able to avoid it altogether.

Secular tenets of social organization embracing the whole civilized world are not dislodged by the events of a decade. Both in Great Britain and in the United States millions of independent business units derived their existence from the principle of *laissez-faire*. Its spectacular failure in one field did not destroy its authority in all. Indeed, its partial eclipse may have even strengthened its hold since it enabled its defenders to argue that the incomplete application of its principles was the reason for every and any difficulty laid to its charge.

This, indeed, is the last remaining argument of economic liberalism today. Its apologists are repeating in endless variations that but for the policies advocated by its critics, liberalism would have delivered the goods; that not the competitive system and the self-regulating market, but interference with that system and interventions with that market are responsible for our ills. And this argument does not find support in innumerable recent infringements of economic freedom only, but also in the indubitable fact that the movement to spread the system of self-regulating markets was met in the second half of the nineteenth century by a persistent countermove obstructing the free working of such an economy.

The economic liberal is thus enabled to formulate a case which links the present with the past in one coherent whole. For who could deny that government intervention in business may undermine confidence?

Who could deny that unemployment would sometimes be less if it were not for out-of-work benefit provided by law? That private business is injured by the competition of public works? That deficit finance may endanger private investments? That paternalism tends to damp business initiative? This being so in the present, surely it was no different in the past. When around the 1870's a general protectionist movement—social and national—started in Europe, who can doubt that it hampered and restricted trade? Who can doubt that factory laws, social insurance, municipal trading, health services, public utilities, tariffs, bounties and subsidies, cartels and trusts, embargoes on immigration, on capital movements, on imports—not to speak of less open restrictions on the movements of men, goods, and payments—must have acted as so many hindrances to the functioning of the competitive system, protracting business depressions, aggravating unemployment, deepening financial slumps, diminishing trade, and damaging severely the self-regulating mechanism of the market? The root of all evil, the liberal insists, was precisely this interference with the freedom of employment, trade and currencies practiced by the various schools of social, national, and monopolistic protectionism since the third quarter of the nineteenth century; but for the unholy alliance of trade unions and labor parties with monopolistic manufacturers and agrarian interests, which in their shortsighted greed joined forces to frustrate economic liberty, the world would be enjoying today the fruits of an almost automatic system of creating material welfare. Liberal leaders never weary of repeating that the tragedy of the nineteenth century sprang from the incapacity of man to remain faithful to the inspiration of the early liberals; that the generous initiative of our ancestors was frustrated by the passions of nationalism and class war, vested interests, and monopolists, and above all, by the blindness of the working people to the ultimate beneficence of unrestricted economic freedom to all human interests, including their own. A great intellectual and moral advance was thus, it is claimed, frustrated by the intellectual and moral weaknesses of the mass of the people; what the spirit of Enlightenment had achieved was put to nought by the forces of selfishness In a nutshell, this is the economic liberal's defense. Unless it is refuted, he will continue to hold the floor in the contest of arguments.

Let us focus the issue. It is agreed that the liberal movement, intent on the spreading of the market system, was met by a protective countermovement tending towards its restriction; such an assumption, indeed, underlies our own thesis of the double movement. But while we assert that the inherent absurdity of the idea of a self-regulating market system would have eventually destroyed society, the liberal accuses the most various elements of having wrecked a great initiative. Unable to adduce evidence of any such concerted effort to thwart the liberal movement, he falls back on the practically irrefutable hypothesis of covert action. This is the myth of the antiliberal conspiracy which in one form or another is common to all liberal interpretations of the events of the 1870's and 1880's. Commonly the rise of nationalism and of socialism is credited with having been the chief agent in that shifting of the scene; manufacturers' associations and monopolists, agrarian interests and trade unions are the villains of the piece. Thus in its most spiritualized form the liberal doctrine hypostasizes the working of some dialectical law in modern society stultifying the endeavors of enlightened reason, while in its crudest version it reduces itself to an attack on political democracy, as the alleged mainspring of interventionism.

The testimony of the facts contradicts the liberal thesis decisively. The antiliberal conspiracy is a pure invention. The great variety of forms in which the "collectivist" countermovement appeared was not due to any preference for socialism or nationalism on the part of concerted interests, but exclusively to the broader range of the vital social interests affected by the expanding market mechanism. This accounts for the all but universal reactions of predominantly practical character called forth by the expansion of that mechanism. Intellectual fashions played no role whatever in this process; there was, accordingly, no room for the prejudice which the liberal regards as the ideological force behind the antiliberal development. Although it is true that the 1870's and 1880's saw the end of orthodox liberalism, and that all crucial problems of the present can be traced back to that period, it is incorrect to say that the change to social and national protectionism was due to any other cause than the manifestation of the weaknesses and perils inherent in a self-regulating market system. This can be shown in more than one way.

First, there is the amazing diversity of the matters on which action was taken. This alone would exclude the possibility of concerted action. Let us cite from a list of interventions which Herbert Spencer compiled in 1884, when charging liberals with having deserted their principles for the sake of "restrictive legislation." [4] The variety of the subjects could hardly be greater. In 1860, authority was given to provide "ana-

4 Spencer, H., *The Man vs. the State*, 1884.

lysts of food and drink to be paid out of local rates"; there followed an Act providing "the inspection of gas works"; an extension of the Mines Act "making it penal to employ boys under twelve not attending schools and unable to read or write." In 1861, power was given "to poor law guardians to enforce vaccination"; local boards were authorized "to fix rates of hire for means of conveyance"; and certain locally formed bodies "had given them powers of taxing the locality for rural drainage and irrigation works, and for supplying water to cattle." In 1862, an Act was passed making illegal "a coal-mine with a single shaft"; an Act giving the Council of Medical Education exclusive right "to furnish a Pharmacopoeia, the price of which is to be fixed by the Treasury." Spencer, horror-struck, filled several pages with an enumeration of these and similar measures. In 1863, came the "extension of compulsory vaccination to Scotland and Ireland." There was also an Act appointing inspectors for the "wholesomeness, or unwholesomeness of food"; a Chimney-Sweeper's Act, to prevent the torture and eventual death of children set to sweep too narrow slots; a Contagious Diseases Act; a Public Libraries Act, giving local powers "by which a majority can tax a minority for their books." Spencer adduced them as so much irrefutable evidence of an antiliberal conspiracy. And yet each of these Acts dealt with some problem arising out of modern industrial conditions and was aimed at the safeguarding of some public interest against dangers inherent either in such conditions or, at any rate, in the market method of dealing with them. To an unbiased mind they proved the purely practical and pragmatic nature of the "collectivist" countermove. Most of those who carried these measures were convinced supporters of *laissez-faire*, and certainly did not wish their consent to the establishment of a fire brigade in London to imply a protest against the principles of economic liberalism. On the contrary, the sponsors of these legislative acts were as a rule uncompromising opponents of socialism, or any other form of collectivism.

Second, the change from liberal to "collectivist" solutions happened sometimes over night and without any consciousness on the part of those engaged in the process of legislative rumination. Dicey adduced the classic instance of the Workmen's Compensation Act dealing with the employers' liability for damage done to his workmen in the course of their employment. The history of the various acts embodying this idea, since 1880, showed consistent adherence to the individualist principle that the responsibility of the employer to his employee must be regulated in a manner strictly identical with that governing his responsibility to others, *e.g.*, strangers. With hardly any change in opinion, in 1897, the employer was suddenly made the insurer of his workmen against any damage incurred in the course of their employment, a "thoroughly collectivistic legislation," as Dicey justly remarked. No better proof could be adduced that no change either in the type of interests involved, or in the tendency of the opinions brought to bear on the matter, caused the supplanting of a liberal principle by an antiliberal one, but exclusively the evolving conditions under which the problem arose and a solution was sought.

Third, there is the indirect, but most striking proof provided by a comparison of the development in various countries of a widely dissimilar political and ideological configuration. Victorian England and the Prussia of Bismarck were poles apart, and both were very much unlike the France of the Third Republic or the Empire of the Hapsburgs. Yet each of them passed through a period of free trade and *laissez-faire*, followed by a period of antiliberal legislation in regard to public health, factory conditions, municipal trading, social insurance, shipping subsidies, public utilities, trade associations, and so on. It would be easy to produce a regular calendar setting out the years in which analogous changes occurred in the various countries. Workmen's compensation was enacted in England in 1880 and 1897, in Germany in 1879, in Austria in 1887, in France in 1899; factory inspection was introduced in England in 1833, in Prussia in 1853, in Austria in 1883; in France in 1874 and 1883; muncipal trading, including the running of public utilities, was introduced by Joseph Chamberlain, a Dissenter and a capitalist, in Birmingham in the 1870's; by the Catholic "Socialist" and Jew-baiter, Karl Lueger, in the Imperial Vienna of the 1890's; in German and French municipalities by a variety of local coalitions. The supporting forces were in some cases violently reactionary and antisocialist as in Vienna, at other times "radical imperialist" as in Birmingham, or of the purest liberal hue as with the Frenchman, Edouard Herriot, Mayor of Lyons. In Protestant England, Conservative and Liberal cabinets labored intermittently at the completion of factory legislation. In Germany, Roman Catholics and Social Democrats took part in its achievement; in Austria, the Church and its most militant supporters; in France, enemies of the Church and ardent anticlericals were responsible for the enactment of almost identical laws. Thus under the most varied slogans, with very different motivations a multitude of parties and social strata put into effect almost exactly the same measures in a series of countries in respect to a large number of complicated subjects. There is, on the face of it, nothing more absurd than to infer that they were secretly actuated by the same ideological preconceptions or narrow group interests as the legend of the antiliberal conspiracy would have it. On the contrary, everything tends to support the assumption that objective reasons of a stringent nature forced the hands of the legislators.

Fourth, there is the significant fact that at various times economic liberals themselves advocated restrictions on the freedom of contract and on *laissez-faire* in a number of well-defined cases of great theoretical and practical importance. Antiliberal prejudice could, naturally, not have been their motive. We have in mind the principle of the association of labor on the one hand, the law of business corporations on the other. The first refers to the right of workers to combine for the purpose of raising their wages; the latter, to the right of trusts, cartels, or other forms of capitalistic combines, to raise prices. It was justly charged in both cases that freedom of contract or *laissez-faire* was being used in restraint of trade. Whether workers' associations to raise wages, or trade associations to raise prices were in question, the principle of *laissez-faire* could be obviously employed by interested parties to narrow the market for labor or other commodities. It is highly significant that in either case consistent liberals from Lloyd George and Theodore Roosevelt to Thurman Arnold and Walter Lippmann subordinated *laissez-faire* to the demand for a free competitive market; they pressed for regulations and restrictions, for penal laws and compulsion, arguing as any "collectivist" would that the freedom of contract was being "abused" by trade unions, or corporations, whichever it was. Theoretically, *laissez-faire* or freedom of contract implied the freedom of workers to withhold their labor either individually or jointly, if they so decided; it implied also the freedom of businessmen to concert on selling prices irrespective of the wishes of the consumers. But in practice such freedom conflicted with the institution of a self-regulating market, and *in such a conflict the self-regulating market was invariably accorded precedence.* In other words, if the needs of a self-regulating market proved incompatible with the demands of *laissez-faire*, the economic liberal turned against *laissez-faire* and preferred— as any antiliberal would have done—the so-called collectivist methods of regulation and restriction. Trade union law as well as antitrust legislation sprang from this attitude. No more conclusive proof could be offered of the inevitability of antiliberal or "collectivist" methods under the conditions of modern industrial society than the fact that even economic liberals themselves regularly used such methods in decisively important fields of industrial organization.

Incidentally, this helps to clarify the true meaning of the term "interventionism" by which economic liberals like to denote the opposite of their own policy, but merely betray confusion of thought. The opposite of interventionism is *laissez-faire* and we have just seen that economic liberalism cannot be identified with *laissez-faire* (although in common parlance there is no harm in using them interchangeably). Strictly, economic liberalism is the organizing principle of a society in which industry is based on the institution of a self-regulating market. True, once such a system is approximately achieved, less intervention of one type is needed. However, this is far from saying that market system and intervention are mutually exclusive terms. For as long as that system is not established, economic liberals must and will unhesitatingly call for the intervention of the state in order to establish it, and once established, in order to maintain it. The economic liberal can, therefore, without any inconsistency call upon the state to use the force of law; he can even appeal to the violent forces of civil war to set up the preconditions of a self-regulating market. In America the South appealed to the arguments of *laissez-faire* to justify slavery; the North appealed to the intervention of arms to establish a free labor market. The accusation of interventionism on the part of liberal writers is thus an empty slogan, implying the denunciation of one and the same set of actions according to whether they happen to approve of them or not. The only principle economic liberals can maintain without inconsistency is that of the self-regulating market, whether it involves them in interventions or not.

To sum up. The countermove against economic liberalism and *laissez-faire* possessed all the unmistakable characteristics of a spontaneous reaction. At innumerable disconnected points it set in without any traceable links between the interests directly affected or any ideological conformity between them. Even in the settlement of one and the same problem as in the case of workmen's compensation, solutions switched over from individualistic to "collectivistic," from liberal to antiliberal, from "*laissez-faire*" to interventionist forms without any change in the economic interest, the ideological influences or political forces in play, merely as a result of the increasing realization of the nature of the problem in question. Also it could be shown that a closely similar change from *laissez-faire* to "collectivism" took place in various countries at a definite stage of their industrial development, pointing to the depth and independence of the underlying causes of the process so superficially credited by economic liberals to changing moods or sundry interests. Finally, analysis reveals that not even radical adherents of economic liberalism could escape the rule which makes *laissez-faire* inapplicable to advanced industrial conditions; for in the critical case of trade union law and antitrust regulations extreme liberals themselves had to call for manifold interventions of the state, in order to secure against monopolistic compacts the preconditions for the working of a self-regulating market. Even free trade and competition required intervention to be workable. The liberal myth of the "collectivist" conspiracy of the 1870's and 1880's is contrary to all the facts.

Our own interpretation of the double movement is, we find, borne out by the evidence. For if market economy was a threat to the human and natural components of the social fabric, as we insisted, what else would one expect than an urge on the part of a great variety of people to press for some sort of protection? This was what we found. Also, one would expect this to happen without any theoretical or intellectual preconceptions on their part, and irrespective of their attitudes towards the principles underlying a market economy. Again, this was the case. Moreover, we suggested that comparative history of governments might offer quasi-experimental support of our thesis if particular interests could be shown to be independent of the specific ideologies present in a number of different countries. For this also we could adduce striking evidence. Finally, the behavior of liberals themselves proved that the maintenance of freedom of trade—in our terms, of a self-regulating market—far from excluding intervention, in effect, demanded such action, and that liberals themselves regularly called for compulsory action on the part of the state as in the case of trade union law and antitrust laws. Thus nothing could be more decisive than the evidence of history as to which of the two contending interpretations of the double movement was correct: that of the economic liberal who maintained that his policy never had a chance, but was strangled by shortsighted trade unionists, Marxist intellectuals, greedy manufacturers, and reactionary landlords; or that of his critics, who can point to the universal "collectivist" reaction against the expansion of market economy in the second half of the nineteenth century as conclusive proof of the peril to society inherent in the utopian principle of a self-regulating market.

13

BIRTH OF THE LIBERAL CREED (Continued): CLASS INTEREST AND SOCIAL CHANGE

THE LIBERAL MYTH of the collectivist conspiracy must be completely dissipated before the true basis of nineteenth century policies can be laid bare. This legend has it that protectionism was merely the result of sinister interest of agrarians, manufacturers, and trade unionists, who selfishly wrecked the automatic machinery of the market. In another form, and, of course, with an opposite political tendency, Marxian parties argued in equally sectional terms. (That the essential philosophy of Marx centered on the totality of society and the noneconomic nature of man is irrelevant here.[1]) Marx himself followed Ricardo in defining classes in economic terms, and economic exploitation was undoubtedly a feature of the bourgeois age.

In popular Marxism this led to a crude class theory of social development. Pressure for markets and zones of influence was simply ascribed to the profit motive of a handful of financiers. Imperialism was explained as a capitalist conspiracy to induce governments to launch wars in the interests of big business. Wars were held to be caused by these interests in combination with armament firms who miraculously gained the capacity to drive whole nations into fatal policies, contrary to their vital interests. Liberals and Marxists agreed, in effect, in deducing the protectionist movement from the force of sectional interests; in accounting for agrarian tariffs by the political pull of reactionary landlords; in making the profit hunger of industrial magnates accountable for the growth of monopolistic forms of enterprise; in presenting war as the result of business rampant.

The liberal economic outlook thus found powerful support in a narrow class theory. Upholding the viewpoint of opposing classes, liberals and Marxists stood for identical propositions. They established a watertight case for the assertion that nineteenth century protectionism

[1] Marx, K., *Nationalökonomie und Philosophie.* In "Der Historische Material ismus," 1932.

was the result of class action, and that such action must have primarily served the economic interests of the members of the classes concerned. Between them they all but completely obstructed an over-all view of market society, and of the function of protectionism in such a society.

Actually, class interests offer only a limited explanation of long-run movements in society. The fate of classes is much more often determined by the needs of society than the fate of society is determined by the needs of classes. Given a definite structure of society, the class theory works; but what if that structure itself undergoes change? A class that has become functionless may disintegrate and be supplanted overnight by a new class or classes. Also, the chances of classes in a struggle will depend upon their ability to win support from outside their own membership, which again will depend upon their fulfillment of tasks set by interests wider than their own. Thus, neither the birth nor the death of classes, neither their aims nor the degree to which they attain them; neither their co-operations nor their antagonisms can be understood apart from the situation of society as a whole.

Now, this situation is created, as a rule, by external causes, such as a change in climate, in the yield of crops, a new foe, a new weapon used by an old foe, the emergence of new communal ends, or, for that matter, the discovery of new methods of achieving the traditional ends. To such a total situation must sectional interests be ultimately related if their function in social development should become clear.

The essential role played by class interests in social change is in the nature of things. For any widespread form of change must affect the various parts of the community in different fashions, if for no other reason than that of differences of geographical location, and of economic and cultural equipment. Sectional interests are thus the natural vehicle of social and political change. Whether the source of the change be war or trade, startling inventions or shifts in natural conditions, the various sections in society will stand for different methods of adjustment (including forcible ones) and adjust their interests in a different way from those of other groups to whom they may seek to give a lead; hence only when one can point to the group or groups that effected a change is it explained *how* that change has taken place. Yet the ultimate cause is set by external forces, and it is for the mechanism of the change only that society relies on internal forces. The "challenge" is to society as a whole; the "response" comes through groups, sections, and classes.

Mere class interests cannot offer, therefore, a satisfactory explanation for any long-run social process. First, because the process in question may decide about the existence of the class itself; second, because the interests of given classes determine only the aims and purposes toward which those classes are striving, not also the success or failure of such endeavors. There is no magic in class interests which would secure to members of one class the support of members of other classes. Yet such support is an everyday occurrence. Protectionism, in fact, is an instance. The problem here was not so much why agrarians, manufacturers, or trade unionists wished to increase their incomes through protectionist action, but why they succeeded in doing so; not why businessmen and workers wished to establish monopolies for their wares, but why they attained their end; not why some groups wished to act in a similar fashion in a number of Continental countries, but why such groups existed in these otherwise dissimilar countries and equally achieved their aims everywhere; not why those who grew corn attempted to sell it dear, but why they regularly succeeded in persuading those who bought the corn to help to raise its price.

Second, there is the equally mistaken doctrine of the essentially economic nature of class interests. Though human society is naturally conditioned by economic factors, the motives of human individuals are only exceptionally determined by the needs of material want-satisfaction. That nineteenth century society was organized on the assumption that such a motivation could be made universal was a peculiarity of the age. It was therefore appropriate to allow a comparatively wide scope to the play of economic motives when analyzing that society. But we must guard against prejudging the issue, which is precisely to what extent such an unusual motivation could be made effective.

Purely economic matters such as affect want-satisfaction are incomparably less relevant to class behavior than questions of social recognition. Want-satisfaction may be, of course, the result of such recognition, especially as its outward sign or prize. But the interests of a class most directly refer to standing and rank, to status and security, that is, they are primarily not economic but social.

The classes and groups which intermittently took part in the general movement towards protectionism after 1870 did not do so primarily on account of their economic interests. The "collectivist" measures enacted in the critical years reveal that only exceptionally was the interest of any single class involved, and if so, that interest could be rarely described as economic. Assuredly no "shortsighted economic interests" were served by an Act authorizing town authorities to take over neglected ornamental spaces; by regulations requiring the cleaning of bakehouses with hot water and soap at least once in six months; or an Act making compulsory the testing of cables and anchors. Such measures simply responded to the needs of an industrial civilization with which market methods were unable to cope. The great majority of these interventions had no direct, and hardly more than an indirect, bearing on incomes. This was true practically of all laws relating to health and homesteads. public amenities and libraries, factory conditions, and social insurance No less was it true of public utilities, education, transportation, and numberless other matters. But even where money values were involved, they were secondary to other interests. Almost invariably professional status, safety and security, the form of a man's life, the breadth of his existence, the stability of his environment were in question. The monetary importance of some typical interventions, such as customs tariffs, or workmen's compensation, should in no way be minimized. But even in these cases nonmonetary interests were inseparable from monetary ones. Customs tariffs which implied profits for capitalists and wages for workers meant, ultimately, security against unemployment, stabilization of regional conditions, assurance against liquidation of industries, and, perhaps most of all, the avoidance of that painful loss of status which inevitably accompanies transference to a job at which a man is less skilled and experienced than at his own.

Once we are rid of the obsession that only sectional, never general, interests can become effective, as well as of the twin prejudice of restricting the interests of human groups to their monetary income, the breadth and comprehensiveness of the protectionist movement lose their mystery. While monetary interests are necessarily voiced solely by the persons to whom they pertain, other interests have a wider constituency. They affect individuals in innumerable ways as neighbors, professional persons, consumers, pedestrians, commuters, sportsmen, hikers, gardeners, patients, mothers, or lovers—and are accordingly capable of representation by almost any type of territorial or functional association such as churches, townships, fraternal lodges, clubs, trade unions, or, most commonly, political parties based on broad principles of adherence. An all too narrow conception of interest must in effect lead to a warped vision of social and political history, and no purely monetary definition of interests can leave room for that vital need for social protection, the representation of which commonly falls to the persons in charge of the general interests of the community—under modern conditions, the governments of the day. Precisely because not the economic but the social interests of different cross sections of the population were threatened by the market, persons belonging to various economic strata unconsciously joined forces to meet the danger. The spread of the market was thus both advanced and obstructed by the action of class forces. Given the need of machine production for the establishment of a market system, the trading classes alone were in the position to take the lead in that early transformation. A new class of entrepreneurs came into being out of the remnants of older classes, in order to take charge of a development which was consonant with the interests of the community as a whole. But if the rise of the industrialists, entrepreneurs, and capitalists was the result of their leading role in the expansionist movement, the defense fell to the traditional landed classes and the nascent working class. And if among the trading community it was the capitalists' lot to stand for the structural principles of the market system, the role of the die-hard defender of the social fabric was the portion of the feudal aristocracy on the one hand, the rising industrial proletariat on the other. But while the landed classes would naturally seek the solution for all evils in the maintenance of the past, the workers were, up to a point, in the position to transcend the limits of a market society and to borrow solutions from the future. This does not imply that the return to feudalism or the proclamation of socialism was amongst the possible lines of action; but it does indicate the entirely different directions in which agrarians and urban working-class forces tended to seek for relief in an emergency. If market economy broke down, as in every major crisis it threatened to do, the landed classes might attempt a return to a military or feudal regime of paternalism, while the factory workers would see the need for the establishment of a co-operative commonwealth of labor. In a crisis "responses" might point towards mutually exclusive solutions. A mere clash of class interests, which otherwise would have been met by compromise, was invested with a fatal significance.

All this should warn us against relying too much on the economic interests of given classes in the explanation of history. Such an approach would tacitly imply the givenness of those classes in a sense in which this is possible only in an indestructible society. It leaves outside its range those critical phases of history, when a civilization has broken down or is passing through a transformation, when as a rule new classes are formed, sometimes within the briefest space of time, out of the ruins of older classes, or even out of extraneous elements like foreign adventurers or outcasts. Frequently, at a historical juncture new classes have been called into being simply by virtue of the demands of the hour. Ultimately, therefore, it is the relation of a class to society as a whole which maps out its part in the drama; and its success is determined by the breadth and variety of the interests, other than its own, which it is able to serve. Indeed, no policy of a narrow class interest can safeguard even that interest well—a rule which allows of but few exceptions. Unless the alternative to the social setup is a plunge into utter destruction, no crudely selfish class can maintain itself in the lead.

In order to fix safely the blame on the alleged collectivist conspiracy, economic liberals must ultimately deny that any need for the protection of society had arisen. Recently they acclaimed views of some scholars who had rejected the traditional doctrine of the Industrial Revolution according to which a catastrophe broke in upon the unfortunate laboring classes of England about the 1790's. Nothing in the nature of a sudden deterioration of standards, according to these writers, ever overwhelmed the common people. They were, on the average, substantially better off after than before the introduction of the factory system, and, as to numbers, nobody could deny their rapid increase. By the accepted yardsticks of economic welfare—real wages and population figures—the Inferno of early capitalism, they maintained, never existed; the working classes, far from being exploited, were economically the gainers and to argue the need for social protection against a system that benefited all was obviously impossible.

Critics of liberal capitalism were baffled. For some seventy years, scholars and Royal Commissions alike had denounced the horrors of the Industrial Revolution, and a galaxy of poets, thinkers, and writers had branded its cruelties. It was deemed an established fact that the masses were being sweated and starved by the callous exploiters of their helplessness; that enclosures had deprived the country folk of their homes and plots, and thrown them on the labor market created by the Poor Law Reform; and that the authenticated tragedies of the small children who were sometimes worked to death in mines and factories offered ghastly proof of the destitution of the masses. Indeed, the familiar explanation of the Industrial Revolution rested on the degree of exploitation made possible by eighteenth century enclosures; on the low wages offered to homeless workers which accounted for the high profits of the cotton industry as well as the rapid accumulation of capital in the hands of the early manufacturers. And the charge against them was exploitation, a boundless exploitation of their fellow citizens that was the root cause of so much misery and debasement. All this was now apparently refuted. Economic historians proclaimed the message that the black shadow that overcast the early decades of the factory system had been dispelled. For how could there be social catastrophe where there was undoubtedly economic improvement?

Actually, of course, a social calamity is primarily a cultural not an economic phenomenon that can be measured by income figures or population statistics. Cultural catastrophes involving broad strata of the common people can naturally not be frequent; but neither are cataclysmic events like the Industrial Revolution—an economic earthquake which transformed within less than half a century vast masses of the inhabitants of the English countryside from settled folk into shiftless migrants. But if such destructive landslides are exceptional in the history of classes, they are a common occurrence in the sphere of culture contacts between peoples of various races. Intrinsically, the conditions are the same. The difference is mainly that a social class forms part of a society inhabiting the same geographical area, while culture contact occurs usually between societies settled in different geographical regions. In both cases the contact may have a devastating effect on the weaker part. Not economic exploitation, as often assumed, but the disintegration of the cultural environment of the victim is then the cause of the degradation. The economic process may, naturally, supply the vehicle of the destruction, and almost invariably economic inferiority will make the weaker yield, but the immediate cause of his undoing is not for that reason economic; it lies in the lethal injury to the institutions in which his social existence is embodied. The result is loss of self-respect and standards, whether the unit is a people or a class, whether the process springs from so-called "culture conflict" or from a change in the position of a class within the confines of a society.

To the student of early capitalism the parallel is highly significant. The condition of some native tribes in Africa today carries an unmistakable resemblance to that of the English laboring classes during the early years of the nineteenth century. The Kaffir of South Africa, a noble savage, than whom none felt socially more secure in his native *kraal,* has been transformed into a human variety of half-domesticated animal dressed in the "unrelated, the filthy, the unsightly rags that not the most degenerated white man would wear," [2] a nondescript being, without self-respect or standards, veritable human refuse. The description recalls the portrait Robert Owen drew of his own work people,

[2] Millin, Mrs. S. G., *The South Africans,* 1926.

when addressing them in New Lanark, telling them to their faces, coolly and objectively as a social researcher might record the facts, why they had become the degraded rabble which they were; and the true cause of their degradation could not be more aptly described than by their existing in a "cultural vacuum"—the term used by an anthropologist [3] to describe the cause of the cultural debasement of some of the valiant black tribes of Africa under the influence of contact with white civilization. Their crafts have decayed, the political and social conditions of their existence have been destroyed, they are dying from boredom, in Rivers' famous phrase, or wasting their lives and substance in dissipation. While their own culture offers them no longer any objectives worthy of effort or sacrifice, racial snobbishness and prejudice bar the way to their adequate participation in the culture of the white intruders.[4] Substitute social bar for color bar and the Two Nations of the 1840's emerge, the Kaffir having been appropriately replaced by the shambling slum dweller of Kingsley's novels.

Some who would readily agree that life in a cultural void is no life at all nevertheless seem to expect that economic needs would automatically fill that void and make life appear livable under whatever conditions. This assumption is sharply contradicted by the result of anthropological research. "The goals for which individuals will work are culturally determined, and are not a response of the organism to an external culturally undefined situation, like a simple scarcity of food," says Dr. Mead. "The process by which a group of savages is converted into gold miners or ship's crew or merely robbed of all incentive to effort and left to die painlessly beside streams still filled with fish, may seem so bizarre, so alien to the nature of society and its normal functioning as to be pathological," yet, she adds, "precisely this will, as a rule, happen to a people in the midst of violent externally introduced, or at least externally produced change. . . ." She concludes: "This rude contact, this uprooting of simple peoples from their *mores*, is too frequent to be undeserving of serious attention on the part of the social historian."

However, the social historian fails to take the hint. He still refuses to see that the elemental force of culture contact, which is now revolutionizing the colonial world, is the same which, a century ago, created the dismal scenes of early capitalism. An anthropologist [5] drew the

---

[3] Goldenweiser, A., *Anthropology*, 1937.

[4] Goldenweiser, A., *ibid.*

[5] Thurnwald, R. C., *Black and White in East Africa; The Fabric of a New Civilization*, 1935.

general inference: "In spite of numerous divergencies there are at the bottom the same predicaments among the exotic peoples today as there were among us decades or centuries ago. The new technical devices, the new knowledge, the new forms of wealth and power enhanced the social mobility, *i.e.*, migration of individuals, rise and fall of families, differentiation of groups, new forms of leadership, new models of life, different valuations." Thurnwald's penetrating mind recognized that the cultural catastrophe of black society today is closely analogous to that of a large part of white society in the early days of capitalism. The social historian alone still misses the point of the analogy.

Nothing obscures our social vision as effectively as the economistic prejudice. So persistently has exploitation been put into the forefront of the colonial problem that the point deserves special attention. Also, exploitation in a humanly obvious sense has been perpetrated so often, so persistently, and with such ruthlessness on the backward peoples of the world by the white man that it would seem to argue utter insensibility not to accord it pride of place in any discussion of the colonial problem. Yet, it is precisely this emphasis put on exploitation which tends to hide from our view the even greater issue of cultural degeneration. If exploitation is defined in strictly economic terms as a permanent inadequacy of ratios of exchange, it is doubtful whether, as a matter of fact, there was exploitation. The catastrophe of the native community is a direct result of the rapid and violent disruption of the basic institutions of the victim (whether force is used in the process or not does not seem altogether relevant). These institutions are disrupted by the very fact that a market economy is foisted upon an entirely differently organized community; labor and land are made into commodities, which, again, is only a short formula for the liquidation of every and any cultural institution in an organic society. Changes in income and population figures are evidently incommensurable with such a process. Who, for instance, would care to deny that a formerly free people dragged into slavery was exploited, though their standard of life, in some artificial sense, may have been improved in the country to which they were sold as compared with what it was in their native bush? And yet nothing would be altered if we assumed that the conquered natives had been left free and not even been made to overpay the cheap cotton goods thrust upon them, and that their starvation was "merely" caused by the disruption of their social institutions.

To cite the famous instance of India. Indian masses in the second half of the nineteenth century did not die of hunger because they were exploited by Lancashire; they perished in large numbers because the

Indian village community had been demolished. That this was brought about by forces of economic competition, namely, the permanent underselling of hand-woven *chaddar* by machine-made piece goods, is doubtless true; but it proves the opposite of economic exploitation, since dumping implies the reverse of surcharge. The actual source of famines in the last fifty years was the free marketing of grain combined with local failure of incomes. Failure of crops was, of course, part of the picture, but despatch of grain by rail made it possible to send relief to the threatened areas; the trouble was that the people were unable to buy the corn at rocketing prices, which on a free but incompletely organized market were bound to be the reaction to a shortage. In former times small local stores had been held against harvest failure, but these had been now discontinued or swept away into the big market. Famine prevention for this reason now usually took the form of public works to enable the population to buy at enhanced prices. The three or four large famines that decimated India under British rule since the Rebellion were thus neither a consequence of the elements, nor of exploitation, but simply of the new market organization of labor and land which broke up the old village without actually resolving its problems. While under the regime of feudalism and of the village community, *noblesse oblige*, clan solidarity, and regulation of the corn market checked famines, under the rule of the market the people could not be prevented from starving according to the rules of the game. The term "exploitation" describes but ill a situation which became really grave only after the East India Company's ruthless monopoly was abolished and free trade was introduced into India. Under the monopolists the situation had been fairly kept in hand with the help of the archaic organization of the countryside, including free distribution of corn, while under free and equal exchange Indians perished by the millions. Economically, India may have been—and, in the long run, certainly was—benefited, but socially she was disorganized and thus thrown a prey to misery and degradation.

In some cases at least, the opposite of exploitation, if we may say so, started the disintegrating culture contact. The forced land allotment to the North American Indians, in 1887, benefited them individually, according to our financial scale of reckoning. Yet the measure all but destroyed the race in its physical existence—the outstanding case of cultural degeneration on record. The moral genius of a John Collier retrieved the position almost half a century later by insisting on the need for a return to tribal landholdings: today the North American

Indian's is in some places, at least, a live community again—and not economic betterment, but *social restoration* wrought the miracle. The shock of a devastating culture contact was recorded by the pathetic birth of the famous Ghost Dance version of the Pawnee Hand Game about 1890, exactly at the time when improving economic conditions made the aboriginal culture of these Red Indians anachronistic. Furthermore, the fact that not even an increasing population—the other economic index—need exclude a cultural catastrophe is equally borne out by anthropological research. Natural rates of increase of population may actually be an index either of cultural vitality or of cultural degradation. The original meaning of the word "proletarian," linking fertility and mendicity, is a striking expression of this ambivalence.

Economistic prejudice was the source both of the crude exploitation theory of early capitalism and of the no less crude, though more scholarly, misapprehension which later denied the existence of a social catastrophe. The significant implication of this latter and more recent interpretation of history was the rehabilitation of *laissez-faire* economy. For if liberal economics did *not* cause disaster, then protectionism, which robbed the world of the benefits of free markets, was a wanton crime. The very term "Industrial Revolution" was now frowned upon as conveying an exaggerated idea of what was essentially a slow process of change. No more had happened, these scholars insisted, than that a gradual unfolding of the forces of technological progress transformed the lives of the people; undoubtedly, many suffered in the course of the change but on the whole the story was one of continuous improvement. This happy outcome was the result of the almost unconscious working of economic forces which did their beneficial work in spite of the interference of impatient parties who exaggerated the unavoidable difficulties of the time. The inference was no less than a denial that danger had threatened society from the new economy. Had the revised history of the Industrial Revolution been true to fact, the protectionist movement would have lacked all objective justification and *laissez-faire* would have been vindicated. The materialistic fallacy in regard to the nature of social and cultural catastrophe thus bolstered the legend that all the ills of the time had been caused by our lapse from economic liberalism.

Briefly, not single groups or classes were the source of the so-called collectivist movement, though the outcome was decisively influenced by the character of the class interests involved. Ultimately, what made things happen were the interests of society as a whole, though their defense fell primarily to one section of the population in preference to another. It appears reasonable to group our account of the protective movement not around class interests but around the social substances imperiled by the market.

The danger points were given by the main directions of the attack. The competitive labor market hit the bearer of labor power, namely, man. International free trade was primarily a threat to the largest industry dependent upon nature, namely, agriculture. The gold standard imperiled productive organizations depending for their functioning on the relative movement of prices. In each of these fields markets were developed, which implied a latent threat to society in some vital aspects of its existence.

Markets for labor, land, and money are easy to distinguish; but it is not so easy to distinguish those parts of a culture the nucleus of which is formed by human beings, their natural surroundings, and productive organizations, respectively. Man and nature are practically *one* in the cultural sphere; and the money aspect of productive enterprise enters only into one socially vital interest, namely, the unity and cohesion of the nation. Thus, while the markets for the fictitious commodities labor, land, and money were distinct and separate, the threats to society which they involved were not always strictly separable.

In spite of this an outline of the institutional development of Western society during the critical eighty years (1834–1914) might refer to each of these danger points in similar terms. For whether man, nature, or productive organization was concerned, market organization grew into a peril, and definite groups or classes pressed for protection. In each case the considerable time lag between English, Continental, and American development had important bearings, and yet by the turn of the century the protectionist countermove had created an analogous situation in all Western countries.

Accordingly, we will deal separately with the defense of man, nature, and productive organization—a movement of self-preservation as the result of which a more closely knit type of society emerged, yet one which stood in danger of total disruption.

14

MARKET AND MAN

To SEPARATE LABOR from other activities of life and to subject it to
the laws of the market was to annihilate all organic forms of existence
and to replace them by a different type of organization, an atomistic
and individualistic one.

Such a scheme of destruction was best served by the application of
the principle of freedom of contract. In practice this meant that the
noncontractual organizations of kinship, neighborhood, profession, and
creed were to be liquidated since they claimed the allegiance of the
individual and thus restrained his freedom. To represent this principle
as one of noninterference, as economic liberals were wont to do, was
merely the expression of an ingrained prejudice in favor of a definite
kind of interference, namely, such as would destroy noncontractual
relations between individuals and prevent their spontaneous re-forma-
tion.

This effect of the establishment of a labor market is conspicuously
apparent in colonial regions today. The natives are to be forced to
make a living by selling their labor. To this end their traditional institutions must be destroyed, and prevented from re-forming, since, as a
rule, the individual in primitive society is not threatened by starvation
unless the community as a whole is in a like predicament. Under the
kraal-land system of the Kaffirs, for instance, "destitution is impossible:
whosoever needs assistance receives it unquestioningly." [1] No Kwakiutl
"ever ran the least risk of going hungry." [2] "There is no starvation in
societies living on the subsistence margin." [3] The principle of freedom
from want was equally acknowledged in the Indian village community
and, we might add, under almost every and any type of social organization up to about the beginning of sixteenth century Europe, when

[1] Mair, L. P., *An African People in the Twentieth Century*, 1934.
[2] Loeb, E. M., *The Distribution and Function of Money in Early Society.* In
"Essays in Anthropology," 1936.
[3] Herskovits, M. J., *The Economic Life of Primitive Peoples*, 1940.

the modern ideas on the poor put forth by the humanist Vives were argued before the Sorbonne. It is the absence of the threat of individual starvation which makes primitive society, in a sense, more human than market economy, and at the same time less economic. Ironically, the white man's initial contribution to the black man's world mainly consisted in introducing him to the uses of the scourge of hunger. Thus the colonists may decide to cut the breadfruit trees down in order to create an artificial food scarcity or may impose a hut tax on the native to force him to barter away his labor. In either case the effect is similar to that of Tudor enclosures with their wake of vagrant hordes. A League of Nations report mentioned with due horror the recent appearance of that ominous figure of the sixteenth century European scene, the "masterless man," in the African bush.[4] During the late Middle Ages he had been found only in the "interstices" of society.[5] Yet he was the forerunner of the nomadic laborer of the nineteenth century.[6]

Now, what the white man may still occasionally practice in remote regions today, namely, the smashing up of social structures in order to extract the element of labor from them, was done in the eighteenth century to white populations by white men for similar purposes. Hobbes' grotesque vision of the State—a human Leviathan whose vast body was made up of an infinite number of human bodies—was dwarfed by the Ricardian construct of the labor market: a flow of human lives the supply of which was regulated by the amount of food put at their disposal. Although it was acknowledged that there existed a customary standard below which no laborer's wages could sink, this limitation also was thought to become effective only if the laborer was reduced to the choice of being left without food or of offering his labor in the market for the price it would fetch. This explains, incidentally, an otherwise inexplicable omission of the classical economists, namely, why only the penalty of starvation, not also the allurement of high wages, was deemed capable of creating a functioning labor market. Here also colonial experience has confirmed theirs. For the higher the wages the smaller the inducement to exertion on the part of the native, who unlike the white man was not compelled by his cultural standards to make as much money as he possibly could. The analogy was all the more striking as the early laborer, too, abhorred the factory, where he

---

[4] Thurnwald, R. C., op. cit.

[5] Brinkmann, C., "Das soziale System des Kapitalismus," Grundriss der Sozial-ökonomik, 1924.

[6] Toynbee, A., Lectures on the Industrial Revolution, 1887, p. 98.

felt degraded and tortured, like the native who often resigned himself to work in our fashion only when threatened with corporal punishment, if not physical mutilation. The Lyons manufacturers of the eighteenth century urged low wages primarily for social reasons.[7] Only an overworked and downtrodden laborer, they argued, would forgo to associate with his comrades and escape the condition of personal servitude under which he could be made to do whatever his master required from him. Legal compulsion and parish serfdom as in England, the rigors of an absolutist labor police as on the Continent, indented labor as in the early Americas were the prerequisites of the "willing worker." But the final stage was reached with the application of "nature's penalty," hunger. In order to release it, it was necessary to liquidate organic society, which refused to permit the individual to starve.

The protection of society, in the first instance, falls to the rulers, who can directly enforce their will. However, it is all too easily assumed by economic liberals that economic rulers tend to be beneficial, while political rulers do not. Adam Smith did not seem to think so when he urged that direct British rule should replace administration through a chartered company in India. Political rulers, he argued, would have parallel interests with the ruled whose wealth would swell their revenue, while the merchant's interests were naturally antagonistic to those of his customers.

By interest and inclination it fell to the landlords of England to protect the lives of the common people from the onrush of the Industrial Revolution. Speenhamland was a moat erected in defense of the traditional rural organization, when the turmoil of change was sweeping the countryside, and, incidentally, making agriculture a precarious industry. In their natural reluctance to bow to the needs of the manufacturing towns, the squires were the first to make a stand in what proved to be a century's losing fight. Yet their resistance was not in vain; it averted ruin for several generations and allowed time for almost complete readjustment. Over a critical span of forty years it retarded economic progress, and when, in 1834, the Reform Parliament abolished Speenhamland, the landlords shifted their resistance to the factory laws. The Church and the manor were now rousing the people against the mill owner whose predominance would make the cry for cheap food irresistible, and thus, indirectly, threaten to sap rents and tithes. Oastler, for one, was "a Churchman, a Tory, and a Protection-

[7] Heckscher, E. F., *op. cit.,* Vol. II, p. 168.

ist";[8] moreover, he was also a Humanitarian. So were also, with vary-ing mixtures of these ingredients of Tory socialism, the other great fighters in the factory movement: Sadler, Southey and Lord Shaftes-bury. But the premonition of threatening pecuniary losses which prompted the bulk of their followers proved only too well grounded: Manchester exporters were soon clamoring for lower wages involving cheaper grain—the repeal of Speenhamland and the growth of the fac-tories actually prepared the way for the success of the Anti-Corn Law agitation, in 1846. Yet, for adventitious reasons, the ruin of agriculture was postponed in England for a whole generation. Meanwhile Disraeli grounded Tory socialism on a protest against the Poor Law Reform Act, and the conservative landlords of England forced radically new techniques of life upon an industrial society. The Ten Hours Bill of 1847, which Karl Marx hailed as the first victory of socialism, was the work of enlightened reactionaries.

The laboring people themselves were hardly a factor in this great movement the effect of which was, figuratively speaking, to allow them to survive the Middle Passage. They had almost as little to say in the determination of their own fate as the black cargo of Hawkins' ships. Yet it was precisely this lack of active participation on the part of the British working class in deciding its own fate that determined the course of English social history and made it, for better or for worse, so different from that of the Continent.

There is a peculiar touch about the undirected excitements, the fumblings and blunders of a nascent class, the true nature of which his-tory has long since revealed. Politically, the British working class was defined by the Parliamentary Reform Act of 1832, which refused them the vote; economically, by the Poor Law Reform Act of 1834, which excluded them from relief and distinguished them from the pauper. For some time to come the industrial working-class-to-be was uncertain whether its salvation did not lie after all in a return to rural existence and conditions of handicraft. In the two decades following Speenhamland its endeavors were focused on the stopping of the free use of machinery either by the enforcement of the apprenticeship clauses of the Statute of Artificers or by direct action as in Luddism. This backward-looking attitude lingered on as an undercurrent all through the Owenite move-ment till the end of the forties, when the Ten Hours Bill, the eclipse of Chartism, and the beginning of the Golden Age of capitalism obliter-

[8] Dicey, A. V., *op. cit.*, p. 226.

ated the vision of the past. Up to that time the British working class *in statu nascendi* was a riddle unto itself; and only if one follows with understanding its half-unconscious stirrings is it possible to gauge the immensity of the loss England suffered through the exclusion of the working class from an equal share in national life. When Owenism and Chartism had burned themselves out, England had become poorer by that substance out of which the Anglo-Saxon ideal of a free society could have been built up for centuries to come.

Even if the Owenite movement had resulted only in inconsiderable local activities, it would have formed a monument to the creative imagination of the race, and even if Chartism had never penetrated beyond the confines of that nucleus which conceived of the idea of a "national holiday" to gain the rights of the people, it would have shown that some of the people were still able to dream their own dreams, and were taking the measure of a society which had forgotten the shape of man. Yet neither the one nor the other was the case. Owenism was not the inspiration of a minute sect, nor was Chartism restricted to a political *élite;* both movements comprised hundreds of thousands of craftsmen and artisans, laborers and working people, and with their vast following ranked among the biggest social movements in modern history. And yet different as they were and similar only in the measure of their failure, they served to prove how inevitable from the first the necessity was of protecting man against the market.

The Owenite Movement originally was neither political nor working class. It represented the cravings of the common people, smitten by the coming of the factory, to discover a form of existence which would make man master of the machine. Essentially, it aimed at what would appear to us as a by-passing of capitalism. Such a formula would, of course, be bound to be somewhat misleading, since the organizing role of capital and the nature of a self-regulating market were still unknown. Yet it expresses perhaps best the spirit of Owen, who emphatically was not an enemy of the machine. In spite of the machine, he believed, man should remain his own employer; the principle of co-operation or "union" would solve the problem of the machine without sacrificing either individual freedom or social solidarity, either man's dignity or his sympathy with his fellows.

The strength of Owenism was that its inspiration was eminently practical, and yet its methods were based on an appreciation of man as a whole. Although the problems were intrinsically those of everyday life such as the quality of food, housing, and education, the level of wages, the avoidance of unemployment, support in sickness and the like, the issues involved were as broad as the moral forces they appealed to. The conviction that, if only the right method was found, man's existence could be restored enabled the roots of the movement to penetrate into that deeper layer where personality itself is formed. There rarely was a less intellectualized social movement of a similar scope; the convictions of those engaged in it imbued even their seemingly most trivial activities with meaning, so that no set creed was needed. Indeed their faith was prophetic, since they insisted on methods of reconstruction which transcended market economy.

Owenism was a religion of industry the bearer of which was the working class.[9] Its wealth of forms and initiatives was unrivaled. Practically, it was the beginning of the modern trade union movement. Co-operative societies were founded, mainly engaged in retail to their members. These were not, of course, regular consumers' co-operatives, but rather stores backed by enthusiasts determined to devote the profits of the venture to the furtherance of Owenite plans, preferably to the establishment of Villages of Co-operation. "Their activities were quite as much educational and propagandist as commercial; their aim was the creation of the New Society by their associated effort." The "Union Shops" erected by members of trade unions were more in the nature of producers' co-operatives, unemployed artisans could find work there, or, in case of strikes, earn some money in lieu of strike pay. In the Owenite "Labour Exchange" the idea of the co-operative store was developed into an institution *sui generis*. At the heart of the Exchange or Bazaar there was reliance on the complementary nature of the crafts; by providing for one another's needs, artisans would emancipate themselves, it was thought, from the ups and downs of the market; this was, later, accompanied by the use of labor notes which had a considerable circulation. Such a device might seem fantastic today; but in Owen's time the character not only of wage labor, but also of bank notes, was still unexplored. Socialism was not essentially different from those projects and inventions with which the Benthamite movement was teeming. Not only the rebellious opposition, but also the respectable middle class was still in an experimental mood. Jeremy Bentham himself invested in Owen's futuristic education scheme in New Lanark, and earned a dividend. The Owenite Societies proper were associations or clubs designed to support plans of Villages of Co-opera-

[9] Cole, G. D. H., *Robert Owen*, 1925, a work on which we have heavily drawn.

tion such as we described in connection with the relief of the poor; this was the origin of the argricultural producers' co-operative, an idea which had a long and distinguished career. The first national producers' organization with syndicalist aims was the Operative Builders' Union, which attempted to regulate the building trade directly by creating "buildings upon the most extensive scale," introducing a currency of its own, and exhibiting the means of realizing "the great association for the emancipation of the productive classes." The industrial producers' co-operatives of the nineteenth century date from this venture. It was from the Builders' Union or Guild and its "Parliament" that the even more ambitious consolidated Trades Union sprang, which for a short time comprised almost a million workers and artisans in its loose federation of trade unions and co-operative societies. Its idea was industrial revolt by peaceful means, which will appear as no contradiction once we remember that in the messianistic dawn of their movement the mere consciousness of their mission was supposed to make the aspirations of the working people irresistible. The martyrs of Tolpuddle belonged to a rural branch of this organization. Propaganda for factory legislation was carried on by Regeneration Societies; while later on ethical societies were founded, the forerunners of the secularist movement. The idea of nonviolent resistance was fully developed in their midst. Like Saint-Simonianism in France, Owenism in England showed all the characteristics of spiritual inspiration; but while Saint-Simon worked for a renaissance of Christianity, Owen was the first opponent of Christianity amongst modern working-class leaders. The consumers' co-operatives of Great Britain which found imitators all over the world were, of course, the most eminently practical offshoot of Owenism. That its impetus was lost—or, rather, was maintained only in the peripheric sphere of the consumers' movement—was the greatest single defeat of spiritual forces in the history of industrial England. Yet a people, which, after the moral debasement of the Speenhamland period, still possessed the resilience required for a creative effort so imaginative and sustained, must have disposed of almost boundless intellectual and emotional vigor.

To Owenism with its claim to man as a whole there still clung something of that medieval inheritance of corporative life which found expression in the Builders' Guild and in the rural scene of its social ideal, the Villages of Co-operation. Although it was the fount of modern socialism, its proposals were not based on the property issue, which

is the legal aspect only of capitalism. In hitting on the new phenomenon of industry, as Saint-Simon had done, it recognized the challenge of the machine. But the characteristic trait in Owenism was that
it insisted on the *social* approach: it refused to accept the division of
society into an economic and political sphere, and, in effect, rejected
political action on that account. The acceptance of a separate economic
sphere would have implied the recognition of the principle of gain and
profit as the organizing force in society. This Owen refused to do.
His genius recognized that the incorporation of the machine was possible only in a new society. The industrial aspect of things was to him
in no way restricted to the economic (this would have implied a marketing view of society which he rejected). New Lanark had taught him
that in a worker's life wages was only one among many factors such as
natural and home surroundings, quality and prices of commodities,
stability of employment, and security of tenure. (The factories of New
Lanark like some other firms before them kept their employees on the
payroll even when there was no work for them to do.) But much more
than that was comprised in the adjustment. The education of children
and adults, provision for entertainment, dance, and music, and the
general assumption of high moral and personal standards of old and
young created the atmosphere in which a new status was attained by
the industrial population as a whole. Thousands of persons from all
over Europe (and even America) visited New Lanark as if it were a
reservation of the future in which had been accomplished the impossible
feat of running a successful factory business with a human population.
Yet Owen's firm paid considerably lower wages than those current in
some neighboring towns. The profits of New Lanark sprang mainly
from the high productivity of labor on shorter hours, due to excellent
organization and rested men, advantages which outweighed the increase in real wages involved in the generous provisions for a decent
life. But the latter alone explain the sentiments of all but adulation
with which his workers clung to Owen. Out of experiences such as these
he extracted the social, that is, wider-than-economic approach to the
problem of industry.

It was another tribute to his insight that in spite of this comprehensive outlook he grasped the incisive nature of the concrete physical
facts dominating the laborer's existence. His religious sense revolted
against the practical transcendentalism of a Hannah More and her
Cheap Repository Tracts. One of them commended the example of a
Lancashire colliery girl. She was taken down the pit, at the age of

nine, to act as drawer with her brother, who was two years younger.[10] "She cheerfully followed him [her father] down into the coal-pit, burying herself in the bowels of the earth, and there at a tender age, without excusing herself on account of her sex, she joined in the same work with the miners, a race of men rough indeed, but highly useful to the community." The father was killed by an accident down the pit in the sight of his children. She then applied for employment as a servant, but there was a prejudice against her because she had been a collier, and her application failed. Fortunately, by that comforting dispensation by which afflictions are turned into blessings, her bearing and patience attracted notice, inquiries were made at the colliery, and she received such a glowing character that she was taken into employment. "This story," the tract concluded, "may teach the poor that they can seldom be in any condition of life so low as to prevent their rising to some degree of independence if they choose to exert themselves, and there can be no situation whatever so mean as to forbid the practice of many noble virtues." The sisters More preferred to work among starving laborers, but refused so much as to be interested in their physical sufferings. They were inclined to solve the physical problem of industrialism by simply conferring status and function on the workers out of the plenitude of their magnanimity. Hannah More insisted that her heroine's father was a highly useful member of the community; the rank of his daughter was recognized by the acknowledgments of her employers. Hannah More believed that no more was needed for a functioning society.[11] Owen turned away from a Christianity which renounced the task of mastering the world of man, and which preferred to extol the imaginary status and function of Hannah More's wretched heroine, instead of facing the awful revelation that transcended the New Testament, of man's condition in a complex society. Nobody can doubt the sincerity which inspired Hannah More's conviction that the more readily the poor acquiesced in their condition of degradation, the more easily they would turn to the heavenly solaces on which alone she relied both for their salvation and for the smooth functioning of a market society in which she firmly believed. But these empty husks of Christianity on which the inner life of the most generous of the upper classes was vegetating contrasted but poorly with the creative faith of

[10] More, H., *The Lancashire Colliery Girl*, May, 1795; cf. Hammond, J. L. and B., *The Town Labourer*, 1917, p. 230.

[11] Cf. Drucker, P. F., *The End of Economic Man*, 1939, p. 93, on the English Evangelicals; and *The Future of Industrial Man*, 1942, pp. 21 and 194 on status and function.

that religion of industry in the spirit of which the common people of England were endeavoring to redeem society. However, capitalism had still a future in store.

The Chartist Movement appealed to a set of impulses so different that its emergence after the practical failure of Owenism and its premature initiatives might have been almost predicted. It was a purely political effort which made a bid for influence on government through constitutional channels; its attempt to put pressure on the government was on the traditional lines of the Reform Movement which had secured the vote to the middle classes. The Six Points of the Charter demanded an effective popular suffrage. The uncompromising rigidity with which such an extension of the vote was rejected by the Reformed Parliament for a third of a century, the use of force in view of the mass support that was manifest for the Charter, the abhorrence in which the liberals of the 1840's held the idea of popular government all prove that the concept of democracy was foreign to the English middle classes. Only when the working class had accepted the principles of a capitalist economy and the trade unions had made the smooth running of industry their chief concern did the middle classes concede the vote to the better situated workers; that is, long after the Chartist Movement had subsided and it had become certain that the workers would not try to use the franchise in the service of any ideas of their own. From the point of view of the spreading of the market forms of existence this may have been justified, since it helped to overcome the obstacles presented by the surviving organic and traditional forms of life among the laboring people. As to the entirely different task of restoring the common people, whose lives had been uprooted in the Industrial Revolution, and inducting them into the fold of a common national culture. it was left undone. Their investment with the vote at a time when irreparable damage had already been inflicted upon their capacity for sharing in leadership, could not retrieve the position. The ruling classes had committed the error of extending the principle of uncompromising class rule to a type of civilization which demanded the cultural and educational unity of the commonwealth if it should be safe from degenerative influences.

The Chartist Movement was political and thus easier to comprehend than Owenism. Yet it is doubtful whether the emotional intensity, or even the extent of that movement can be realized without some imaginative reference to the times. The years 1789 and 1830 had made revolution a regular institution in Europe; in 1848, the date of the Paris rising was actually forecast in Berlin and London with a precision more usual in regard to the opening of a fair than to a social upheaval, and "follow-up" revolutions broke out promptly in Berlin, Vienna, Budapest, and some towns of Italy. In London also there was high tension, for everybody, including the Chartists themselves, expected violent action to compel Parliament to grant the vote to the people. (Less than 15 per cent of adult males were entitled to vote.) Never in all the history of England was there a comparable concentration of force put in readiness for the defense of law and order than on April 12, 1848; hundreds of thousands of citizens were prepared in the capacity of special constables to turn their arms against the Chartists on that day. The Paris Revolution came too late to carry a popular movement in England to victory. By that time the spirit of revolt roused by the Poor Law Reform Act as well as by the sufferings of the Hungry Forties was waning; the wave of rising trade was boosting employment, and capitalism began to deliver the goods. The Chartists dispersed peacefully. Their case was not even considered by Parliament until a later date, when their application was defeated by a five-to-one majority in the House of Commons. In vain had millions of signatures been collected. In vain had the Chartists behaved as law-abiding citizens. Their Movement was ridiculed out of existence by the victors. Thus ended the greatest political effort of the people of England to constitute that country a popular democracy. A year or two later Chartism was all but forgotten.

The Industrial Revolution reached the Continent half a century later. There the working class had not been forced off the land by an enclosure movement; rather, the allurements of higher wages and urban life made the semiservile agricultural laborer desert the manor and migrate to the town, where he consorted with the traditional lower middle class, and had a chance of acquiring an urban tone. Far from feeling debased, he felt elevated by his new environment. Doubtless housing conditions were abominable, alcoholism and prostitution were rampant among the lower strata of town laborers as late as the beginning of the twentieth century. Yet there was no comparison between the moral and cultural catastrophe of the English cottager or copyholder of decent ancestry, who found himself hopelessly sinking in the social and physical mire of the slums of some factory neighborhood and the Slovakian or, for that matter, Pomeranian agricultural laborer changing almost overnight from a stable-dwelling peon into an industrial worker in a modern metropolis. An Irish or Welsh day laborer or Western Highlander might have had a similar experience when slouching through the alleys of early Manchester or Liverpool; but the English yeoman's son or the evicted cottager certainly did not feel his status raised. Yet not only had the recently emancipated peasant lout of the Continent a fair chance of rising into the lower middle classes of craftsmen and traders with their ancient cultural traditions, but even the bourgeoisie, which socially towered above him, was politically in the same boat, being almost as removed from the ranks of the actual ruling class as he was himself. Against feudal aristocracy and Roman episcopacy the forces of the rising middle and working classes were closely allied. The intelligentsia, particularly the university students, cemented the union between these two classes in their common attack on absolutism and privilege. In England the middle classes, whether squires and merchants as in the seventeenth century, or farmers and tradesmen as in the nineteenth, were strong enough to vindicate their rights alone, and not even in their near-revolutionary effort in 1832 did they look to the laborers for support. Moreover, the English aristocracy unfailingly assimilated the wealthiest of the newcomers and broadened the top ranks of the social hierarchy, while on the Continent the still semifeudal aristocracy did not inter-marry with the sons and daughters of the bourgeoisie, and the absence of the institution of primogeniture hermetically insulated them from the other classes. Every successful step towards equal rights and liberties thus benefited Continental middle and working classes alike. Since 1830, if not since 1789, it was part of the Continental tradition that the working class would help to fight the battles of the bourgeoisie against feudalism, if only—as the saying ran—to be cheated by the middle class of the fruits of victory. But whether the working class won or lost, its experience was enhanced, and its aims raised to a political level. This was what was meant by becoming class conscious. Marxian ideologies crystallized the outlook of the urban worker, who had been taught by circumstances to use his industrial and political strength as a weapon of high policy. While the British workers developed an incomparable experience in the personal and social problems of unionism, including the tactics and strategy of industrial action, and left national politics to their betters, the Central European worker became a political socialist, used to handle problems of statecraft—primarily, it is true, those which concerned his own interests, such as factory laws and social legislation.

If there was a time-lag of some half a century between the industrialization of Great Britain and that of the Continent, there was a very much greater lag between the establishment of national unity. Italy and Germany arrived only during the second half of the nineteenth century at that stage of unification which England achieved centuries before, and smaller Eastern Europe states reached even later. In this process of state building the working classes played a vital part, which further enhanced their political experience. In the industrial age such a process could not fail to comprise social policy. Bismarck made a bid for unification of the Second Reich through the introduction of an epochal scheme of social legislation. Italian unity was speeded up by the nationalization of the railways. In the Austro-Hungarian monarchy, that congeries of races and peoples, the Crown itself repeatedly appealed to the laboring classes for support in the work of centralization and imperial unity. In this wider sphere also, through their influence on legislation, the socialist parties and trade unions found many openings for serving the interests of the industrial worker.

Materialistic preconceptions have blurred the outlines of the working-class problem. British writers have found it difficult to comprehend the terrible impression that early capitalistic conditions in Lancashire made on Continental observers. They pointed to the even lower standard of life of many Central European artisans in the textile industries, whose conditions of work were often perhaps just as bad as those of their English comrades. Yet such a comparison obscured the salient point, which was precisely the rise in the social and political status of the laborer on the Continent in contrast to a fall in that status in England. The Continental laborer had not passed through the degrading pauperization of Speenhamland nor was there any parallel in his experience to the scorching fires of the New Poor Law. From the status of a villein he changed—or rather rose—to that of a factory worker, and very soon to that of an enfranchised and unionized worker. Thus he escaped the cultural catastrophe which followed in the wake of the Industrial Revolution in England. Moreover, the Continent was industrialized at a time when adjustment to the new productive techniques had already become possible, thanks, almost exclusively, to the imitation of English methods of social protection.[12]

[12] Knowles, L., The Industrial and Commercial Revolution in Great Britain During the 19th Century, 1926.

The Continental worker needed protection not so much against the impact of the Industrial Revolution—in the social sense there never was such a thing on the Continent—as against the normal action of factory and labor market conditions. He achieved it mainly by the help of legislation, while his British comrades relied more on voluntary association—trade unions—and their power to monopolize labor. Social insurance came, relatively, very much sooner on the Continent than in England. The difference was readily explained by the Continental's political bent, and by the comparatively early extension of the vote to the working masses on the Continent. While economically the difference between compulsory and voluntary methods of protection—legislation versus unionism—can be easily overrated, politically its consequences were great. On the Continent trade unions were a creation of the political party of the working class; in England the political party was a creation of the trade unions. While on the Continent unionism became more or less socialist, in England even political socialism remained essentially trade unionist. Universal suffrage, therefore, which in England tended to increase national unity, had sometimes the opposite effect on the Continent. There, rather than in England, did Pitt's and Peel's, Tocqueville's and Macaulay's misgivings come true that popular government would involve a danger to the economic system.

Economically, English and Continental methods of social protection led to almost identical results. They achieved what had been intended: the disruption of the market for that factor of production known as labor power. Such a market could serve its purpose only if wages fell parallel with prices. In human terms such a postulate implied for the worker extreme instability of earnings, utter absence of professional standards, abject readiness to be shoved and pushed about indiscriminately, complete dependence on the whims of the market. Mises justly argued that if workers "did not act as trade unionists, but reduced their demands and changed their locations and occupations according to the requirements of the labor market, they could eventually find work." This sums up the position under a system based on the postulate of the commodity character of labor. It is not for the commodity to decide where it should be offered for sale, to what purpose it should be used, at what price it should be allowed to change hands, and in what manner it should be consumed or destroyed. "It has occurred to no one," this consistent liberal wrote, "that lack of wages would be a better term than lack of employment, for what the

unemployed person misses is not work but the remuneration of work."
Mises was right, though he should not have claimed originality; 150
years prior to him Bishop Whately said: "When a man begs for work
he asks not for work but for wages." Yet, it is true that technically
speaking "unemployment in the capitalist countries is due to the fact
that the policy both of the government and of the trade unions aims at
maintaining a level of wages which is out of harmony with the existing
productivity of labor." For how could there be unemployment, Mises
asked, but for the fact that the workers are "not willing to work at the
wages they could get in the labor market for the particular work they
were able and willing to perform?" This makes clear what the employers' demand for mobility of labor and flexibility of wages really
means: precisely that which we circumscribed above as a market in
which human labor is a commodity.

The natural aim of all social protection was to destroy such an
institution and make its existence impossible. Actually, the labor
market was allowed to retain its main function only on condition that
wages and conditions of work, standards and regulations should be
such as would safeguard the human character of the alleged commodity, labor. To argue that social legislation, factory laws, unemployment insurance, and, above all, trade unions have not interfered
with the mobility of labor and the flexibility of wages, as is sometimes
done, is to imply that those institutions have entirely failed in their
purpose, which was exactly that of interfering with the laws of supply
and demand in respect to human labor, and removing it from the orbit
of the market.

15

MARKET AND NATURE

WHAT WE CALL LAND is an element of nature inextricably interwoven with man's institutions. To isolate it and form a market out of it was perhaps the weirdest of all undertakings of our ancestors.

Traditionally, land and labor are not separated; labor forms part of life, land remains part of nature, life and nature form an articulate whole. Land is thus tied up with the organizations of kinship, neighborhood, craft, and creed—with tribe and temple, village, gild, and church. One Big Market, on the other hand, is an arrangement of economic life which includes markets for the factors of production. Since these factors happen to be indistinguishable from the elements of human institutions, man and nature, it can be readily seen that market economy involves a society the institutions of which are subordinated to the requirements of the market mechanism.

The proposition is as utopian in respect to land as in respect to labor. The economic function is but one of many vital functions of land. It invests man's life with stability; it is the site of his habitation; it is a condition of his physical safety; it is the landscape and the seasons. We might as well imagine his being born without hands and feet as carrying on his life without land. And yet to separate land from man and organize society in such a way as to satisfy the requirements of a real-estate market was a vital part of the utopian concept of a market economy.

Again, it is in the field of modern colonization that the true significance of such a venture becomes manifest. Whether the colonist needs land as a site for the sake of the wealth buried in it, or whether he merely wishes to constrain the native to produce a surplus of food and raw materials, is often irrelevant; nor does it make much difference whether the native works under the direct supervision of the colonist or only under some form of indirect compulsion, for in every and any case the social and cultural system of native life must be first shattered.

There is close analogy between the colonial situation today and that of Western Europe a century or two ago. But the mobilization of land which in exotic regions may be compressed into a few years or decades may have taken as many centuries in Western Europe. The challenge came from the growth of other than purely commercial forms of capitalism. There was, starting in England with the Tudors, agricultural capitalism with its need for an individualized treatment of the land, including conversions and enclosures. There was industrial capitalism which—in France as in England—was primarily rural and needed sites for its mills and laborers' settlements, since the beginning of the eighteenth century. Most powerful of all, though affecting more the use of the land than its ownership, there was the rise of industrial towns with their need for practically unlimited food and raw material supplies in the nineteenth century.

Superficially, there was little likeness in the responses to these challenges, yet they were stages in the subordination of the surface of the planet to the needs of an industrial society. The first stage was the commercialization of the soil, mobilizing the feudal revenue of the land. The second was the forcing up of the production of food and organic raw materials to serve the needs of a rapidly growing industrial population on a national scale. The third was the extension of such a system of surplus production to overseas and colonial territories. With this last step land and its produce were finally fitted into the scheme of a self-regulating world market.

Commercialization of the soil was only another name for the liquidation of feudalism which started in Western urban centers as well as in England in the fourteenth century and was concluded some five hundred years later in the course of the European revolutions, when the remnants of villeinage were abolished. To detach man from the soil meant the dissolution of the body economic into its elements so that each element could fit into that part of the system where it was most useful. The new system was first established alongside the old which it tried to assimilate and absorb, by securing a grip on such soil as was still bound up in precapitalistic ties. The feudal sequestration of the land was abolished. "The aim was the elimination of all claims on the part of neighborhood or kinship organizations, especially those of virile aristocratic stock, as well as of the Church—claims, which exempted land from commerce or mortgage." [1] Some of this was achieved by individual force and violence, some by revolution from

---

[1] Brinkmann, C., "Das soziale System des Kapitalismus," *Grundriss der Sozialökonomik,* 1924.

above or below, some by war and conquest, some by legislative action, some by administrative pressure, some by spontaneous small-scale action of private persons over long stretches of time. Whether the dislocation was swiftly healed or whether it caused an open wound in the body social depended primarily on the measures taken to regulate the process. Powerful factors of change and adjustment were introduced by the governments themselves. Secularization of Church lands, for instance, was one of the fundaments of the modern state up to the time of the Italian *Risorgimento* and, incidentally, one of the chief means of the ordered transference of land into the hands of private individuals.

The biggest single steps were taken by the French Revolution and by the Benthamite reforms of the 1830's and 1840's. "The condition most favorable to the prosperity of agriculture exists," wrote Bentham, "when there are no entails, no unalienable endowments, no common lands, no right of redemptions, no tithes. . . ." Such freedom in dealing with property, and especially property in land, formed an essential part of the Benthamite conception of individual liberty. To extend this freedom in one way or another was the aim and effect of legislation such as the Prescriptions Acts, the Inheritance Act, the Fines and Recoveries Act, the Real Property Act, the general Enclosure Act of 1801 and its successors,[2] as well as the Copyhold Acts from 1841 up to 1926. In France and much of the Continent the Code Napoléon instituted middle-class forms of property, making land a commerciable good and making mortgage a private civil contract.

The second step, overlapping the first, was the subordination of land to the needs of a swiftly expanding urban population. Although the soil cannot be physically mobilized, its produce can, if transportation facilities and the law permit. *"Thus the mobility of goods to some extent compensates the lack of interregional mobility of the factors*; or (what is really the same thing) trade mitigates the disadvantages of the unsuitable geographical distribution of the productive facilities."* [3] Such a notion was entirely foreign to the traditional outlook. "Neither with the ancients, nor during the early Middle Ages—this should be emphatically asserted—were the goods of every day life regularly bought and sold." [4] Surpluses of grain were supposed to

---

[2] Dicey, A. V., *op. cit.*, p. 226.
[3] Ohlin, B., *Interregional and International Trade*, 1935, p. 42.
[4] Bücher, K., *Entstehung der Volkswirtschaft*, 1904. Cf. also Penrose, E. F., *Population Theories and Their Application*, 1934, quotes Longfield, 1834, for the first mention of the idea that movements of commodities may be regarded as substitutes for movements of the factors of production.

provision the neighborhood, especially the local town; corn markets up to the fifteenth century had a strictly local organization. But the growth of towns induced landlords to produce primarily for sale on the market and—in England—the growth of the metropolis compelled authorities to loosen the restrictions on the corn trade and allow it to become regional, though never national.

Eventually agglomeration of the population in the industrial towns of the second half of the eighteenth century changed the situation completely—first on a national, then on a world scale.

To effect this change was the true meaning of free trade. The mobilization of the produce of the land was extended from the neighboring countryside to tropical and subtropical regions—the industrial-agricultural division of labor was applied to the planet. As a result, peoples of distant zones were drawn into the vortex of change the origins of which were obscure to them, while the European nations became dependent for their everyday activities upon a not yet ensured integration of the life of mankind. With free trade the new and tremendous hazards of planetary interdependence sprang into being.

The scope of social defense against all-round dislocation was as broad as the front of attack. Though common law and legislation speeded up change at times, at others they slowed it down. However, common law and statute law were not necessarily acting in the same direction at any given time.

In the advent of the labor market common law played mainly a positive part—the commodity theory of labor was first stated emphatically not by economists but by lawyers. On the issue of labor combinations and the law of conspiracy, too, the common law favored a free labor market, though this meant restricting the freedom of association of organized workers.

But, in respect to land, the common law shifted its role from encouraging change to opposing it. During the sixteenth and seventeenth centuries, more often than not common law insisted on the owner's right to improve his land profitably even if this involved grave dislocation in habitations and employment. On the Continent this process of mobilization involved, as we know, the reception of Roman law, while in England common law held its own and succeeded in bridging the gap between restricted medieval property rights and modern individual property without sacrificing the principle of judge-made law vital to constitutional liberty. Since the eighteenth century, on the other hand, common law in land acted as a conserver of the past in the face of modernizing legislation. But eventually, the Benthamites had their way, and, between 1830 and 1860, freedom of contract was extended to the land. This powerful trend was reversed only in the 1870's when legislation altered its course radically. The "collectivist" period had begun.

The inertia of the common law was deliberately enhanced by statutes expressly passed in order to protect the habitations and occupations of the rural classes against the effects of freedom of contract. A comprehensive effort was launched to ensure some degree of health and salubrity in the housing of the poor, providing them with allotments, giving them a chance to escape from the slums and to breathe the fresh air of nature, the "gentleman's park." Wretched Irish tenants and London slum dwellers were rescued from the grip of the laws of the market by legislative acts designed to protect their habitations against the juggernaut, improvement. On the Continent it was mainly statute law and administrative action that saved the tenant, the peasant, the agricultural laborer from the most violent effects of urbanization. Prussian conservatives such as Rodbertus, whose Junker socialism influenced Marx, were blood brothers to the Tory-Democrats of England.

Presently, the problem of protection arose in regard to the agricultural populations of whole countries and continents. International free trade, if unchecked, must necessarily eliminate ever-larger compact bodies of agricultural producers.[5] This inevitable process of destruction was very much aggravated by the inherent discontinuity in the development of modern means of transportation, which are too expensive to be extended into new regions of the planet unless the prize to be gained is high. Once the great investments involved in the building of steamships and railroads came to fruition, whole continents were opened up and an avalanche of grain descended upon unhappy Europe. This was contrary to classical prognostication. Ricardo had erected it into an axiom that the most fertile land was settled first. This was turned to scorn in a spectacular manner when the railways found more fertile land in the antipodes. Central Europe, facing utter destruction of its rural society, was forced to protect its peasantry by introducing corn laws.

But if the organized states of Europe could protect themselves

[5] Borkenau, F., *The Totalitarian Enemy*, 1939, Chapter "Towards Collectivism."

against the backwash of international free trade, the politically unorganized colonial peoples could not. The revolt against imperialism
was mainly an attempt on the part of exotic peoples to achieve the
political status necessary to shelter themselves from the social dislocations caused by European trade policies. The protection that the
white man could easily secure for himself, through the sovereign status
of his communities was out of reach of the colored man as long as he
lacked the prerequisite, political government.

The trading classes sponsored the demand for mobilization of the
land. Cobden set the landlords of England aghast with his discovery
that farming was "business" and that those who were broke must clear
out. The working classes were won over to free trade as soon as it
became apparent that it made food cheaper. Trade unions became the
bastions of anti-agrarianism and revolutionary socialism branded the
peasantry of the world an indiscriminate mass of reactionaries. International division of labor was doubtless a progressive creed; and its
opponents were often recruited from amongst those whose judgment
was vitiated by vested interests or lack of natural intelligence. The
few independent and disinterested minds who discovered the fallacies
of unrestricted free trade were too few to make any impression.

And yet their consequences were no less real for not being consciously recognized. In effect, the great influence wielded by landed
interests in Western Europe and the survival of feudal forms of life in
Central and Eastern Europe during the nineteenth century are readily
explained by the vital protective function of these forces in retarding
the mobilization of the land. The question was often raised: what
enabled the feudal aristocracy of the Continent to maintain their sway
in the middle-class state once they had shed the military, judicial, and
administrative functions to which they owed their ascendency? The
theory of "survivals" was sometimes adduced as an explanation,
according to which functionless institutions or traits may continue to
exist by virtue of inertia. Yet it would be truer to say that no institution ever survives its function—when it appears to do so, it is because
it serves in some other function, or functions, which *need not include
the original one.* Thus feudalism and landed conservatism retained
their strength as long as they served a purpose that happened to be that
of restricting the disastrous effects of the mobilization of land. By this
time it had been forgotten by free traders that land formed part of the
territory of the country, and that the territorial character of sovereignty

was not merely a result of sentimental associations, but of massive facts, including economic ones. "In contrast to the nomadic peoples, the cultivator commits himself to improvements *fixed in a particular place*. Without such improvements human life must remain elementary, and little removed from that of animals. And how large a role have these fixtures played in human history! It is they, the cleared and cultivated lands, the houses, and the other buildings, the means of communication, the multifarious plant necessary for production, including industry and mining, all the permanent and immovable improvements that tie a human community to the locality where it is. They cannot be improvised, but must be built up gradually by generations of patient effort, and the community cannot afford to sacrifice them and start afresh elsewhere. Hence that *territorial* character of sovereignty, which permeates our political conceptions." [6] For a century these obvious truths were ridiculed.

The economic argument could be easily expanded so as to include the conditions of safety and security attached to the integrity of the soil and its resources—such as the vigor and stamina of the population, the abundance of food supplies, the amount and character of defense materials, even the climate of the country which might suffer from the denudation of forests, from erosions and dust bowls, all of which, ultimately, depend upon the factor land, yet none of which respond to the supply-and-demand mechanism of the market. Given a system entirely dependent upon market functions for the safeguarding of its existential needs, confidence will naturally turn to such forces outside the market system which are capable of ensuring common interests jeopardized by that system. Such a view is in keeping with our appreciation of the true sources of class influence: instead of trying to explain developments that run counter to the general trend of the time by the (unexplained) influence of reactionary classes, we prefer to explain the influence of such classes by the fact that they, even though incidentally, stand for developments only seemingly contrary to the general interest of the community. That their own interests are often all too well served by such a policy offers only another illustration of the truth that classes manage to profit disproportionately from these services that they may render to the commonalty.

An instance was offered by Speenhamland. The squire who ruled the village struck upon a way of slowing down the rise in rural wages and the threatening dislocation of the traditional structure of village

[6] Hawtrey, R. G., *The Economic Problem*, 1933.

life. In the long run, the method chosen was bound to have the most nefarious results. Yet the squires would not have been able to maintain their practices, unless by doing so they had assisted the country as a whole to meet the ground swell of the Industrial Revolution.

On the continent of Europe, again, agrarian protectionism was a necessity. But the most active intellectual forces of the age were engaged in an adventure which happened to shift their angle of vision so as to hide from them the true significance of the agrarian plight. Under the circumstances, a group able to represent the endangered rural interests could gain an influence out of proportion to their numbers. The protectionist countermovement actually succeeded in stabilizing the European countryside and in weakening that drift towards the towns which was the scourge of the time. Reaction was the beneficiary of a socially useful function which it happened to perform. The identical function which allowed reactionary classes in Europe to make play with traditional sentiments in their fight for agrarian tariffs was responsible in America about a half century later for the success of the TVA and other progressive social techniques. The same needs of society which benefited democracy in the New World strengthened the influence of the aristocracy in the Old.

Opposition to mobilization of the land was the sociological background of that struggle between liberalism and reaction that made up the political history of Continental Europe in the nineteenth century. In this struggle, the military and the higher clergy were allies of the landed classes, who had almost completely lost their more immediate functions in society. These classes were now available for any reactionary solution of the *impasse* to which market economy and its corollary, constitutional government, threatened to lead since they were not bound by tradition and ideology to public liberties and parliamentary rule.

Briefly, economic liberalism was wedded to the liberal state, while landed interests were not—this was the source of their permanent political significance on the Continent, which produced the crosscurrents of Prussian politics under Bismarck, fed clerical and militarist *revanche* in France, ensured court influence for the feudal aristocracy in the Hapsburg empire, made Church and Army the guardians of crumbling thrones. Since the connection outlasted the critical two generations once laid down by John Maynard Keynes as the practical alternative to eternity, land and landed property were now credited with a congenital bias for reaction. Eighteenth century England with its Tory free traders and agrarian pioneers was as forgotten as the Tudor engrossers and their revolutionary methods of making money from the land; the Physiocratic landlords of France and Germany with their enthusiasm for free trade were obliterated in the public mind by the modern prejudice of the everlasting backwardness of the rural scene. Herbert Spencer, with whom one generation sufficed as a sample of eternity, simply identified militarism with reaction. The social and technological adaptability recently shown by the Nipponese, the Russian, or the Nazi army would have been inconceivable to him.

Such thoughts were narrowly time-bound. The stupendous industrial achievements of market economy had been bought at the price of great harm to the substance of society. The feudal classes found therein an occasion to retrieve some of their lost prestige by turning advocates of the virtues of the land and its cultivators. In literary romanticism Nature had made its alliance with the Past; in the agrarian movement of the nineteenth century feudalism was trying not unsuccessfully to recover its past by presenting itself as the guardian of man's natural habitat, the soil. If the danger had not been genuine, the stratagem could not have worked.

But Army and Church gained prestige also by being available for the "defense of law and order," which now became highly vulnerable, while the ruling middle class was not fitted to ensure this requirement of the new economy. The market system was more allergic to rioting than any other economic system we know. Tudor governments relied on riots to call attention to local complaints; a few ringleaders might be hanged, otherwise no harm was done. The rise of the financial market meant a complete break with such an attitude; after 1797 rioting ceases to be a popular feature of London life, its place is gradually taken by meetings at which, at least in principle, the hands are counted which otherwise would be raining blows.[7] The Prussian king who proclaimed that to keep the peace was the subject's first and foremost duty, became famous for this paradox; yet very soon it was a commonplace. In the nineteenth century breaches of the peace, if committed by armed crowds, were deemed an incipient rebellion and an acute danger to the state; stocks collapsed and there was no bottom

[7] Trevelyan, G. M., *History of England*, 1926, p. 533. "England under Walpole, was still an aristocracy, tempered by rioting." Hannah More's "repository" song, "The Riot" was written "in ninety-five, a year of scarcity and alarm"—it was the year of Speenhamland. Cf. *The Repository Tracts*, Vol. I, New York, 1835. Also *The Library*, 1940, fourth series, Vol. XX, p. 295, on "Cheap Repository Tracts (1795-98)."

in prices. A shooting affray in the streets of the metropolis might destroy a substantial part of the nominal national capital. And yet the middle classes were unsoldierly; popular democracy prided itself on making the masses vocal; and, on the Continent, the bourgeoisie still clung to the recollections of its revolutionary youth when it had itself faced a tyrannic aristocracy on the barricades. Eventually, the peasantry, least contaminated by the liberal virus, were reckoned the only stratum that would stand in their persons "for law and order." One of the functions of reaction was understood to be to keep the working classes in their place, so that markets should not be thrown into panic. Though this service was only very infrequently required, the availability of the peasantry as the defenders of property rights was an asset to the agrarian camp.

The history of the 1920's would be otherwise inexplicable. When, in Central Europe, the social structure broke down under the strain of war and defeat, the working class alone was available for the task of keeping things going. Everywhere power was thrust upon the trade unions and Social Democratic parties: Austria, Hungary, even Germany, were declared republics although no active republican party had ever been known to exist in any of these countries before. But hardly had the acute danger of dissolution passed and the services of the trade unions become superfluous than the middle classes tried to exclude the working classes from all influence on public life. This is known as the counterrevolutionary phase of the postwar period. Actually, there was never any serious danger of a Communist regime since the workers were organized in parties and unions actively hostile to the Communists. (Hungary had a Bolshevik episode literally forced upon the country when defense against French invasion left no alternative to the nation.) The peril was not Bolshevism, but disregard of the rules of market economy on the part of trade unions and working-class parties, in an emergency. For under a market economy otherwise harmless interruptions of public order and trading habits might constitute a lethal threat [8] since they could cause the breakdown of the economic regime upon which society depended for its daily bread. This explained the remarkable shift in some countries from a supposedly imminent dictatorship of the industrial workers to the actual dictatorship of the peasantry. Right through the twenties the peasantry deter-

---

[8] Hayes, C., *A Generation of Materialism, 1870-1890*, remarks that "most of the individual states, at least in Western and Central Europe, now possessed a seemingly superlative internal stability."

mined economic policy in a number of states in which they normally played but a modest role. They now happened to be the only class available to maintain law and order in the modern high-strung sense of the term.

The fierce agrarianism of postwar Europe was a side light on the preferential treatment accorded to the peasant class for political reasons. From the Lappo movement in Finland to the Austrian *Heimwehr* the peasants proved the champions of market economy; this made them politically indispensable. The scarcity of food in the first postwar years to which their ascendency was sometimes credited had little to do with this. Austria, for instance, in order to benefit the peasants financially, had to lower her food standards by maintaining duties for grain, though she was heavily dependent upon imports for her food requirements. But the peasant interest had to be safeguarded at all cost even though agrarian protectionism might mean misery to the town dwellers and an unreasonably high cost of production to the exporting industries. The formerly uninfluential class of peasants gained in this manner an ascendency quite disproportionate to their economic importance. Fear of Bolshevism was the force which made their political position impregnable. And yet that fear, as we saw, was not fear of a working-class dictatorship—nothing faintly similar was on the horizon—but rather the dread of a paralysis of market economy, unless all forces were eliminated from the political scene that, under duress, might set aside the rules of the market game. As long as the peasants were the only class able to eliminate these forces, their prestige stood high and they could hold the urban middle class in ransom. As soon as the consolidation of the power of the state and— even before that—the forming of the urban lower middle class into storm troops by the fascists, freed the bourgeoisie from dependence upon the peasantry, the latter's prestige was quickly deflated. Once the "internal enemy" in town and factory had been neutralized or subdued, the peasantry was relegated to its former modest position in industrial society.

The big landowners' influence did not share in this eclipse. A more constant factor worked in their favor—the increasing military importance of agricultural self-sufficiency. The Great War had brought the basic strategic facts home to the public, and thoughtless reliance on the world market gave way to a panicky hoarding of food-producing capacity. The "reagrarianization" of Central Europe started by the Bolshevik scare was completed in the sign of autarchy. Besides the argument of the "internal enemy" there was now the argument of the "external enemy." Liberal economists, as usual, saw merely a romantic aberration induced by unsound economic doctrines, where in reality towering political events were awakening even the simplest minds to the irrelevance of economic considerations in the face of the approaching dissolution of the international system. Geneva continued its futile attempts to convince the peoples that they were hoarding against imaginary perils, and that if only all acted in unison free trade could be restored and would benefit all. In the curiously credulous atmosphere of the time many took for granted that the solution of the economic problem (whatever that may mean) would not only assuage the threat of war but actually avert that threat forever. A hundred years' peace had created an insurmountable wall of illusions which hid the facts. The writers of that period excelled in lack of realism. The nation-state was deemed a parochial prejudice by A. J. Toynbee, sovereignty a ridiculous illusion by Ludwig von Mises, war a mistaken calculation in business by Norman Angell. Awareness of the essential nature of the problems of politics sank to an unprecedented low point.

Free trade which, in 1846, had been fought and won on the Corn Laws, was eighty years later fought over again and this time lost on the same issue. The problem of autarchy haunted market economy from the start. Accordingly, economic liberals exorcised the specter of war and naïvely based their case on the assumption of an indestructible market economy. It went unnoticed that their arguments merely showed how great was the peril of a people which relied for its safety on an institution as frail as the self-regulating market. The autarchy movement of the twenties was essentially prophetic: it pointed to the need for adjustment to the vanishing of an order. The Great War had shown up the danger and men acted accordingly; but since they acted ten years later, the connection between cause and effect was discounted as unreasonable. "Why protect oneself against passed dangers?" was the comment of many contemporaries. This faulty logic befogged not only an understanding of autarchy but, even more important, that of fascism. Actually, both were explained by the fact that, once the common mind has received the impress of a danger, fear remains latent, as long as its causes are not removed.

We claimed that the nations of Europe never overcame the shock of the war experience which unexpectedly confronted them with the perils of interdependence. In vain was trade resumed, in vain did swarms of international conferences display the idylls of peace, and dozens of governments declare for the principle of freedom of trade— no people could forget that unless they owned their food and raw material sources themselves or were certain of military access to them, neither sound currency nor unassailable credit would rescue them from helplessness. Nothing could be more logical than the consistency with which this fundamental consideration shaped the policy of communities. The source of the peril was not removed. Why then expect fear to subside?

A similar fallacy tricked those critics of fascism—they formed the great majority—who described fascism as a freak devoid of all political *ratio*. Mussolini, it was said, claimed to have averted Bolshevism in Italy, while statistics proved that for more than a year before the March on Rome the strike wave had subsided. Armed workers, it was conceded, occupied the factories in 1921. But was that a reason for disarming them in 1923, when they had long climbed down again from the walls where they had mounted guard? Hitler claimed he had saved Germany from Bolshevism. But could it not be shown that the flood of unemployment which preceded his chancellorship had ebbed away before his rise to power? To claim that he averted that which no longer existed when he came, as was argued, was contrary to the law of cause and effect, which must also hold in politics.

Actually, in Germany as in Italy, the story of the immediate postwar period proved that Bolshevism had not the slightest chance of success. But it also showed conclusively that in an emergency the working class, its trade unions and parties, might disregard the rules of the market which established freedom of contract and the sanctity of private property as absolutes—a possibility which must have the most deleterious effects on society, discouraging investments, preventing the accumulation of capital, keeping wages on an unremunerative level, endangering the currency, undermining foreign credit, weakening confidence and paralyzing enterprise. Not the illusionary danger of a communist revolution, but the undeniable fact that the working classes were in the position to force possibly ruinous interventions, was the source of the latent fear which, at a crucial juncture, burst forth in the fascist panic.

The dangers to man and nature cannot be neatly separated. The reactions of the working class and the peasantry to market economy both led to protectionism, the former mainly in the form of social legislation and factory laws, the latter in agrarian tariffs and land laws. Yet there was this important difference : in an emergency, the farmers and peasants of Europe defended the market system, which the working-class policies endangered. While the crisis of the inherently unstable system was brought on by both wings of the protectionist movement, the social strata connected with the land were inclined to compromise with the market system, while the broad class of labor did not shrink from breaking its rules and challenging it outright.

16

MARKET AND PRODUCTIVE ORGANIZATION

EVEN CAPITALIST business itself had to be sheltered from the unrestricted working of the market mechanism. This should dispose of the suspicion which the very terms "man" and "nature" sometimes awaken in sophisticated minds, who tend to denounce all talk about protecting labor and land as the product of antiquated ideas if not as a mere camouflaging of vested interests.

Actually, in the case of productive enterprise as in that of man and nature the peril was real and objective. The need for protection arose on account of the manner in which the supply of money was organized under a market system. Modern central banking, in effect, was essentially a device developed for the purpose of offering protection without which the market would have destroyed its own children, the business enterprises of all kinds. Eventually, however, it was this form of protection which contributed most immediately to the downfall of the international system.

While the perils threatening land and labor from the maelstrom of the market are fairly obvious, the dangers to business inherent in the monetary system are not as readily apprehended. Yet if profits depend upon prices, then the monetary arrangements upon which prices depend must be vital to the functioning of any system motivated by profits. While, in the long run, changes in selling prices need not affect profits, since costs will move up and down correspondingly, this is not true in the short run, since there must be a time-lag before contractually fixed prices change. Among them is the price of labor which, together with many other prices, would naturally be fixed by contract. Hence, if the price level was falling for monetary reasons over a considerable time, business would be in danger of liquidation accompanied by the dissolution of productive organization and massive destruction of capital. Not low prices, but falling prices were the trouble. Hume became the founder of the quantity theory of money with his discovery that business remains unaffected if the amount of money is halved since prices will simply adjust to half their former level. He forgot that business might be destroyed in the process.

This is the easily understandable reason why a system of commodity money, such as the market mechanism tends to produce without outside interference, is incompatible with industrial production. Commodity money is simply a commodity which happens to function as money, and its amount, therefore, cannot, in principle, be increased at all, except by diminishing the amount of the commodities not functioning as money. In practice commodity money is usually gold or silver, the amount of which can be increased, but not by much, within a short time. But the expansion of production and trade unaccompanied by an increase in the amount of money must cause a fall in the price level—precisely the type of ruinous deflation which we have in mind. Scarcity of money was a permanent, grave complaint with seventeenth century merchant communities. Token money was developed at an early date to shelter trade from the enforced deflations that accompanied the use of specie when the volume of business swelled. No market economy was possible without the medium of such artificial money.

The real difficulty arose with the need for stable foreign exchanges and the consequent introduction of the gold standard, about the time of the Napoleonic Wars. Stable exchanges became essential to the very existence of English economy; London had become the financial center of a growing world trade. Yet nothing else but commodity money could serve this end for the obvious reason that token money, whether bank or fiat, cannot circulate on foreign soil. Hence, the gold standard—the accepted name for a system of international commodity money—came to the fore.

But for domestic purposes, as we know, specie is an inadequate money just because it is a commodity and its amount cannot be increased at will. The amount of gold available may be increased by a few per cent over a year, but not by as many dozen within a few weeks, as might be required to carry a sudden expansion of transactions. In the absence of token money business would have to be either curtailed or carried on at very much lower prices, thus inducing a slump and creating unemployment.

In its simplest form the problem was this: commodity money was vital to the existence of foreign trade; token money, to the existence of domestic trade. How far did they agree with each other?

Under nineteenth century conditions foreign trade and the gold standard had undisputed priority over the needs of domestic business. The working of the gold standard required the lowering of domestic prices whenever the exchange was threatened by depreciation. Since deflation happens through credit restrictions, it follows that the working of commodity money interfered with the working of the credit system. This was a standing danger to business. Yet, to discard token money altogether and restrict currency to commodity money was entirely out of the question, since such a remedy would have been worse than the disease.

Central banking mitigated this defect of credit money greatly. By centralizing the supply of credit in a country, it was possible to avoid the wholesale dislocation of business and employment involved in deflation and to organize deflation in such a way as to absorb the shock and spread its burden over the whole country. The bank in its normal function was cushioning the immediate effects of gold withdrawals on the circulation of notes as well as of the diminished circulation of notes on business.

The bank might use various methods. Short-term loans might bridge the gap caused by short-run losses of gold, and avoid the need for credit restrictions altogether. But even when restrictions of credit were inevitable, as was often the case, the bank's action had a buffer effect: The raising of the bank rate as well as open-market operations spread the effects of restrictions to the whole community while shifting the burden of the restrictions to the strongest shoulders.

Let us envisage the crucial case of transferring one-sided payments from one country to another, such as might be caused by a shift in demand from domestic to foreign types of food. The gold that now has to be sent abroad in payment for the imported food would otherwise be used for inland payments, and its absence must cause a falling off of domestic sales and a consequent drop in prices. We will call this type of deflation "transactional," since it spreads from individual firm to firm according to their fortuitous business dealings. Eventually, the spread of deflation will reach the exporting firms and thus achieve the export surplus which represents "real" transfer. But the harm and damage caused to the community at large will be much greater than that which was strictly necessary to achieve such an export surplus. For there are always firms just short of being able to export, which need only the inducement of a slight reduction of costs to "go over the top," and such a reduction can be most economically achieved by spreading the deflation thinly over the whole of the business community.

This precisely was one of the functions of the central bank. The broad pressure of its discount and open-market policy forced domestic prices down more or less equally, and enabled "export-near" firms to resume or increase exports, while only the least efficient firms would have to liquidate. "Real" transfer would thus have been achieved at the cost of a much smaller amount of dislocation than would have been needed to attain the same export surplus by the irrational method of haphazard and often catastrophic shocks transmitted through the narrow channels of "transactional deflation."

That in spite of these devices to mitigate the effects of deflation, the outcome was, nevertheless, again and again a complete disorganization of business and consequent mass unemployment, is the most powerful of all the indictments of the gold standard.

The case of money showed a very real analogy to that of labor and land. The application of the commodity fiction to each of them led to its effective inclusion into the market system, while at the same time grave dangers to society developed. With money, the threat was to productive enterprise, the existence of which was imperiled by any fall in the price level caused by use of commodity money. Here also protective measures had to be taken, with the result that the self-steering mechanism of the market was put out of action.

Central banking reduced the automatism of the gold standard to a mere pretense. It meant a centrally managed currency; manipulation was substituted for the self-regulating mechanism of supplying credit, even though the device was not always deliberate and conscious. More and more it was recognized that the international gold standard could be made self-regulating only if the single countries relinquished central banking. The one consistent adherent of the pure gold standard who actually advocated this desperate step was Ludwig von Mises; his advice, had it been heeded, would have transformed national economies into a heap of ruins.

Most of the confusion existing in monetary theory was due to the separation of politics and economics, this outstanding characteristic of market society. For more than a century, money was regarded as a purely economic category, a commodity used for the purpose of indirect exchange. If gold was the commodity so preferred, a gold standard was in being. (The attribute "international" in connection with that standard was meaningless, since for the economist, no nations existed; transactions were carried on not between nations but between individuals, whose political allegiance was as irrelevant as the color of their hair.) Ricardo indoctrinated nineteenth century England with the conviction that the term "money" meant a medium of exchange, that bank notes were a mere matter of convenience, their utility consisting in their being easier to handle than gold, but that their value derived from the certainty that their possession provided us with the means of possessing ourselves at any time of the commodity itself, gold. It followed that the national characer of currencies was of no consequence, since they were but different tokens representing the same commodity. And if it was injudicious for a government to make any effort to possess itself of gold (since the distribution of that commodity regulated itself on the world market just as that of any other), it was even more injudicious to imagine that the nationally different tokens were of any relevance to the welfare and prosperity of the countries concerned.

Now the institutional separation of the political and economic spheres had never been complete, and it was precisely in the matter of currency that it was necessarily incomplete; the state, whose Mint seemed merely to certify the weight of coins, was in fact the guarantor of the value of token money, which it accepted in payment for taxes and otherwise. This money was *not* a means of exchange, it was a means of payment; it was not a commodity, it was purchasing power; far from having utility itself, it was merely a counter embodying a quantified claim to things that might be purchased. Clearly, a society in which distribution depended upon the possession of such tokens of purchasing power was a construction entirely different from market economy.

We are not dealing here, of course, with pictures of actuality, but with conceptual patterns used for the purposes of clarification. No market economy separated from the political sphere is possible; yet it was such a construction which underlay classical economics since David Ricardo and apart from which its concepts and assumptions were incomprehensible. Society, according to this "lay-out," consisted of bartering individuals possessing an outfit of commodities—goods, land, labor, and their composites. Money was simply one of the commodities bartered more often than another and, hence, acquired for the purpose of use in exchange. Such a "society" may be unreal; yet it contains the bare bones of the construction from which the classical economists started.

An even less complete picture of actuality is offered by a purchasing-power economy.[1] Yet some of its features resemble our actual society much more closely than the paradigm of market economy. Let us try to imagine a "society" in which every individual is endowed with a definite amount of purchasing power, enabling him to claim goods each item of which is provided with a price tag. Money in such an economy is not a commodity; it has no usefulness in itself; its only use is to purchase goods to which price tags are attached, very much as they are in our shops today.

While the commodity money theorem was far superior to its rival in the nineteenth century, when institutions conformed in many essentials to the market pattern, since the beginning of the twentieth century the conception of purchasing power gained steadily. With the disintegration of the gold standard, commodity money practically ceased to exist, and it was only natural that the purchasing power concept of money should replace it.

To turn from mechanisms and concepts to the social forces in play, it is important to realize that the ruling classes themselves lent their support to the management of the currency through the central bank. Such management was not, of course, regarded as an interference with the institution of the gold standard; on the contrary, it was part of the rules of the game under which the gold standard was supposed to function. Since maintenance of the gold standard was axiomatic and the central banking mechanism was never allowed to act in such a way as to make a country go off gold, but, on the contrary, the supreme directive of the bank was always and under all conditions to stay on gold, no question of principle seemed to be involved. But this was so only as long as the movements of the price level involved were the paltry 2–3 per cent, at the most, that separated the so-called gold points. As soon as the movement of the internal price level necessary to keep the exchanges stable was much larger, when it jumped to 10 per cent or 30 per cent, the situation was entirely changed. Such downward movements of the price level would spread misery and destruction. The fact that currencies were managed became of prime importance, since it meant that central banking methods were a matter of policy *i.e.*, something the body politic might have to decide about. Indeed, the great institutional significance of central banking lay in the fact that

[1] The underlying theory has been elaborated by F. Schafer, Wellington, New Zealand.

monetary policy was thereby drawn into the sphere of politics. The consequences could not be other than far reaching.

They were twofold. In the domestic field, monetary policy was only another form of interventionism, and clashes of economic classes tended to crystallize around this issue so intimately linked with the gold standard and balanced budgets. Internal conflicts in the thirties, as we will see, often centered on this issue which played an important part in the growth of the antidemocratic movement.

In the foreign field, the role of national currencies was of overwhelming importance, though this fact was but little recognized at the time. The ruling philosophy of the nineteenth century was pacifist and internationalist; "in principle" all educated people were free traders, and, with qualifications which appear ironically modest today, they were no less so in practice. The source of this outlook was, of course, economic; much genuine idealism sprang from the sphere of barter and trade—by a supreme paradox man's selfish wants were validating his most generous impulses. But since the 1870's an emotional change was noticeable though there was no corresponding break in the dominant ideas. The world continued to believe in internationalism and interdependence, while acting on the impulses of nationalism and self-sufficiency. Liberal nationalism was developing into national liberalism, with its marked leanings towards protectionism and imperialism abroad, monopolistic conservatism at home. Nowhere was the contradiction as sharp and yet as little conscious as in the monetary realm. For dogmatic belief in the international gold standard continued to enlist men's stintless loyalties, while at the same time token currencies were established, based on the sovereignty of the various central banking systems. Under the aegis of international principles, impregnable bastions of a new nationalism were being unconsciously erected in the shape of the central banks of issue.

In truth, the new nationalism was the corollary of the new internationalism. The international gold standard could not be borne by the nations whom it was supposed to serve, unless they were secured against the dangers with which it threatened the communities adhering to it. Completely monetarized communities could not have stood the ruinous effects of abrupt changes in the price level necessitated by the maintenance of stable exchanges unless the shock was cushioned by the means of an independent central banking policy. The national token currency was the certain safeguard of this relative security since it allowed the central bank to act as a buffer between the internal and the external economy. If the balance of payment was threatened with illiquidity, reserves and foreign loans would tide over the difficulty; if an altogether new economic balance had to be created involving a fall in the domestic price level, the restriction of credit could be spread in the most rational fashion, eliminating the inefficient, and putting the burden on the efficient. Absence of such a mechanism would have made it impossible for any advanced country to stay on gold without devastating effects as to its welfare, whether in terms of production, income, or employment.

If the trading class was the protagonist of market economy, the banker was the born leader of that class. Employment and earnings depended upon the profitability of business, but the profitability of business depended upon stable exchanges and sound credit conditions, both of which were under the care of the banker. It was part of his creed that the two were inseparable. A sound budget and stable internal credit conditions presupposed stable foreign exchanges; also exchanges could not be stable unless domestic credit was safe and the financial household of the state in equilibrium. Briefly, the banker's twin trust comprised sound domestic finance and external stability of the currency. That is why bankers as a class were the last to notice it when both had lost their meaning. There is indeed nothing surprising either in the dominating influence of international bankers in the twenties, nor in their eclipse in the thirties. In the twenties, the gold standard was still regarded as *the* precondition of a return to stability and prosperity, and consequently no demand raised by its professional guardians, the bankers, was deemed too burdensome, if only it promised to secure stable exchange rates; when, after 1929, this proved impossible, the imperative need was for a stable internal currency and nobody was as little qualified to provide it as the banker.

In no field was the breakdown of market economy as abrupt as in that of money. Agrarian tariffs interfering with the importing of the produce of foreign lands broke up free trade; the narrowing and regulating of the labor market restricted bargaining to that which the law left to the parties to decide. But neither in the case of labor nor in that of land was there a formal sudden and complete rift in the market mechanism such as happened in the field of money. There was nothing comparable in the other markets to the relinquishing of the gold standard by Great Britain on September 21, 1931; nor even to the subsidiary event of America's similar action, in June, 1933. Though by that time the Great Depression which began in 1929 had swept away the major part of world trade, this meant no change in methods, nor did it affect the ruling ideas. But final failure of the gold standard was the final failure of market economy.

Economic liberalism had started a hundred years before, and had been met by a protectionist countermove, which now broke into the last bastion of market economy. A new set of ruling ideas superseded the world of the self-regulating market. To the stupefaction of the vast majority of contemporaries, unsuspected forces of charismatic leadership and autarchist isolationism broke forth and fused societies into new forms.

17

SELF-REGULATION IMPAIRED

IN THE HALF CENTURY 1879–1929, Western societies developed into closely knit units, in which powerful disruptive strains were latent. The more immediate source of this development was the impaired self-regulation of market economy. Since society was made to conform to the needs of the market mechanism, imperfections in the functioning of that mechanism created cumulative strains in the body social.

Impaired self-regulation was an effect of protectionism. There is a sense, of course, in which markets are always self-regulating, since they tend to produce a price which clears the market; this, however, is true of all markets, whether free or not. But as we have already shown, a self-regulating market *system* implies something very different, namely, markets for the elements of production—labor, land, and money. Since the working of such markets threatens to destroy society, the self-preserving action of the community was meant to prevent their establishment or to interfere with their free functioning, once established.

America has been adduced by economic liberals as conclusive proof of the ability of a market economy to function. For a century, labor, land, and money were traded in the States with complete freedom, yet no measures of social protection were allegedly needed, and apart from customs tariffs, industrial life continued unhampered by government interference.

The explanation, of course, is simple: it is free labor, land, and money. Up to the 1890's the frontier was open and free land lasted; up to the Great War the supply of low standard labor flowed freely; [1] and up to the turn of the century there was no commitment to keep foreign exchanges stable. A free supply of land, labor, and money continued to be available; consequently no self-regulating market system was in existence. As long as these conditions prevailed, neither man, nor nature, nor business organization needed protection of the kind that only government intervention can provide.

[1] Penrose, E. F., *op. cit.* The Malthusian law is valid only under the assumption that the supply of land is limited.

As soon as these conditions ceased to exist, social protection set in. As the lower ranges of labor could not any more be freely replaced from an inexhaustible reservoir of immigrants, while its higher ranges were unable to settle freely on the land; as the soil and natural resources became scarce and had to be husbanded; as the gold standard was introduced in order to remove the currency from politics and to link domestic trade with that of the world, the United States caught up with a century of European development: protection of the soil and its cultivators, social security for labor through unionism and legislation, and central banking—all on the largest scale—made their appearance. Monetary protectionism came first: the establishment of the Federal Reserve System was intended to harmonize the needs of the gold standard with regional requirements; protectionism in respect to labor and land followed. A decade of prosperity in the twenties sufficed to bring on a depression so fierce that in its course the New Deal started to build a moat around labor and land, wider than any Europe had known. Thus America offered striking proof, both positive and negative, of our thesis that social protection was the accompaniment of a supposedly self-regulating market.

At the same time protectionism everywhere was producing the hard shell of the emerging unit of social life. The new entity was cast in the national mold, but had otherwise only little resemblance to its predecessors, the easygoing nations of the past. The new crustacean type of nation expressed its identity through national token currencies safeguarded by a type of sovereignty more jealous and absolute than anything known before. These currencies were also spotlighted from outside, since it was of them that the international gold standard (the chief instrument of world economy) was constructed. If money now avowedly ruled the world, that money was stamped with a national die.

Such emphasis on nations and currencies would have been incomprehensible to liberals, whose minds habitually missed the true characteristics of the world they were living in. If the nation was deemed by them an anachronism, national currencies were reckoned not even worthy of attention. No self-respecting economist of the liberal age doubted the irrelevance of the fact that different pieces of paper were called differently on different sides of political frontiers. Nothing was simpler than to change one denomination for another by the use of the exchange market, an institution which could not fail to function since, luckily, it was not under the control of the state or the politician

Western Europe was passing through a new Enlightenment and high amongst its bugbears ranked the "tribalistic" concept of the nation, whose alleged sovereignty was to liberals an outcrop of parochial thinking. Up to the 1930's the economic Baedeker included the certain information that money was only an instrument of exchange and thus inessential by definition. The blind spot of the marketing mind was equally insensitive to the phenomena of the nation *and* of money. The free trader was a nominalist in regard to both.

This connection was highly significant, yet it passed unnoticed at the time. Off and on, critics of free-trade doctrines as well as critics of orthodox doctrines on money arose, but there was hardly anyone who recognized that these two sets of doctrines were stating the same case in different terms and that if one was false the other was equally so. William Cunningham or Adolph Wagner showed up cosmopolitan free-trade fallacies, but did not link them with money; on the other hand, Macleod or Gesell attacked classical money theories while adhering to a cosmopolitan trading system. The constitutive importance of the currency in establishing the nation as the decisive economic and political unit of the time was as thoroughly overlooked by the writers of liberal Enlightenment as the existence of history had been by their eighteenth century predecessors. Such was the position upheld by the most brilliant economic thinkers from Ricardo to Wieser, from John Stuart Mill to Marshall and Wicksell, while the common run of the educated were brought up to believe that preoccupation with the economic problem of the nation or of the currency marked a person with the stigma of inferiority. To combine these fallacies in the monstrous proposition that national currencies played a vital part in the institutional mechanism of our civilization would have been judged a pointless paradox, devoid of sense and meaning.

Actually, the new national unit and the new national currency were inseparable. It was currency which provided national and international systems with their mechanics and introduced into the picture those features which resulted in the abruptness of the break. The monetary system on which credit was based had become the life line of both national and international economy.

Protectionism was a three-pronged drive. Land, labor, and money, each played their part, but while land and labor were linked to definite even though broad social strata, such as the workers or the peasantry, monetary protectionism was, to a greater extent, a national factor, often fusing diverse interests into a collective whole. Though monetary policy, too, could divide as well as unite, objectively the monetary system was the strongest among the economic forces integrating the nation.

Labor and land accounted, primarily, for social legislation and corn duties, respectively. Farmers would protest against burdens that benefited the laborer and raised wages, while laborers would object to any increase in food prices. But once corn laws and labor laws were in force—in Germany since the early eighties—it would become difficult to remove the one without removing the other. Between agricultural and industrial tariffs, the relationship was even closer. Since the idea of all-round protectionism had been popularized by Bismarck (1879), the political alliance of landowners and industrialists for the reciprocal safeguarding of tariffs had been a feature of German politics; tariff logrolling was as common as the setting up of cartels in order to secure private benefits from tariffs.

Internal and external, social and national protectionism tended to fuse.[2] The rising cost of living induced by corn laws invited the manufacturer's demand for protective tariffs, which he rarely failed to utilize as an implement of cartel policy. Trade unions naturally insisted on higher wages to compensate for increased costs of living, and could not well object to such customs tariffs as permitted the employer to meet an inflated wage bill. But once the accountancy of social legislation had been based on a wage level conditioned by tariffs, employers could not in fairness be expected to carry the burden of such legislation unless they were assured of continued protection. Incidentally, this was the slender factual basis of the charge of collectivist conspiracy allegedly responsible for the protectionist movement. But this mistakes effect for cause. The origins of the movement were spontaneous and widely dispersed, but once started it could not, of course, fail to create parallel interests which were committed to its continuation.

More important than similarity of interests was the uniform spread of actual conditions created by the combined effects of such measures. If life in different countries was different, as had always been the case, the disparity could now be traced to definite legislative and administrative acts of a protective intent, since conditions of production and labor were now mainly dependent on tariffs, taxation, and social laws. Even before the United States and the British dominions restricted immigration, the number of emigrants from the United Kingdom dwindled, in spite of severe unemployment, admittedly on account of the much improved social climate of the mother country.

[2] Carr, E. H., *The Twenty Years' Crisis, 1919–1939,* 1940.

But if customs tariffs and social laws produced an artificial climate, monetary policy created what amounted to veritable artificial weather conditions varying day by day and affecting every member of the community in his immediate interests. The integrating power of monetary policy surpassed by far that of the other kinds of protectionism, with their slow and cumbersome apparatus, for the influence of monetary protection was ever active and ever changing. What the businessman, the organized worker, the housewife pondered, what the farmer who was planning his crop, the parents who were weighing their children's chances, the lovers who were waiting to get married, resolved in their minds when considering the favor of the times, was more directly determined by the monetary policy of the central bank than by any other single factor. And if this was true even with a stable currency, it became incomparably truer when the currency was unstable, and the fatal decision to inflate or deflate had to be taken. Politically, the nation's identity was established by the government; economically it was vested in the central bank.

Internationally, the monetary system assumed, if possible, even greater importance. The freedom of money was, paradoxically enough, a result of restrictions on trade. For the more numerous became the obstacles to the movement of goods and men across frontiers, the more effectively had the freedom of payments to be safeguarded. Short-term money moved at an hour's notice from any point of the globe to another; the modalities of international payments between governments and between private corporations or individuals were uniformly regulated; the repudiation of foreign debts, or attempts to tamper with budgetary guarantees, even on the part of backward governments, was deemed an outrage, and was punished by relegation of those unworthy of credit to the outer darkness. In all matters relevant to the world monetary system, similar institutions were established everywhere, such as representative bodies, written constitutions defining their jurisdiction and regulating the publication of budgets, the promulgation of laws, the ratification of treaties, the methods of incurring financial obligations, the rules of public accountancy, the rights of foreigners, the jurisdiction of courts, the domicile of bills of exchange, and thus, by implication, the status of the bank of issue, of foreign bondholders, of creditors of all description. This involved conformity in the use of bank notes and specie, of postal regulations, and in stock exchange and banking methods. No government, except perhaps the most powerful, could afford to disregard the taboos of money. For international purposes the currency was the nation; and no nation could for any length of time exist outside the international scheme.

In contrast to men and goods, money was free from all hampering measures and continued to develop its capacity to transact business at any distance at any time. The more difficult it became to shift actual objects, the easier it became to transmit claims to them. While trade in commodities and services was slowed down and its balance swayed precariously, the balance of payments was almost automatically kept liquid with the help of short-term loans that flitted over the globe, and funding operations that only faintly took note of visible trade. Payments, debts, and claims remained unaffected by the mounting barriers erected against the exchange of goods; the rapidly growing elasticity and catholicity of the international monetary mechanism was compensating, in a way, for the ever-contracting channels of world trade. When, by the early thirties, world trade was down to a trickle, international short-term lending attained un unheard-of degree of mobility. As long as the mechanism of international capital movements and short credits functioned, no disequilibrium of actual trade was too great to be overcome by methods of bookkeeping. Social dislocation was avoided with the help of credit movements; economic imbalance was righted by financial means.

In the last resort, impaired self-regulation of the market led to political intervention. When the trade cycle failed to come round and restore employment, when imports failed to produce exports, when bank reserve regulations threatened business with a panic, when foreign debtors refused to pay, governments had to respond to the strain. In an emergency the unity of society asserted itself through the medium of intervention.

How far the state was induced to interfere depended on the constitution of the political sphere and on the degree of economic distress. As long as the vote was restricted and only the few exerted political influence, interventionism was a much less urgent problem than it became when universal suffrage made the state the organ of the ruling million—the identical million who, in the economic realm, had often to carry in bitterness the burden of the ruled. And as long as employment was plentiful, incomes were secure, production was continuous, living standards were dependable, and prices were stable, interventionist pressure was naturally less than it became when protracted slumps made industry a wreckage of unused tools and frustrated effort.

Internationally, also, political methods were used to supplement the imperfect self-regulation of the market. Ricardian trade and currency theory vainly ignored the difference in status existing between the various countries owing to their different wealth-producing capacity, exporting facilities, trading, shipping, and banking experience. In the liberal theory, Great Britain was merely another atom in the universe of trade and ranked precisely on the same footing as Denmark and Guatemala. Actually, the world counted a limited number of countries, divided into lending countries and borrowing countries, exporting countries and practically self-sufficient ones, countries with varied exports and such as depended for their imports and foreign borrowing on the sale of a single commodity like wheat or coffee. Such differences could be ignored by theory, but their consequences could not be equally disregarded in practice. Frequently overseas countries found themselves unable to discharge their foreign debts, or their currencies depreciated, endangering their solvency; sometimes they decided to right the balance by political means and interfered with the property of foreign investors. In none of these cases could processes of economic self-healing be relied upon, though according to classical doctrine those processes would unfailingly reimburse the creditor, restore the currency and safeguard the foreigner against the recurrence of similar losses. But this would have required that the countries concerned should be more or less equal participants in a system of world division of labor, which was emphatically not the case. It was idle to expect that invariably the country whose currency slumped would automatically increase its exports, and thereby restore its balance of payments, or that its need for foreign capital would compel it to compensate the foreigner and resume the service of its debt. Increased sales of coffee or nitrates, for instance, might knock the bottom out of the market, and repudiation of a usurious foreign debt would appear preferable to a depreciation of the national currency. The world market mechanism could not afford to run such risks. Instead, gunboats were dispatched on the spot and the defaulting government, whether fraudulent or not, faced with the alternative of bombardment or settlement. No other method was available to enforce payment, avoid great losses, and keep the system going. A similar practice was used to induce colonial peoples to recognize the advantages of trade, when the theoretically unfailing argument of mutual advantage was not promptly—or perhaps not at all—grasped by the natives. Even more evident was the need for interventionist methods, if the region in question happened to be rich in raw materials required for European manufactures, while no pre-established harmony ensured the emergence of a craving after European manufactures on the part of the natives whose natural wants had previously taken an entirely different direction. Of course, none of these difficulties was supposed to arise under an allegedly self-regulating system. But the more often repayments were made only under the threat of armed intervention, the more often trade routes were kept open only with the help of gunboats, the more often trade followed the flag, while the flag followed the needs of invading governments, the more patent it became that political instruments had to be used in order to maintain equilibrium in world economy.

18

DISRUPTIVE STRAINS

FROM SUCH UNIFORMITY of underlying institutional arrangements derived the intriguing similarity in the pattern of events which in the half century 1879–1929 was spread out over an enormous expanse.

An endless variety of personalities and backgrounds, mentalities and historical antecedents gave local color and topical emphasis to the vicissitudes of many countries, and yet, over the greater part of the world civilization was of the same fabric. This affinity transcended that of the culture traits common to peoples using similar tools, enjoying similar amusements, and rewarding effort with similar prizes. Rather, the similarity concerned the function of concrete events in the historical context of life, the time-bound component of collective existence. An analysis of these typical strains and stresses should reveal much of the mechanism that produced the singularly uniform pattern of history during this period.

The strains can be readily grouped according to the main institutional spheres. In the domestic economy the most varied symptoms of disequilibrium—like decline of production, employment, and earnings —shall be represented here by the typical scourge of *unemployment*. In domestic politics there was the struggle and deadlock of social forces, which we shall typify by *tension of classes*. Difficulties in the field of international economics, which centered around the so-called balance of payment and comprised a falling off of exports, unfavorable terms of trade, dearth of imported raw materials, and losses on foreign investments, we shall designate as a group by a characteristic form of strain, namely, *pressure on exchanges*. Lastly, tensions in international politics will be subsumed under *imperialist rivalries*.

Now let us consider a country which, in the course of a business depression, is stricken by unemployment. It is easy to see that all measures of economic policy which the banks may decide upon in order to create employment are limited by the exigencies of stable exchanges. The banks will not be able to expand or further extend credits to industry, without appealing to the central bank which, on its part, will refuse to follow suit since the safety of the currency requires the opposite course. On the other hand, if the strain spreads from industry to state— trade unions might induce affiliated political parties to raise the issue in the parliament—the scope of any policy of relief or public works will be limited by the requirements of budgetary equilibrium, another pre-condition of stable exchanges. The gold standard will thus check the action of the Treasury as effectively as that of the bank of issue, and the legislature will find itself confronted with identically the same limitations that applied to industry.

Within the compass of the nation the strain of unemployment might, of course, be borne alternatively in the industrial or the govern-mental zone. If in a particular instance the crisis was overcome by a deflationary pressure on wages, then, it might be said, the burden fell primarily on the economic sphere. If, however, that painful measure was avoided with the help of public works subsidized from death duties, the brunt of the tension would fall on the political sphere (the same would be the case if the decrease in wages was forced upon the trade unions by some governmental measure in defiance of acquired rights). In the first instance—deflationary pressure on wages—the tension remained within the market zone, and was expressed in a shift of in-comes transmitted by a change in prices; in the latter instance—public works or trade union restrictions—there was a shift in legal status or in taxation which affected primarily the political position of the group concerned.

Further, the strain of unemployment might have spread outside the confines of the nation and affected foreign exchanges. This might hap-pen whether political or economic methods of combating unemploy-ment had been used. Under the gold standard—which we all the time assume to be in force—any governmental measure that caused a budgetary deficit might start a depreciation of the currency; if, on the other hand, unemployment was being fought by the expansion of bank credit, rising domestic prices would hit exports and affect the balance of payment in that way. In either case exchanges would slump and the country feel the pressure on its currency.

Alternatively, the strain which sprang from unemployment might induce foreign tension. In the case of a weak country this had some-times the gravest consequences for its international position. Its status deteriorated, its rights were disregarded, foreign control was foisted upon it, its national aspirations were foiled. In the case of strong states the pressure might be deflected into a scramble for foreign markets, colonies, zones of influence, and other forms of imperialist rivalry.

The strains emanating from the market were thus shifting to and fro between market and the other main institutional zones, sometimes affecting the working of the field of government, sometimes that of the gold standard or that of the balance-of-power system, as the case might be. Each field was comparatively independent of the others and tended towards an equilibrium of its own; whenever this balance was not achieved, the imbalance spread over into the other spheres. It was the relative autonomy of the sphere that caused the strains to accumulate and to generate tensions which eventually exploded in more or less stereotyped forms. While in imagination the nineteenth century was engaged in constructing the liberal utopia, in reality it was handing over things to a definite number of concrete institutions the mechanisms of which ruled the day.

The nearest approach to the realization of the true position was perhaps the rhetorical query of an economist who, as late as 1933, arraigned the protectionist policies of *"the overwhelming majority of governments."* Can a policy, he asked, be right which is being unanimously condemned by all experts as utterly mistaken, grossly fallacious, and contrary to all principles of economic theory? His answer was an unconditional "No." [1] But in vain would one seek in liberal literature for anything in the nature of an explanation for the patent facts. An unending stream of abuse of the governments, politicians, and statesmen whose ignorance, ambition, greed, and shortsighted prejudice were supposedly responsible for the consistently followed policies of protectionism in an "overwhelming majority" of countries was the only answer. Rarely was as much as a reasoned argument on the subject to be found. Not since the Schoolmen's defiance of the empirical facts of science was sheer prejudice displayed in so fearful array. The only intellectual response was to supplement the myth of the protectionist conspiracy by the myth of imperialist craze.

The liberal argument, in so far as it became articulate, asserted that sometime in the early 1880's imperialist passions began to stir in the Western countries, and destroyed the fruitful work of economic thinkers by their emotional appeal to tribal prejudice. These sentimental policies gradually gathered strength and finally led to World War I. After the Great War the forces of Enlightenment had another chance of restoring the reign of reason but an unexpected outburst of imperialism,

[1] Haberler, G., *Der internationale Handel*, 1933, p. vi.

especially on the part of the small new countries, later on also of the "have-nots," such as Germany, Italy, and Japan, upset the wagon of progress. The "crafty animal," the politician, had defeated the brain centers of the race—Geneva, Wall Street, and the City of London.

In this piece of popular political theology imperialism stands for the old Adam. States and empires are held to be congenitally imperialist; they will eat up their neighbors without any moral compunctions. The latter half of the contention is true, but not the former. While imperialism, when and where it appears, does not wait on rational or moral justification for expansion, it is contrary to fact that states and empires are always expansionist. Territorial associations are not necessarily eager to extend their boundaries; neither cities, nor states, nor empires stand under such compulsion. To argue the opposite is to mistake some typical situations for a general law. In effect, contrary to popular preconceptions, modern capitalism started with a long period of contractionism; only late in its career did the turn towards imperialism happen.

Anti-imperialism was initiated by Adam Smith, who thereby not only anticipated the American Revolution but also the Little England movement of the following century. The reasons for the break were economic: the rapid expansion of markets started by the Seven Years' War made empires go out of fashion. While geographical discoveries, combined with comparatively slow means of transportation, favored overseas plantations, fast communications turned colonies into an expensive luxury. Another factor unfavorable to plantations was that exports now eclipsed imports in significance; the ideal of the buyer's market gave way to the seller's market, an aim attainable now by the simple means of underselling one's competitors, including, eventually, the colonists themselves. Once the Atlantic seaboard colonies were lost, Canada hardly managed to have herself retained in the Empire (1837); even a Disraeli advocated the liquidation of the West African possessions; the Orange State vainly offered to join the empire; and some islands in the Pacific, regarded today as pivots of world strategy, were consistently refused admission. Free traders and protectionists, liberals and ardent Tories joined in the popular conviction that colonies were a wasting asset destined to become a political and financial liability. Anybody who talked colonies in the century between 1780 and 1880 was looked upon as an adherent of the *ancien régime*. The middle class denounced war and conquest as dynastic machinations, and pandered to pacifism (François Quesnay had been the first to claim for *laissez-faire* the laurels of peace). France and Germany followed in England's wake. The former slowed down her rate of expansion appreciably, and even her imperialism was now more Continental than colonial. Bismarck contemptuously declined to pay the price of one single life for the Balkans and put all his influence behind anticolonial propaganda. Such was governmental attitude at the time when capitalistic companies were invading whole continents; when the East India Company had been dissolved at the insistence of eager Lancashire exporters, and anonymous piece-goods dealers replaced in India the resplendent figures of Warren Hastings and Clive. The governments held aloof. Canning ridiculed the notion of intervention on behalf of gambling investors and overseas speculators. The separation of politics and economics now spread into international affairs. While Queen Elizabeth had been loath to distinguish too strictly between her private income and privateer's income, Gladstone would have branded it a calumny that British foreign policy was being put at the service of foreign investors. To allow state power and trading interests to fuse was not a nineteenth century idea; on the contrary, early Victorian statesmen had proclaimed the independence of politics and economics as a maxim of international behavior. Only in narrowly defined cases were diplomatic representatives supposed to be active on behalf of the private interests of their nationals, and the surreptitious extension of these occasions was publicly denied, and if proven, reprimanded accordingly. Not only at home but also abroad, the principle of nonintervention of the state in the affairs of private business was maintained. The home government was not supposed to intervene in private trade, nor were foreign offices expected to regard private interests abroad otherwise than on broad national lines. Investments were overwhelmingly agricultural and located at home; foreign investments were still deemed a gamble, and the frequent total losses incurred by investors were regarded as amply compensated for by the scandalous terms of usurious lending.

The change came suddenly, and this time simultaneously in all leading Western countries. While Germany repeated England's domestic development only after a lag of half a century, external events of world scope would necessarily affect all trading countries alike. Such an event was the increase in the rhythm and volume of international trade as well as the universal mobilization of land, implied in the mass transportation of grain and agricultural raw materials from one part of the planet to another, at a fractional cost. This economic earthquake dislocated the lives of dozens of millions in rural Europe. Within a few years free trade was a matter of the past, and the further expansion of market economy took place under utterly new conditions.

These conditions themselves were set by the "double movement." The pattern of international trade which was now spreading at an accelerated rate was crossed by the introduction of protectionist institutions designed to check the all-round action of the market. The agrarian crisis and the Great Depression of 1873–86 had shaken confidence in economic self-healing. From now onward the typical institutions of market economy could usually be introduced only if accompanied by protectionist measures, all the more so because since the late 1870's and early 1880's nations were forming themselves into organized units which were apt to suffer grievously from the dislocations involved in any sudden adjustment to the needs of foreign trade or foreign exchanges. The supreme vehicle of the expansion of market economy, the gold standard, was thus usually accompanied by the simultaneous introduction of the typical protectionist policies of the age such as social legislation and customs tariffs.

On this point also the traditional liberal version of the collectivist conspiracy was not true to fact. The free trade and gold standard system was not wantonly wrecked by selfish tariff mongers and by softhearted social laws; on the contrary, the coming of the gold standard itself hastened the spreading of these protectionist institutions, which were the more welcome the more burdensome fixed exchanges were. From this time onward tariffs, factory laws, and an active colonial policy were prerequisites of a stable external currency (Great Britain with her vast industrial superiority was the exception which proved the rule). Only when these prerequisites were given could the methods of market economy now be safely introduced. Where such methods were forced upon a helpless people in absence of protective measures, as in exotic and semicolonial regions, unspeakable suffering ensued.

Herein we hold the key to the seeming paradox of imperialism— the economically inexplicable and therefore allegedly irrational refusal of countries to trade together indiscriminately, and their aiming instead at the acquisition of overseas and exotic markets. What made countries act in this manner was simply the fear of consequences similar to those which the powerless peoples were unable to avert. The difference was merely that while the tropical population of the wretched colony was thrown into utter misery and degradation, often to the point of physical extinction, the Western country's refusal was induced by the danger of a smaller peril but still sufficiently real to be avoided at almost all cost. That the threat, as in the case of colonies, was not essentially economic made no difference; there was no reason, apart from prejudice, to seek the measure of social dislocation in economic magnitudes. Indeed, to expect that a community would remain indifferent to the scourge of unemployment, the shifting of industries and occupations and to the moral and psychological torture accompanying them, merely because economic effects, in the long run, might be negligible, was to assume an absurdity.

The nation was just as often the passive recipient as the active initiator of strain. If some external event weighed heavily on the country, its internal mechanism functioned in the usual way, shifting the pressure from the economic to the political zone or *vice versa*. Significant instances occurred in the postwar period. For some Central European countries defeat created highly artificial conditions which included fierce external pressure in the shape of reparations. During more than a decade the German domestic scene was dominated by a shifting of the external burden between industry and state—between wages and profits on the one hand, social benefits and taxes on the other. The nation as a whole was the bearer of reparations, and the domestic position changed according to the manner in which the country—government and business combined—tackled the job. National solidarity was thus anchored in the gold standard, which made the maintenance of the external value of the currency a paramount obligation. The Dawes Plan was expressly devised to safeguard the German currency. The Young Plan made the same condition absolute. But for the obligation to keep the external value of the *reichsmark* unimpaired, the course of German home affairs during this period would be unintelligible. Collective responsibility for the currency created the indestructible framework within which business and parties, industry and state adjusted to the strain. Yet what a defeated Germany had to put up with as a result of a lost war, all peoples up to the Great War had endured voluntarily, namely, the artificial integration of their countries through the pressure of stable exchanges. Only resignation to the inevitable laws of the market could explain the proud acquiescence with which the cross was borne.

It might be objected that this outline is the result of sustained oversimplification. Market economy did not start in a day, nor did the three markets run a pace like a troika, nor did protectionism have parallel effects in all markets, and so on. This, of course, is true; only, it misses the point at issue.

Admittedly, economic liberalism merely created a novel mechanism out of more or less developed markets; it unified various types of already existing markets, and co-ordinated their functions in a single whole. Also, the separation of labor and land was, by that time, well on the way, and so was the development of markets for money and credit. All along the line the present was linked with the past, and nowhere was a break to be found.

Yet institutional change, such is its nature, started to operate abruptly. The critical stage was reached with the establishment of a labor market in England, in which workers were put under the threat of starvation if they failed to comply with the rules of wage labor. As soon as this drastic step was taken, the mechanism of the self-regulating market sprang into gear. Its impact on society was so violent that, almost instantly, and without any prior change in opinion, powerful protective reactions set in.

Also, in spite of their widely different nature and origin, the markets for the various elements of industry now showed a parallel development. This could have hardly been otherwise. The protection of man, nature, and productive organization amounted to an interference with markets for labor and land as well as for the medium of exchange, money, and thereby, *ipso facto*, impaired the self-regulation of the system. Since the purpose of the intervention was to rehabilitate the lives of men and their environment, to give them some security of status, intervention necessarily aimed at reducing the flexibility of wages and the mobility of labor, giving stability to incomes, continuity to production, introducing public control of national resources, and the management of currencies in order to avoid unsettling changes in the price level.

The Depression of 1873–86 and the agrarian distress of the seventies increased the strain permanently. At the beginning of the Depression Europe had been in the heyday of free trade. The new German Reich had forced upon France the most-favored-nation clause between herself and the latter country, committed herself to the removal of tariffs on pig iron, and introduced the gold standard. By the end of the Depression, Germany had surrounded herself with protective tariffs, established a general cartel organization, set up an all-round social insurance system, and was practicing high-pressure colonial policies. Prussianism, which had been a pioneer of free trade, was evidently as

little responsible for the change to protectionism as it was for the introduction of "collectivism." The United States had even higher tariffs
than the Reich and was just as "collectivistic" in its own way; it subsidized long-range railway building heavily and developed the elephan-
tine formation of the trusts.

All Western countries followed the same trend, irrespective of national mentality and history.[2] With the international gold standard
the most ambitious market scheme of all was put into effect, implying
absolute independence of markets from national authorities. World
trade now meant organization of life on the planet under a self-regulating market, comprising labor, land, and money, with the gold standard
as the guardian of this gargantuan automaton. Nations and peoples
were mere puppets in a show utterly beyond their control. They
shielded themselves from unemployment and instability with the help
of central banks and customs tariffs, supplemented by migration laws.
These devices were designed to counteract the destructive effects of
free trade plus fixed currencies, and to the degree in which they
achieved this purpose they interfered with the play of those mechanisms. Although each single restriction had its beneficiaries whose
super-profits or -wages were a tax on all other citizens, it was often only
the *amount* of the tax that was unjustified, not also protection itself.
In the long run there was an all-round drop in prices which benefited
all.

Whether protection was justified or not, a debility of the world
market system was brought to light by the effects of interventions. The
import tariffs of one country hampered the exports of another and
forced it to seek for markets in politically unprotected regions. Economic imperialism was mainly a struggle between the Powers for the
privilege of extending their trade into politically unprotected markets.
Export pressure was reinforced by a scramble for raw material supplies
caused by the manufacturing fever. Governments lent support to their
nationals engaged in business in backward countries. Trade and the
flag were racing in one another's wake. Imperialism and half-conscious
preparation for autarchy were the bent of Powers which found themselves more and more dependent upon an increasingly unreliable system of world economy. And yet rigid maintenance of the integrity of
the international gold standard was imperative. This was one institutional source of disruption.

A similar contradiction operated inside the national boundaries.

[2] G. D. H. Cole calls the seventies "by far the most active period for social
legislation of the entire 19th century."

Protectionism helped to transform competitive markets into monopolistic ones. Less and less could markets be described as autonomous and automatic mechanisms of competing atoms. More and more were individuals replaced by associations, men and capital united to noncompeting groups. Economic adjustment became slow and difficult. The self-regulation of markets was gravely hampered. Eventually, unadjusted price and cost structures prolonged depressions, unadjusted equipment retarded the liquidation of unprofitable investments, unadjusted price and income levels caused social tension. And whatever the market in question—labor, land, or money—the strain would transcend the economic zone and the balance would have to be restored by political means. Nevertheless, the institutional separation of the political from the economic sphere was constitutive to market society and had to be maintained whatever the tension involved. This was the other source of disruptive strain.

We are nearing the conclusion of our narrative. Yet a considerable part of our argument remains to be unfolded. For even if we have succeeded in proving beyond any doubt that at the heart of the transformation there was the failure of the market utopia, it is still incumbent upon us to show in what manner actual events were determined by this cause.

In a sense, this is an impossible undertaking, since history is not shaped by any single factor. Yet in spite of all its wealth and variety, the flow of history has its recurrent situations and alternatives which account for the broad similarity in the texture of the events of an age. We need not trouble about the fringe of unpredictable eddies, if we can account to some degree for the regularities which governed currents and countercurrents under typical conditions.

In the nineteenth century such conditions were given by the mechanism of the self-regulating market, the requirements of which had to be met by national and international life. From that mechanism two peculiarities of civilization followed: its rigid determinism and its economic character. Contemporary outlook tended to link the two and to assume that the determinism derived from the nature of economic motivation, according to which individuals were expected to pursue their monetary interests. In point of fact there was no connection between the two. The "determinism" so prominent in many details was simply the outcome of the mechanism of a market society with its predictable alternatives, the stringency of which was erroneously attributed to the strength of materialistic motivations. The supply-demand-price system will always balance, whatever the motives of the individuals, and economic motives *per se* are notoriously much less effective with most people than so-called emotional ones.

Mankind was in the grip, not of new motives, but of new mechanisms. Briefly, the strain sprang from the zone of the market; from there it spread to the political sphere, thus comprising the whole of society. But within the single nations the tension remained latent as long as world economy continued to function. Only when the last of its surviving institutions, the gold standard, dissolved was the stress within the nations finally released. Different as their responses to the new situation were, essentially they represented adjustments to the disappearance of the traditional world economy; when it disintegrated, market civilization itself was engulfed. This explains the almost unbelievable fact that a civilization was being disrupted by the blind action of soulless institutions the only purpose of which was the automatic increase of material welfare.

But how did the inevitable actually happen? How was it translated into the political events which are the core of history? Into this final phase of the fall of market economy the conflict of class forces entered decisively.

PART THREE

Transformation In Progress

19

POPULAR GOVERNMENT AND MARKET ECONOMY

WHEN IN THE 1920's the international system failed, the almost forgotten issues of early capitalism reappeared. First and foremost among them stood that of popular government.

The fascist attack on popular democracy merely revived the issue of political interventionism that haunted the history of market economy, since that issue was hardly more than another name for the separation of the economic from the political sphere.

The interventionist issue was first brought to a head with regard to labor by Speenhamland and the New Poor Law on the one hand, Parliamentary Reform and the Chartist Movement on the other. In regard to land and money the importance of interventionism was hardly smaller, even though clashes were less spectacular. On the Continent, similar difficulties in respect to labor, land, and money arose with a time-lag which brought conflicts to bear on an industrially more modern but socially less unified environment. Everywhere the separation of the economic and the political sphere was the result of the same type of development. In England as on the Continent the starting points were the establishment of a competitive labor market and the democratization of the political state.

Speenhamland has been justly described as a preventive act of intervention, obstructing the creation of a labor market. The battle for an industrial England was first fought and, for the time being, lost on Speenhamland. In this struggle the slogan of interventionism was coined by the classical economists and Speenhamland branded an artificial interference with an actually nonexistent market order. Townsend, Malthus, and Ricardo erected upon the flimsy foundation of Poor Law conditions the edifice of classical economics, the most formidable conceptual instrument of destruction ever directed against an outworn order. Yet for another generation the allowance system protected the confines of the village against the attraction of high urban wages. By the middle 1820's, Huskisson and Peel were broadening the avenues of foreign trade, export of machinery was permitted, the embargo on wool exports was raised, shipping restrictions were abolished, emigration was eased, while the formal revocation of the Statute of Artificers on apprenticeship and on wage assessments was followed by the repeal of the Anti-Combination Laws. And still the demoralizing Speenhamland Law was spreading from county to county, deterring the laborer from honest work, and making the very concept of an independent working man an incongruity. Though the time for a labor market had come, its birth was prevented by the squires' "law."

The Reform Parliament at once set out to abolish the allowance system. The New Poor Law which achieved this end has been called the most important act of social legislation ever carried by the House of Commons. Yet the core of the Bill was simply the repeal of Speenhamland. Nothing could prove more decisively that by this time the bare absence of intervention in the labor market was recognized as a fact of constitutive importance for the whole future structure of society. So much as to the economic source of the tension.

As to the political, the Parliamentary Reform of 1832 achieved a peaceful revolution. By the Poor Law Amendment of 1834 the social stratification of the country was altered, and some of the basic facts of English life were reinterpreted along radically new lines. The New Poor Law abolished the general category of *the poor,* the "honest poor," or "laboring poor"—terms against which Burke had inveighed. The former *poor* were now divided into physically helpless paupers whose place was in the workhouse, and independent workers who earned their living by laboring for wages. This created an entirely new category of the poor, the unemployed, who made their appearance on the social scene. While the pauper, for the sake of humanity, should be relieved, the unemployed, for the sake of industry, should *not* be relieved. That the unemployed worker was innocent of his fate did not matter. The point was not whether he might or might not have found work had he only really tried, but that unless he was in danger of famishing with only the abhorred workhouse for an alternative, the wage system would break down, thus throwing society into misery and chaos. That this meant penalizing the innocent was recognized. The perversion of cruelty consisted precisely in emancipating the laborer for the avowed purpose of making the threat of destruction through hunger effective. This procedure makes intelligible that dismal feeling of desolation which speaks to us from the works of the classical economists. But to lock the doors safely upon the supernumeraries who were now caged in the confines of the labor market, government was put under a self-denying ordinance to the effect that—in Harriet Martineau's words—to provide any relief to the innocent victims was on the part of the state a "violation of the rights of the people."

When the Chartist Movement demanded entrance for the disinherited into the precincts of the state, the separation of economics and politics ceased to be an academic issue and became the irrefragable condition of the existing system of society. It would have been an act of lunacy to hand over the administration of the New Poor Law with its scientific methods of mental torture to the representatives of the self-same people for whom that treatment was designed. Lord Macaulay was only consistent when he demanded in the House of Lords in one of the most eloquent speeches ever made by a great liberal the unconditional rejection of the Chartist petition in the name of the institution of property on which all civilization rested. Sir Robert Peel called the Charter an impeachment of the Constitution. The more viciously the labor market contorted the lives of the workers, the more insistently they clamored for the vote. The demand for popular government was the political source of the tension.

Under these conditions constitutionalism gained an utterly new meaning. Until then constitutional safeguards against unlawful interference with the rights of property were directed only against arbitrary acts from above. Locke's vision did not transcend the limits of landed and commercial property, and aimed merely at excluding high-handed acts of the Crown such as the secularizations under Henry VIII, the robbing of the Mint under Charles I, or the "stop" of the Exchequer under Charles II. Separation of government from business, in John Locke's sense, was achieved in an exemplary fashion in the charter of an independent Bank of England in 1694. Commercial capital had won its tilt against the Crown.

A hundred years later not commercial but industrial property was to be protected, and not against the Crown but against the people. Only by misconception could seventeenth century meanings be applied to nineteenth century situations. The separation of powers, which Montesquieu (1748) had meanwhile invented, was now used to separate the people from power over their own economic life. The American Constitution, shaped in a farmer-craftsman's environment by a leadership forewarned by the English industrial scene, isolated the economic sphere entirely from the jurisdiction of the Constitution, put private property thereby under the highest conceivable protection, and created the only legally grounded market society in the world. In spite of universal suffrage, American voters were powerless against owners.[1]

In England it became the unwritten law of the Constitution that the working class must be denied the vote. The Chartist leaders were jailed; their adherents, numbered in millions, were derided by a legislature representing a bare fraction of the population, and the mere demand for the ballot was often treated as a criminal act by the author-ties. Of the spirit of compromise allegedly characteristic of the British system—a later invention—there was no sign. Not before the working class had passed through the Hungry Forties and a docile generation had emerged to reap the benefits of the Golden Age of capitalism; not before an upper layer of skilled workers had developed their unions and parted company with the dark mass of poverty-stricken laborers; not before the workers had acquiesced in the system which the New Poor Law was meant to enforce upon them was their better-paid stratum allowed to participate in the nation's councils. The Chartists had fought for the right to stop the mill of the market which ground the lives of the people. But the people were granted rights only when the awful adjustment had been made. Inside and outside England, from Macaulay to Mises, from Spencer to Sumner, there was not a militant liberal who did not express his conviction that popular democracy was a danger to capitalism.

The experience of the labor issue was repeated on the currency issue. Here also the 1920's were foreshadowed by the 1790's. Bentham was the first to recognize that inflation and deflation were interventions with the right of property: the former a tax on, the latter an interference with, business.[2] Ever since then labor and money, unemployment and inflation have been politically in the same category. Cobbett denounced the gold standard together with the New Poor Law; Ricardo stood for both, and with very similar arguments, labor as well as money being commodities and the government having no right to interfere with either. Bankers who opposed the introduction of the gold standard, like Atwood of Birmingham, found themselves on the same side with socialists, like Owen. And a century later Mises

---

[1] Hadley, A. T., *Economics: An Account of the Relations between Private Property and Public Welfare*, 1896.

[2] Bentham, J., *Manual of Political Economy*, p. 44, on inflation as "forced frugality"; p. 45 (footnote) as "indirect taxation." Cf. also *Principles of Civil Code*, Ch. 15.

was still reiterating that labor and money were no more a concern of the government than any other commodity on the market. In eighteenth century, prefederation America, cheap money was the equivalent to Speenhamland, that is, an economically demoralizing concession made by government to popular clamor. The French Revolution and its assignats showed that the people might smash the currency, and the history of the American states did not help to dispel that suspicion. Burke identified American democracy with currency troubles and Hamilton feared not only factions but also inflation. But while in nineteenth century America the bickerings of populists and greenback parties with Wall Street magnates were endemic, in Europe the charge of inflationism became an effective argument against democratic legislatures only in the 1920's, with far-reaching political consequences.

Social protection and interference with the currency were not merely analogous but often identical issues. Since the establishment of the gold standard, the currency was just as much endangered by a rising wage level as by direct inflation—both might diminish exports and eventually depress exchanges. This simple connection between the two basic forms of intervention became the fulcrum of politics in the twenties. Parties concerned for the safety of the currency protested as much against threatening budget deficits as against cheap money policies, thus opposing "treasury inflation" as much as "credit inflation," or, in more practical terms, denouncing social burdens *and* high wages, trade unions *and* labor parties. Not the form, but the essence mattered, and who could doubt but that unrestricted unemployment benefits might be as effective in upsetting the balance of the budget as too low a rate of interest in inflating prices—and with the same nefarious consequences for the exchanges? Gladstone had made the budget the conscience of the British nation. With lesser peoples, a stable currency might take the place of the budget. But the result was closely similar. Whether wages or social services had to be cut, the consequences of not cutting them were inescapably set by the mechanism of the market. From the point of view of this analysis, the National Government of 1931 in Great Britain performed in a modest way the same function as the American New Deal. Both these were moves of adjustment of single countries in the great transformation. But the British instance had the advantage of being free of complicating factors, such as civil strifes or ideological conversions, thus showing up the decisive features more clearly.

Since 1925 the position of Great Britain's currency had been unsound. The return to gold was not accompanied by a corresponding adjustment of the price level, which was distinctly above world parity. Very few people were conscious of the absurdity of the course on which government and Bank, parties and trade unions had jointly embarked. Snowden, Chancellor of the Exchequer in Labor's first government (1924), was a gold standard addict if ever there was one, yet he failed to realize that by undertaking to restore the pound he had committed his party either to shoulder a fall in wages or to go into the wilderness. Seven years later Labor was forced—by Snowden himself—to do both. By autumn, 1931, the continuous drain of depression was telling on the pound. In vain had the collapse of the General Strike, in 1926, ensured against a further increase in the wage level—it did not prevent a rise in the financial burden of social services, especially through unconditional unemployment benefit. There was no need for a banker's "ramp" (though ramp there was) to impress upon the nation the alternative of sound currency and sound budgets on the one hand, improved social services and a depreciated currency on the other—whether the depreciation was caused by high wages and falling exports or simply by deficit spending. In other words, there had to be either a cut in the social services or a fall in the exchanges. Since Labor was unable to decide for either—a cut was contrary to trade union policy and going off gold would have been deemed a sacrilege—Labor was shoved out of office, and the traditional parties cut the social services *and*, eventually, went off gold. Unconditional unemployment benefit was scrapped; a means test was introduced. At the same time the political traditions of the country underwent a significant change. The two-party system was suspended and no precipitation was shown to restore it. Twelve years later it was still in eclipse, with all signs against an early comeback. Without any tragic loss of welfare or of freedom the country, by suspending the gold standard, had taken a decisive step towards a transformation. During World War II this was accompanied by changes in the methods of liberal capitalism. However, these latter were not meant to be permanent and did not, therefore, remove the country from the danger zone.

In all important European countries a similar mechanism was active and with very much the same effects. In Austria in 1923, in Belgium and France in 1926, in Germany in 1931, Labor Parties had to quit office in order to "save the currency." Statesmen like Seipel, Francqui, Poincaré, or Brüning eliminated Labor from government, reduced social services, and tried to break the resistance of the unions to wage adjustments. Invariably the danger was to the currency, and with equal regularity the responsibility was fixed on inflated wages and unbalanced budgets. Such a simplification hardly does justice to the variety of problems involved which comprised almost every question of economic and financial policy, including those of foreign trade, agriculture, and industry. Yet the more closely we consider these questions the clearer it must become that eventually currency and budget focused the issues pending between employers and the employees, with the rest of the population swinging in to the support of the one or the other of the leading groups.

The so-called Blum experiment (1936) offered another instance. Labor was in government, but on condition that no embargo on gold exports be imposed. The French New Deal never had a chance since the government was tied on the crucial question of currency. The case is conclusive since in France as in England, once labor had been made innocuous, the middle-class parties gave up the defense of the gold standard without further ado. These examples show how crippling the effect of the sound currency postulate was on popular policies.

The American experience taught the same lesson, in another way. The New Deal could not have been launched without going off gold, though foreign exchange actually mattered but little. Under the gold standard the leaders of the financial market are entrusted, in the nature of things, with the safeguarding of stable exchanges and sound internal credit on which government finance largely depends. The banking organization is thus in the position to obstruct any domestic move in the economic sphere which it happens to dislike, whether its reasons are good or bad. In terms of politics, on currency and credit, governments must take the advice of the bankers, who alone can know whether any financial measure would or would not endanger the capital market and the exchanges. That social protectionism did not in this case result in a deadlock was due to the fact that the United States went off gold in time. For although the technical advantages of this move were slight (and the reasons given by the Administration were, as so often, very poor), the political dispossession of Wall Street was the result of this step. The financial market governs by panic. The eclipse of Wall Street in the thirties saved the United States from a social catastrophe of the Continental type.

However, only in the United States, with its independence from world trade and its excessively strong currency position, was the gold standard chiefly a matter of domestic politics. In other countries, going off gold involved no less than dropping out of world economy. Perhaps the only exception was Great Britain, whose share in world trade was so large that she had been able to lay down the modalities under which the international monetary system should work, thus shifting the burden of the gold standard largely to other shoulders. In countries like Germany, France, Belgium, and Austria, none of these conditions existed. With them destruction of the currency meant cutting loose from the outer world and thereby sacrificing industries dependent upon imported raw materials, disorganizing foreign trade upon which employment rested, and all this without a chance of forcing a similar degree of depreciation on their purveyors and thus evading the internal consequences of a fall in the gold value of the currency, as Great Britain had done.

Exchanges were the highly effective arm of the lever that was pressing on the wage level. Before exchanges brought matters to a head, usually the wage issue was increasing the tension under the surface. But what the laws of the market often could not force upon reluctant wage earners, the foreign exchange mechanism most effectively performed. The currency indicator made visible to all the unfavorable effects that interventionist trade union policies had on the market mechanism (the inherent weaknesses of which, including the trade cycle, were now taken for granted).

Indeed, the utopian nature of a market society cannot be better illustrated than by the absurdities in which the commodity fiction in regard to labor must involve the community. The strike, this normal bargaining weapon of industrial action, was more and more frequently felt to be a wanton interruption of socially useful work, which, at the same time, diminished the social dividend out of which, ultimately, wages must come. Sympathy strikes were resented, general strikes were regarded as a threat to the existence of the community. Actually, strikes in vital services and public utilities held the citizens in ransom while involving them in the labyrinthine problem of the true functions of a labor market. Labor is supposed to find its price on the market, any other price than that so established being uneconomical. As long as labor lives up to this responsibility, it will behave as an element in the supply of that which it is, the commodity "labor," and will refuse to sell below the price which the buyer can still afford to pay. Consistently followed up, this means that the chief obligation of labor is to be almost continually on strike. The proposition could not be outbidden for sheer absurdity, yet it is only the logical inference from the commodity theory of labor. The source of the incongruity of theory and practice is, of course, that labor is not really a commodity, and that if labor was withheld merely in order to ascertain its exact price (just as an increase in supply of all other commodities is withheld in similar circumstances) society would very soon dissolve for lack of sustenance. It is remarkable that this consideration is very rarely, if ever, mentioned in the discussion of the strike issue on the part of liberal economists.

Returning to reality: the strike method of fixing wages would be disastrous in any type of society, not to mention our own, which prides itself on its utilitarian rationality. Actually, the worker has no security in his job under a system of private enterprise, a circumstance which involved a grave deterioration in his status. Add to this the threat of mass unemployment, and the function of trade unions becomes morally and culturally vital to the maintenance of minimum standards for the majority of the people. Yet clearly any method of intervention that offers protection to the workers must obstruct the mechanism of the self-regulating market, and eventually diminish the very fund of consumers' goods that provides them with wages.

By inherent necessity the root problems of market society reappeared: interventionism and currency. They became the center of politics in the twenties. Economic liberalism and socialist interventionism turned upon the different answers given to them.

Economic liberalism made a supreme bid to restore the self-regulation of the system by eliminating all interventionist policies which interfered with the freedom of markets for land, labor, and money. It undertook no less than to solve, in an emergency, the secular problem involved in the three fundamental principles of free trade, a free labor market, and a freely functioning gold standard. It became, in effect, the spearhead of a heroic attempt to restore world trade, remove all avoidable hindrances to the mobility of labor, and reconstruct stable exchanges. This last aim had precedence over the rest. For unless confidence in the currencies was restored, the mechanism of the market could not function, in which case it was illusory to expect governments to refrain from protecting the lives of their people by all the means at their disposal. In the nature of things, these means were, primarily, tariffs and social laws designed to secure food and employment, that is, precisely the type of intervention which made a self-regulating system unworkable.

There was also another, more immediate, reason to put the restoration of the international monetary system first: in the face of disorganized markets and unstable exchanges international credit was playing an increasingly vital part. Before the Great War international capital movements (other than those connected with long-term investments) merely helped to keep the balance of payment liquid, but were strictly limited even in this function by economic considerations. Credit was given only to such as seemed deserving of confidence on business grounds. Now the position was reversed: debts had been created on political grounds such as reparations, and loans were given on semi-political grounds, in order to make reparation payments possible. But loans were also given for reasons of economic policy, in order to stabilize world prices or to restore the gold standard. The credit mechanism was being used by the relatively sound part of world economy to bridge the gaps in the relatively disorganized parts of that economy, irrespective of the conditions of production and trade. Balances of payment, budgets, exchanges were made to balance artificially in a number of countries with the help of a supposedly all-powerful international credit mechanism. This mechanism itself was based on the expectation of a return to stable exchanges, which again was synonymous with a return to gold. An elastic band of amazing strength helped to maintain the semblance of unity in a dissolving economic system; but whether the band would stand the strain depended upon a timely return to gold.

The achievement of Geneva was remarkable in its way. Had the aim not been intrinsically impossible, it would have been surely attained, so able, sustained, and single-minded was the attempt. As matters stood, no intervention was probably more disastrous in its results than that of Geneva. Just because it always appeared to be almost successful, it aggravated enormously the effects of the ultimate failure. Between 1923, when the German mark was pulverized within a few months, and the beginning of 1930, when all the important currencies of the world were on gold, Geneva used the international credit mechanism to shift the burden of the incompletely stabilized economies of Eastern Europe, first, to the shoulders of the Western victors, second, from there to the even broader shoulders of the United States of America.[3] The collapse came in America in the course of the usual

[3] Polanyi, K., "Der Mechanismus der Weltwirtschaftskrise." *Der Österreichische Volkswirt*, 1933 (Supplement).

business cycle, but by the time it came, the financial web created by Geneva and Anglo-Saxon banking entangled the economy of the planet in that awful capsize.

But even more was involved. During the twenties, according to Geneva, questions of social organization had to be wholly subordinated to the needs of the restoration of the currency. Deflation was the primary need; domestic institutions had to adjust as best they might. For the time being, even the restoration of free internal markets and of the liberal state had to be postponed. For in the words of the Gold Delegation, deflation had failed "to affect certain classes of goods and services, and failed, therefore, to bring about a stable new equilibrium." Governments had to intervene in order to reduce prices of monopoly articles, to reduce agreed wage schedules, and cut rents. The deflationist's ideal came to be a "free economy under a strong government"; but while the phrase on government meant what it said, namely, emergency powers and suspension of public liberties, "free economy" meant in practice the opposite of what it said, namely, governmentally adjusted prices and wages (though the adjustment was made with the express purpose of restoring the freedom of the exchanges and free internal markets). Primacy of exchanges involved no less a sacrifice than that of free markets and free governments—the two pillars of liberal capitalism. Geneva thus represented a change in aim, but no change in methods: while the inflationary governments condemned by Geneva subordinated the stability of the currency to stability of incomes and employment, the deflationary governments put in power by Geneva used no fewer interventions in order to subordinate the stability of incomes and employment to the stability of the currency. In 1932, the Report of the Gold Delegation of the League of Nations declared that with the return of the exchange uncertainty the main monetary achievement of the last decade had been eliminated. What the Report did not say was that in the course of these vain deflationary efforts free markets had *not* been restored though free governments *had* been sacrificed. Though opposed in theory to interventionism and inflation alike, economic liberals had chosen between the two and set the sound-currency ideal above that of nonintervention. In so doing they followed the logic inherent in a self-regulating economy. Yet such a course of action tended to spread the crisis, it burdened finance with the unbearable strain of massive economic dislocations, and it heaped up the deficits of the various national economies to the point where a disruption of the remnants of international division of labor became inevitable. The stubbornness with which economic liberals, for a critical decade, had, in the service of deflationary policies, supported authoritarian interventionism, merely resulted in a decisive weakening of the democratic forces which might otherwise have averted the fascist catastrophe. Great Britain and the United States—masters not servants of the currency—went off gold in time to escape this peril.

Socialism is, essentially, the tendency inherent in an industrial civilization to transcend the self-regulating market by consciously subordinating it to a democratic society. It is the solution natural to the industrial workers who see no reason why production should not be regulated directly and why markets should be more than a useful but subordinate trait in a free society. From the point of view of the community as a whole, socialism is merely the continuation of that endeavor to make society a distinctively human relationship of persons which in Western Europe was always associated with Christian traditions. From the point of view of the economic system, it is, on the contrary, a radical departure from the immediate past, in so far as it breaks with the attempt to make private money gains the general incentive to productive activities, and does not acknowledge the right of private individuals to dispose of the main instruments of production. This is, ultimately, why the reform of capitalist economy by socialist parties is difficult even when they are determined not to interfere with the property system. For the mere possibility that they might decide to do so undermines that type of confidence which in liberal economy is vital, namely, absolute confidence in the continuity of the titles to property. While the actual content of property rights might undergo redefinition at the hands of legislation, assurance of formal continuity is essential to the functioning of the market system.

Since the Great War two changes have taken place which affect the position of socialism. First, the market system proved unreliable to the point of almost total collapse, a deficiency that had not been expected even by its critics; second, a socialist economy was established in Russia, representing an altogether new departure. Though the conditions under which this venture took place made it inapplicable to Western countries, the very existence of Soviet Russia proved an incisive influence. True, she had turned to socialism in the absence of industries, a literate population, and democratic traditions—all three of which, according to Western ideas, were preconditions of socialism. These differences made her methods and solutions inapplicable elsewhere, but did not prevent socialism from becoming a world power. On the Continent workers' parties had always been socialist in outlook and any reform they wished to achieve was, as a matter of course, suspect of serving socialist aims. In quiet times such a suspicion would have been unjustified ; socialist working-class parties were, on the whole, committed to the reform of capitalism, not to its revolutionary overthrow. But the position was different in an emergency. Then, if normal methods were insufficient, abnormal ones would be tried, and with a workers' party such methods might involve a disregard of property rights. Under the stress of imminent danger workers' parties might strike out for measures which were socialistic or at least appeared as such to the militant adherents of private enterprise. And the very hint would suffice to throw markets into confusion and start a universal panic.

Under conditions such as these the routine conflict of interests between employers and employees took on an ominous character. While a divergence of economic interests would normally end in compromise, the separation of the economic and the political spheres in society tended to invest such clashes with grave consequences to the community. The employers were the owners of the factories and mines and thus directly responsible for carrying on production in society (quite apart from their personal interest in profits). In principle, they would have the backing of all in their endeavor to keep industry going. On the other hand, the employees represented a large section of society ; their interests also were to an important degree coincident with those of the community as a whole. They were the only available class for the protection of the interests of the consumers, of the citizens, of human beings as such, and, under universal suffrage, their numbers would give them a preponderance in the political sphere. However, the legislature, like industry, had its formal functions to perform in society. Its members were entrusted with the forming of the communal will, the direction of public policy, the enactment of long-term programs at home and abroad. No complex society could do without functioning legislative and executive bodies of a political kind. A clash of group interests that resulted in paralyzing the organs of industry or state— either of them, or both—formed an immediate peril to society.

Yet precisely this was the case in the twenties. Labor entrenched itself in parliament where its numbers gave it weight, capitalists built industry into a fortress from which to lord the country. Popular bodies answered by ruthlessly intervening in business, disregarding the needs of the given form of industry. The captains of industry were subverting the population from allegiance to their own freely elected rulers, while democratic bodies carried on warfare against the industrial system on which everybody's livelihood depended. Eventually, the moment would come when both the economic and the political systems were threatened by complete paralysis. Fear would grip the people, and leadership would be thrust upon those who offered an easy way out at whatever ultimate price. The time was ripe for the fascist solution.

20

HISTORY IN THE GEAR OF SOCIAL CHANGE

IF EVER THERE WAS a political movement that responded to the needs of an objective situation and was not a result of fortuitous causes it was fascism. At the same time, the degenerative character of the fascist solution was evident. It offered an escape from an institutional deadlock which was essentially alike in a large number of countries, and yet, if the remedy were tried, it would everywhere produce sickness unto death. That is the manner in which civilizations perish.

The fascist solution of the *impasse* reached by liberal capitalism can be described as a reform of market economy achieved at the price of the extirpation of all democratic institutions, both in the industrial and in the political realm. The economic system which was in peril of disruption would thus be revitalized, while the people themselves were subjected to a re-education designed to denaturalize the individual and make him unable to function as the responsible unit of the body politic.[1] This re-education, comprising the tenets of a political religion that denied the idea of the brotherhood of man in all its forms, was achieved through an act of mass conversion enforced against recalcitrants by scientific methods of torture.

The appearance of such a movement in the industrial countries of the globe, and even in a number of only slightly industrialized ones, should never have been ascribed to local causes, national mentalities, or historical backgrounds as was so consistently done by contemporaries. Fascism had as little to do with the Great War as with the Versailles Treaty, with Junker militarism as with the Italian temperament. The movement appeared in defeated countries like Bulgaria and in victorious ones like Jugoslavia, in countries of Northern temperament like Finland and Norway and of Southern temperament like Italy and Spain, in countries of Aryan race like England, Ireland, or Belgium and non-Aryan race like Japan, Hungary or Palestine, in countries of

[1] Polanyi, K., "The Essence of Fascism." In *Christianity and the Social Revolution*, 1935.

237

Catholic traditions like Portugal and in Protestant ones like Holland, in soldierly communities like Prussia and civilian ones like Austria, in old cultures like France and new ones like the United States and the Latin-American countries. In fact, there was no type of background—of religious, cultural, or national tradition—that made a country immune to fascism, once the conditions for its emergence were given.

Moreover, there was a striking lack of relationship between its material and numerical strength and its political effectiveness. The very term "movement" was misleading since it implied some kind of enrollment or personal participation of large numbers. If anything was characteristic of fascism it was its independence of such popular manifestations. Though usually aiming at a mass following, its potential strength was reckoned not by the numbers of its adherents but by the influence of the persons in high position whose good will the fascist leaders possessed, and whose influence in the community could be counted upon to shelter them from the consequences of an abortive revolt, thus taking the risks out of revolution.

A country approaching the fascist phase showed symptoms among which the existence of a fascist movement proper was not necessarily one. At least as important signs were the spread of irrationalistic philosophies, racialist esthetics, anticapitalistic demagogy, heterodox currency views, criticism of the party system, widespread disparagement of the "regime," or whatever was the name given to the existing democratic set-up. In Austria the so-called universalist philosophy of Othmar Spann, in Germany the poetry of Stephan George and the cosmogonic romanticism of Ludwig Klages, in England D. H. Lawrence's erotic vitalism, in France Georges Sorel's cult of the political myth were among its extremely diverse forerunners. Hitler was eventually put in power by the feudalist clique around President Hindenburg, just as Mussolini and Primo de Rivera were ushered into office by their respective sovereigns. Yet Hitler had a vast movement to support him; Mussolini had a small one; Primo de Rivera had none. In no case was an actual revolution against constituted authority launched; fascist tactics were invariably those of a sham rebellion arranged with the tacit approval of the authorities who pretended to have been overwhelmed by force. These are the bare outlines of a complex picture in which room would have to be made for figures as diverse as the Catholic free-lance demagogue in industrial Detroit, the "Kingfish" in backward Louisiana, Japanese army conspirators, and Ukrainian anti-Soviet saboteurs. Fascism was an ever given political possibility, an almost instantaneous emotional reaction in every industrial community since the 1930's. One may call it a "move" in preference to a "movement," to indicate the impersonal nature of the crisis the symptoms of which were frequently vague and ambiguous. People often did not feel sure whether a political speech or a play, a sermon or a public parade, a metaphysics or an artistic fashion, a poem or a party program was fascist or not. There were no accepted criteria of fascism, nor did it possess conventional tenets. Yet one significant feature of all its organized forms was the abruptness with which they appeared and faded out again, only to burst forth with violence after an indefinite period of latency. All this fits into the picture of a social force that waxed and waned according to the objective situation.

What we termed, for short, "fascist situation" was no other than the typical occasion of easy and complete fascist victories. All at once, the tremendous industrial and political organizations of labor and of other devoted upholders of constitutional freedom would melt away, and minute fascist forces would brush aside what seemed until then the overwhelming strength of democratic governments, parties, trade unions. If a "revolutionary situation" is characterized by the psychological and moral disintegration of all forces of resistance to the point where a handful of scantily armed rebels were enabled to storm the supposedly impregnable strongholds of *reaction,* then the "fascist situation" was its complete parallel except for the fact that here the bulwarks of *democracy and constitutional liberties* were stormed and their defenses found wanting in the same spectacular fashion. In Prussia, in July, 1932, the legal government of the Social Democrats, entrenched in the seat of legitimate power, capitulated to the mere threat of unconstitutional violence on the part of Herr von Papen. Some six months later Hitler possessed himself peacefully of the highest positions of power, whence he at once launched a revolutionary attack of wholesale destruction against the institutions of the Weimar Republic and the constitutional parties. To imagine that it was the strength of the movement which created situations such as these, and not to see that it was the situation that gave birth in this case to the movement, is to miss the outstanding lesson of the last decades.

Fascism, like socialism, was rooted in a market society that refused to function. Hence, it was world-wide, catholic in scope, universal in application; the issues transcended the economic sphere and begot a general transformation of a distinctively social kind. It radiated into almost every field of human activity whether political or economic,

cultural, philosophic, artistic, or religious. And up to a point it co-
alesced with local and topical tendencies. No understanding of the
history of the period is possible unless we distinguish between the underlying fascist move and the ephemeral tendencies with which that move
fused in different countries.

In the Europe of the twenties two such tendencies figured promi-
nently and overlay the fainter but vastly more comprehensive pattern
of fascism: counterrevolution and nationalist revisionism. Their immediate starting point was the Treaties and the postwar revolutions.
Though strictly conditioned, and limited to their specific objectives,
they were easily confounded with fascism.

Counterrevolutions were the usual backswing of the political pendulum towards a state of affairs that had been violently disturbed.
Such moves have been typical in Europe at least since the English
Commonwealth, and had but limited connection with the social processes of their time. In the twenties numerous situations of this kind
developed, since the upheavals that destroyed more than a dozen
thrones in Central and Eastern Europe were partly due to the backwash
of defeat, not to the forward move of democracy. The job of counterrevolution was mainly political and fell as a matter of course to the
dispossessed classes and groups such as dynasties, aristocracies, churches,
heavy industries, and the parties affiliated with them. The alliances
and clashes of conservatives and fascists during this period concerned
mainly the share that should go to the fascists in the counterrevolutionary undertaking. Now, fascism was a revolutionary tendency directed as
much against conservatism as against the competing revolutionary
force of socialism. That did not preclude the fascists from seeking
power in the political field by offering their services to the counterrevolution. On the contrary, they claimed ascendency chiefly by virtue of
the alleged impotence of conservatism to accomplish that job, which
was unavoidable if socialism was to be barred. The conservatives,
naturally, tried to monopolize the honors of the counterrevolution and,
actually, as in Germany, accomplished it alone. They deprived the
working-class parties of influence and power, without giving in to the
Nazi. Similarly, in Austria, the Christian Socialists—a conservative
party—largely disarmed the workers (1927) without making any
concession to the "revolution from the right." Even where fascist
participation in the counterrevolution was unavoidable, "strong" governments were established which relegated fascism to the limbo. This
happened in Esthonia in 1929, in Finland in 1932, in Latvia in 1934.
Pseudo-liberal regimes broke the power of fascism for the time, in

Hungary in 1922, and in Bulgaria in 1926. In Italy alone were the conservatives unable to restore work-discipline in industry without providing the fascists with a chance of gaining power.

In the militarily defeated countries, but also in the "psychologically" defeated Italy, the national problem loomed large. Here a task was set the stringency of which could not be denied. Deeper than all other issues cut the permanent disarmament of the defeated countries; in a world in which the only existing organization of international law, international order, and international peace rested on the balance of power, a number of countries had been made powerless without any intimation of the kind of system that would replace the old. The League of Nations represented, at the best, an improved system of balance of power, but was actually not even on the level of the late Concert of Europe, since the prerequisite of a general diffusion of power was now lacking. The nascent fascist movement put itself almost everywhere into the service of the national issue; it could hardly have survived without this "pick-up" job.

Yet, it used this issue only as a stepping stone; at other times it struck the pacifist and isolationist note. In England and the United States it was allied with appeasement; in Austria the *Heimwehr* co-operated with sundry Catholic pacifists; and Catholic fascism was anti-nationalist, on principle. Huey Long needed no border conflict with Mississippi or Texas to launch his fascist movement from Baton Rouge. Similar movements in Holland and Norway were nonnationalist to the point of treason—Quisling may have been a name for a good fascist, but was certainly not one for a good patriot.

In its struggle for political power fascism is entirely free to disregard or to use local issues, at will. Its aim transcends the political and economic framework: it is social. It puts a political religion into the service of a degenerative process. In its rise it excludes only a very few emotions from its orchestra; yet once victorious it bars from the band wagon all but a very small group of motivations, though again extremely characteristic ones. Unless we distinguish closely between this pseudo intolerance on the road to power and the genuine intolerance in power, we can hardly hope to understand the subtle but decisive difference between the sham-nationalism of some fascist movements during the revolution, and the specifically imperialistic nonnationalism which they developed after the revolution.[2]

While conservatives were as a rule successful in carrying the domes-

[2] Heymann, H., *Plan for Permanent Peace*, 1941. Cf. Brüning's letter of January 8th, 1940

tic counterrevolutions alone, they were but rarely able to bring the national-international problem of their countries to an issue. Brüning maintained in 1940 that German reparations and disarmament had been solved by him before the "clique around Hindenburg" decided to put him out of office and to hand over power to the Nazis, the reason for their action being that they did not want the honors to go to him.[3] Whether, in a very limited sense, this was so or not seems immaterial, since the question of Germany's equality of status was *not* restricted to technical disarmament, as Brüning implied, but included the equally vital question of demilitarization; also, it was not really possible to disregard the strength which German diplomacy drew from the existence of Nazi masses sworn to radical nationalist policies. Events proved conclusively that Germany's equality of status could not have been attained without a revolutionary departure, and it is in this light that the awful responsibility of Nazism, which committed a free and equal Germany to a career of crime, becomes apparent. Both in Germany and in Italy fascism could seize power only because it was able to use as its lever unsolved national issues, while in France as in Great Britain fascism was decisively weakened by its antipatriotism. Only in small and naturally dependent countries could the spirit of subservience to a foreign power prove an asset to fascism.

By accident only, as we see, was European fascism in the twenties connected with national and counterrevolutionary tendencies. It was a case of symbiosis between movements of independent origin, which reinforced one another and created the impression of essential similarity, while being actually unrelated.

In reality, the part played by fascism was determined by one factor: the condition of the market system.

During the period 1917–23 governments occasionally sought fascist help to restore law and order: no more was needed to set the market system going. Fascism remained undeveloped.

In the period 1924–29, when the restoration of the market system seemed ensured, fascism faded out as a political force altogether.

After 1930 market economy was in a general crisis. Within a few years fascism was a world power.

The first period 1917–23 produced hardly more than the term. In a number of European countries—such as Finland, Lithuania, Esthonia, Latvia, Poland, Roumania, Bulgaria, Greece, and Hungary— agrarian or socialist revolutions had taken place, while in others—

[3] Rauschning, H., *The Voice of Destruction*, 1940.

among them Italy, Germany, and Austria—the industrial working class had gained political influence. Eventually counterrevolutions restored the domestic balance of power. In the majority of countries the peasantry turned against the urban workers; in some countries fascist movements were started by officers and gentry, who gave a lead to the peasantry; in others, as in Italy, the unemployed and the petite bourgeoisie formed into fascist troops. Nowhere was any other issue than that of law and order mooted, no question of radical reform was raised; in other words, no sign of a fascist revolution was apparent. These movements were fascist only in form, that is to say only in so far as civilian bands, so-called irresponsible elements, made use of force and violence with the connivance of persons in authority. The antidemocratic philosophy of fascism was already born, but was not as yet a political factor. Trotsky gave a voluminous report on the situation in Italy on the eve of the Second Congress of the Comintern, in 1920, but did not even mention fascism, although *fasci* had been in existence for some time. It took another ten years or more before Italian fascism, long since established in the government of the country, developed anything in the nature of a distinctive social system.

In 1924 and after, Europe and the United States were the scene of a boisterous boom that drowned all concern for the soundness of the market system. Capitalism was proclaimed restored. Both Bolshevism and fascism were liquidated except in peripheric regions. The Comintern declared the consolidation of capitalism a fact; Mussolini eulogized liberal capitalism; all important countries except Great Britain were on the upgrade. The United States enjoyed a legendary prosperity, and the Continent was doing almost as well. Hitler's *putsch* had been quashed; France had evacuated the Ruhr; the *Reichsmark* was restored as by miracle; the Dawes Plan had taken politics out of reparations; Locarno was in the offing; and Germany was starting out on seven fat years. Before the end of 1926 the gold standard ruled again from Moscow to Lisbon.

It was in the third period—after 1929—that the true significance of fascism became apparent. The deadlock of the market system was evident. Until then fascism had been hardly more than a trait in Italy's authoritarian government, which otherwise differed but little from those of a more traditional type. It now emerged as an alternative solution of the problem of an industrial society. Germany took the lead in a revolution of European scope and the fascist alignment provided her struggle for power with a dynamics which soon embraced five continents. History was in the gear of social change.

An adventitious but by no means accidental event started the destruction of the international system. A Wall Street slump grew to huge dimensions and was followed by Great Britain's decision to go off gold and, another two years later, by a similar move on the part of the United States. Concurrently, the Disarmament Conference ceased to meet, and, in 1934, Germany left the League of Nations.

These symbolic events ushered in an epoch of spectacular change in the organization of the world. Three powers, Japan, Germany, and Italy, rebelled against the *status quo* and sabotaged the crumbling institutions of peace. At the same time the factual organization of world economy refused to function. The gold standard was at least temporarily put out of action by its Anglo-Saxon creators; under the guise of default, foreign debts were repudiated; capital markets and world trade dwindled away. The political *and* the economic system of the planet disintegrated conjointly.

Within the nations themselves the change was no less thorough. Two-party systems were superseded by one-party governments, sometimes by national governments. However, external similarities between dictatorship countries and countries which retained a democratic public opinion merely served to emphasize the superlative importance of free institutions of discussion and decision. Russia turned to socialism under dictatorial forms. Liberal capitalism disappeared in the countries preparing for war like Germany, Japan, and Italy, and, to a lesser extent, also in the United States and Great Britain. But the emerging regimes of fascism, socialism, and the New Deal were similar only in discarding *laissez-faire* principles.

While history was thus started on its course by an event external to all, the single nations reacted to the challenge according to whither they were bound. Some were averse to change; some went a long way to meet it when it came; some were indifferent. Also, they sought for solutions in various directions. Yet from the point of view of market economy these often radically different solutions merely represented given alternatives.

Among those determined to make use of a general dislocation to further their own interests was a group of dissatisfied Powers for whom the passing of the balance-of-power system, even in its weakened form of the League, appeared to offer a rare chance. Germany was now eager to hasten the downfall of traditional world economy, which still provided international order with a foothold, and she anticipated the collapse of that economy, so as to have the start of her opponents. She deliberately cut loose from the international system of capital, commodity, and currency so as to lessen the hold of the outer world upon her when she would deem it convenient to repudiate her political obligations. She fostered economic autarchy to ensure the freedom required for her far-reaching plans. She squandered her gold reserves, destroyed her foreign credit by gratuitous repudiation of her obligations and even, for a time, wiped out her favorable foreign trade balance. She easily managed to camouflage her true intentions since neither Wall Street nor the City of London nor Geneva suspected that the Nazis were actually banking on the final dissolution of nineteenth century economy. Sir John Simon and Montagu Norman firmly believed that eventually Schacht would restore orthodox economics in Germany, which was acting under duress and which would return to the fold, if she were only assisted financially. Illusions such as these survived in Downing Street up to the time of Munich and after. While Germany was thus greatly assisted in her conspirative plans by her ability to adjust to the dissolution of the traditional system, Great Britain found herself severely handicapped by her adherence to that system.

Although England had temporarily gone off gold, her economy and finance continued to be based on the principles of stable exchanges and sound currency. Hence, the limitations under which she found herself in respect to rearmament. Just as German autarchy was an outcome of military and political considerations that sprang from her intent to forestall a general transformation, Britain's strategy and foreign policy were constricted by her conservative financial outlook. The strategy of limited warfare reflected the view of an island emporium, which regards itself safe as long as its Navy is strong enough to secure the supplies that its sound money can buy in the Seven Seas. Hitler was already in power when, in 1933, Duff Cooper, a die-hard, defended the cuts in the army budget of 1932 as made "in the face of the national bankruptcy, which was then thought to be an even greater danger than having an inefficient fighting service." More than three years later Lord Halifax maintained that peace could be had by economic adjustments and that there should be no interference with trade since this would make such adjustments more difficult. In the very year of Munich, Halifax and Chamberlain still formulated Britain's policy in terms of "silver bullets" and the traditional American loans for Germany. Indeed, even after Hitler had crossed the Rubicon and had occupied Prague, Lord Simon approved in the House of Commons of Montagu Norman's part in the handing over of the Czech gold reserves to Hitler. It was Simon's conviction that the integrity of the gold standard, to the restoration of which his statesmanship was dedicated, outweighed all other considerations. Contemporaries believed that Simon's action was the result of a determined policy of appeasement. Actually, it was an homage to the spirit of the gold standard, which continued to govern the outlook of the leading men of the City of London on strategic as well as on political matters. In the very week of the outbreak of the war the Foreign Office, in answer to a verbal communication of Hitler to Chamberlain, formulated Britain's policy in terms of the traditional American loans for Germany.[4] England's military unpreparedness was mainly the result of her adherence to gold standard economics.

Germany at first reaped the advantages of those who kill that which is doomed to die. Her start lasted as long as the liquidation of the outworn system of the nineteenth century permitted her to keep in the lead. The destruction of liberal capitalism, of the gold standard, and of absolute sovereignties was the incidental result of her marauding raids. In adjusting to an isolation sought by herself and, later, in the course of her slave dealer's expeditions, she developed tentative solutions to some problems of the transformation.

Her greatest political asset, however, lay in her ability to compel the countries of the world into an alignment against Bolshevism. She made herself the foremost beneficiary of the transformation by taking the lead in that solution of the problem of market economy which for a long time appeared to enlist the unconditional allegiance of the propertied classes, and indeed not always of these alone. Under the liberal and Marxist assumption of the primacy of economic class interests, Hitler was bound to win. But the social unit of the nation proved, in the long run, even more relevant than the economic unit of class.

Russia's rise also was linked with her role in the transformation. From 1917 to 1929 the fear of Bolshevism was no more than the fear of disorder which might fatally hamper the restoration of a market economy which could not function except in an atmosphere of unqualified confidence. In the following decade socialism became a reality in Russia. The collectivization of the farms meant the supersession of market economy by co-operative methods in regard to the decisive

[4] *British Blue Book*, No. 74, Cmd. 6106, 1939.

factor of land. Russia, which had been merely a seat of revolutionary agitation directed towards the capitalistic world, now emerged as the representative of a new system which could replace market economy.

It is not usually realized that the Bolsheviks, though ardent socialists themselves, stubbornly refused to "establish socialism in Russia." Their Marxist convictions alone would have precluded such an attempt in a backward agrarian country. But apart from the entirely exceptional episode of so-called "War Communism" in 1920, the leaders adhered to the position that the world revolution must start in industrialized Western Europe. Socialism in one country would have appeared to them a contradiction in terms, and when it became reality, the Old Bolsheviks rejected it almost to a man. Yet it was precisely this departure which proved an amazing success.

Looking back upon a quarter century of Russian history it appears that what we call the Russian Revolution really consisted of two separate revolutions, the first of which embodied traditional Western European ideals, while the second formed part of the utterly new development of the thirties. The Revolution of 1917–24 was indeed the *last* of the political upheavals in Europe that followed the pattern of the English Commonwealth and of the French Revolution; the revolution that started with the collectivization of the farms, about 1930, was the *first* of the great social changes that transformed our world in the thirties. For the first Russian Revolution achieved the destruction of absolutism, feudal land tenure, and racial oppression— a true heir to the ideals of 1789; the second Revolution established a socialist economy. When all is said, the first was merely a Russian event—it fulfilled a long process of Western development on Russian soil—while the second formed part of a simultaneous universal transformation.

Seemingly in the twenties Russia stood apart from Europe and was working out her own salvation. A closer analysis might disprove this appearance. For among the factors which forced upon her a decision in the years between the two revolutions was the failure of the international system. By 1924 "War Communism" was a forgotten incident and Russia had re-established a free domestic grain market, while maintaining state control of foreign trade and key industries. She was now bent on increasing her foreign trade, which depended mainly on exports of grain, timber, furs, and some other organic raw materials, the prices of which were slumping heavily in the course of the agrarian depression which preceded the general break in trade. Russia's inability to develop an export trade on favorable terms restricted her imports of machinery and hence the establishment of a national industry; this, again, affected the terms of barter between town and countryside—the so-called "scissors"—unfavorably, thus increasing the antagonism of the peasantry to the rule of the urban workers. In this way the disintegration of world economy increased the strain on the makeshift solutions of the agrarian question in Russia, and hastened the coming of the kolkhoz. The failure of the traditional political system of Europe to provide safety and security worked in the same direction since it induced the need for armaments, thus enhancing the burdens of high-pressure industrialization. The absence of the nineteenth century balance-of-power system, as well as the inability of the world market to absorb Russia's agricultural produce, forced her reluctantly into the paths of self-sufficiency. Socialism in one country was brought about by the incapacity of market economy to provide a link between all countries; what appeared as Russian autarchy was merely the passing of capitalist internationalism.

The failure of the international system let loose the energies of history—the rails were set by the tendencies inherent in a market society.

21

FREEDOM IN A COMPLEX SOCIETY

NINETEENTH CENTURY civilization was not destroyed by the external or internal attack of barbarians; its vitality was not sapped by the devastations of World War I nor by the revolt of a socialist proletariat or a fascist lower middle class. Its failure was not the outcome of some alleged laws of economics such as that of the falling rate of profit or of underconsumption or overproduction. It disintegrated as the result of an entirely different set of causes: the measures which society adopted in order not to be, in its turn, annihilated by the action of the self-regulating market. Apart from exceptional circumstances such as existed in North America in the age of the open frontier, the conflict between the market and the elementary requirements of an organized social life provided the century with its dynamics and produced the typical strains and stresses which ultimately destroyed that society. External wars merely hastened its destruction.

After a century of blind "improvement" man is restoring his "habitation." If industrialism is not to extinguish the race, it must be subordinated to the requirements of man's nature. The true criticism of market society is not that it was based on economics—in a sense, every and any society must be based on it—but that its economy was based on self-interest. Such an organization of economic life is entirely unnatural, in the strictly empirical sense of *exceptional*. Nineteenth century thinkers assumed that in his economic activity man strove for profit, that his materialistic propensities would induce him to choose the lesser instead of the greater effort and to expect payment for his labor; in short, that in his economic activity he would tend to abide by what they described as economic rationality, and that all contrary behavior was the result of outside interference. It followed that markets were natural institutions, that they would spontaneously arise if only men were let alone. Thus, nothing could be more normal than an economic system consisting of markets and under the sole control of market prices, and a human society based on such markets appeared, therefore, as the goal of all progress. Whatever the desirability or undesirability of such a society on moral grounds, its practicability—this was axiomatic—was grounded in the immutable characteristics of the race.

Actually, as we now know, the behavior of man both in his primitive state and right through the course of history has been almost the opposite from that implied in this view. Frank H. Knight's "no specifically human motive is economic" applies not only to social life in general, but even to economic life itself. The tendency to barter, on which Adam Smith so confidently relied for his picture of primitive man, is not a common tendency of the human being in his economic activities, but a most infrequent one. Not only does the evidence of modern anthropology give the lie to these rationalistic constructs, but the history of trade and markets also has been completely different from that assumed in the harmonistic teachings of nineteenth century sociologists. Economic history reveals that the emergence of national markets was in no way the result of the gradual and spontaneous emancipation of the economic sphere from governmental control. On the contrary, the market has been the outcome of a conscious and often violent intervention on the part of government which imposed the market organization on society for noneconomic ends. And the self-regulating market of the nineteenth century turns out on closer inspection to be radically different from even its immediate predecessor in that it relied for its regulation on economic self-interest. *The congenital weakness of nineteenth century society was not that it was industrial but that it was a market society.* Industrial civilization will continue to exist when the utopian experiment of a self-regulating market will be no more than a memory.

Yet the shifting of industrial civilization onto a new nonmarketing basis seems to many a task too desperate to contemplate. They fear an institutional vacuum or, even worse, the loss of freedom. Need these perils prevail?

Much of the massive suffering inseparable from a period of transition is already behind us. In the social and economic dislocation of our age, in the tragic vicissitudes of the depression, fluctuations of currency, mass unemployment, shiftings of social status, spectacular destruction of historical states, we have experienced the worst. Unwittingly we have been paying the price of the change. Far as mankind still is from having adapted itself to the use of machines, and great as the pending changes are, the restoration of the past is as impossible as the transferring of our troubles to another planet. Instead of eliminating the demonic forces of aggression and conquest, such a futile attempt would actually ensure the survival of those forces, even after their utter military defeat. The cause of evil would become endowed with the advantage, decisive in politics, of representing the possible, in opposition to that which is impossible of achievement however good it may be of intention.

Nor does the collapse of the traditional system leave us in the void. Not for the first time in history may makeshifts contain the germs of great and permanent institutions.

Within the nations we are witnessing a development under which the economic system ceases to lay down the law to society and the primacy of society over that system is secured. This may happen in a great variety of ways, democratic and aristocratic, constitutionalist and authoritarian, perhaps even in a fashion yet utterly unforeseen. The future in some countries may be already the present in others, while some may still embody the past of the rest. But the outcome is common with them all: the market system will no longer be self-regulating, even in principle, since it will not comprise labor, land, and money.

To take labor out of the market means a transformation as radical as was the establishment of a competitive labor market. The wage contract ceases to be a private contract except on subordinate and accessory points. Not only conditions in the factory, hours of work, and modalities of contract, but the basic wage itself, are determined outside the market; what role accrues thereby to trade unions, state, and other public bodies depends not only on the character of these institutions but also on the actual organization of the management of production. Though in the nature of things wage differentials must (and should) continue to play an essential part in the economic system, other motives than those directly involved in money incomes may outweigh by far the financial aspect of labor.

To remove land from the market is synonymous with the incorporation of land with definite institutions such as the homestead, the co-operative, the factory, the township, the school, the church, parks, wild life preserves, and so on. However widespread individual ownership of farms will continue to be, contracts in respect to land tenure need deal with accessories only, since the essentials are removed from the jurisdiction of the market. The same applies to staple foods and organic raw materials, since the fixing of prices in respect to them is not left to the market. That for an infinite variety of products com-

petitive markets continue to function need not interfere with the constitution of society any more than the fixing of prices outside the market
for labor, land, and money interferes with the costing-function of
prices in respect to the various products. The nature of property, of
course, undergoes a deep change in consequence of such measures since
there is no longer any need to allow incomes from the title of property
to grow without bounds, merely in order to ensure employment, production, and the use of resources in society.

The removal of the control of money from the market is being
accomplished in all countries in our day. Unconsciously, the creation
of deposits effected this to a large extent, but the crisis of the gold
standard in the twenties proved that the link between commodity
money and token money had by no means been severed. Since the introduction of "functional finance" in all important states, the directing
of investments and the regulation of the rate of saving have become
government tasks.

To remove the elements of production—land, labor, and money—
from the market is thus a uniform act only from the viewpoint of the
market, which was dealing with them as if they were commodities.
From the viewpoint of human reality that which is restored by the
disestablishment of the commodity fiction lies in all directions of the
social compass. In effect, the disintegration of a uniform market
economy is already giving rise to a variety of new societies. Also, the
end of market society means in no way the absence of markets. These
continue, in various fashions, to ensure the freedom of the consumer,
to indicate the shifting of demand, to influence producers' income, and
to serve as an instrument of accountancy, while ceasing altogether to
be an organ of economic self-regulation.

In its international methods, as in these internal methods, nineteenth century society was constricted by economics. The realm of
fixed foreign exchanges was coincident with civilization. As long as the
gold standard and—what became almost its corollary—constitutional
regimes were in operation, the balance of power was a vehicle of
peace. The system worked through the instrumentality of those Great
Powers, first and foremost Great Britain, who were the center of world
finance, and pressed for the establishment of representative government
in less advanced countries. This was required as a check on the
finances and currencies of debtor countries with the consequent need
for controlled budgets, such as only responsible bodies can provide.
Though, as a rule, such considerations were not consciously present in
the minds of statesmen, this was the case only because the requirements

of the gold standard ranked as axiomatic. The uniform world pattern of monetary and representative institutions was the result of the rigid economy of the period.

Two principles of nineteenth century international life derived their relevance from this situation: anarchistic sovereignty and "justified" intervention in the affairs of other countries. Though apparently contradictory, the two were interrelated. Sovereignty, of course, was a purely political term, for under unregulated foreign trade and the gold standard governments possessed no powers in respect to international economics. They neither could nor would bind their countries in respect to monetary matters—this was the legal position. Actually, only countries which possessed a monetary system controlled by central banks were reckoned sovereign states. With the powerful Western countries this unlimited and unrestricted national monetary sovereignty was combined with its complete opposite, an unrelenting pressure to spread the fabric of market economy and market society elsewhere. Consequently, by the end of the nineteenth century the peoples of the world were institutionally standardized to a degree unknown before.

This system was hampering both on account of its elaborateness *and* its universality. Anarchistic sovereignty was a hindrance to all effective forms of international co-operation, as the history of the League of Nations strikingly proved; and enforced uniformity of domestic systems hovered as a permanent threat over the freedom of national development, especially in backward countries and sometimes even in advanced, but financially weak countries. Economic co-operation was limited to private institutions as rambling and ineffective as free trade, while actual collaboration between peoples, that is, between governments, could never even be envisaged.

The situation may well make two apparently incompatible demands on foreign policy: it will require closer co-operation between friendly countries than could even be contemplated under nineteenth century sovereignty, while at the same time the existence of regulated markets will make national governments more jealous of outside interference than ever before. However, with the disappearance of the automatic mechanism of the gold standard, governments will find it possible to drop the most obstructive feature of absolute sovereignty, the refusal to collaborate in international economics. At the same time it will become possible to tolerate willingly that other nations shape their domestic institutions according to their inclinations, thus transcending the pernicious nineteenth century dogma of the necessary uniformity of domestic regimes within the orbit of world economy. Out of the ruins of the

Old World, cornerstones of the New can be seen to emerge: economic collaboration of governments *and* the liberty to organize national life at will. Under the constrictive system of free trade neither of these possibilities could have been conceived of, thus excluding a variety of methods of co-operation between nations. While under market economy and the gold standard the idea of federation was justly deemed a nightmare of centralization and uniformity, the end of market economy may well mean effective co-operation with domestic freedom.

The problem of freedom arises on two different levels: the institutional and the moral or religious. On the institutional level it is a matter of balancing increased against diminished freedoms; no radically new questions are encountered. On the more fundamental level the very possibility of freedom is in doubt. It appears that the means of maintaining freedom are themselves adulterating and destroying it. The key to the problem of freedom in our age must be sought on this latter plane. Institutions are embodiments of human meaning and purpose. We cannot achieve the freedom we seek, unless we comprehend the true significance of freedom in a complex society.

On the institutional level, regulation both extends and restricts freedom; only the balance of the freedoms lost and won is significant. This is true of juridical and actual freedoms alike. The comfortable classes enjoy the freedom provided by leisure in security; they are naturally less anxious to extend freedom in society than those who for lack of income must rest content with a minimum of it. This becomes apparent as soon as compulsion is suggested in order to more justly spread out income, leisure and security. Though restriction applies to all, the privileged tend to resent it, as if it were directed solely against themselves. They talk of slavery, while in effect only an extension to the others of the vested freedom they themselves enjoy is intended. Initially, there may have to be reduction in their own leisure and security, and, consequently, their freedom so that the level of freedom throughout the land shall be raised. But such a shifting, reshaping and enlarging of freedoms should offer no ground whatsoever for the assertion that the new condition must necessarily be less free than was the old.

Yet there are freedoms the maintenance of which is of paramount importance. They were, like peace, a by-product of nineteenth-century economy, and we have come to cherish them for their own sake. The institutional separation of politics and economics, which proved a deadly danger to the substance of society, almost automatically produced freedom at the cost of justice and security. Civic liberties, private enterprise and wage-system fused into a pattern of life which favored moral freedom and independence of mind. Here again, juridical and actual freedoms merged into a common fund, the elements of which cannot be neatly separated. Some were the corollary of evils like unemployment and speculator's profits; some belonged to the most precious traditions of Renaissance and Reformation. We must try to maintain by all means in our power these high values inherited from the market-economy which collapsed. This, assuredly, is a great task. Neither freedom nor peace could be institutionalized under that economy, since its purpose was to create profits and welfare, not peace and freedom. We will have consciously to strive for them in the future if we are to possess them at all; they must become chosen aims of the societies towards which we are moving. This may well be the true purport of the present world effort to make peace and freedom secure. How far the will to peace can assert itself once the interest in peace which sprang from nineteenth-century economy has ceased to operate will depend upon our success in establishing an international order. As to personal liberty, it will exist to the degree in which we will deliberately create new safeguards for its maintenance and, indeed, extension. In an established society, the right to nonconformity must be institutionally protected. The individual must be free to follow his conscience without fear of the powers that happen to be entrusted with administrative tasks in some of the fields of social life. Science and the arts should always be under the guardianship of the republic of letters. Compulsion should never be absolute; the "objector" should be offered a niche to which he can retire, the choice of a "second-best" that leaves him a life to live. Thus will be secured the right to nonconformity as the hallmark of a free society.

Every move towards integration in society should thus be accompanied by an increase of freedom; moves towards planning should comprise the strengthening of the rights of the individual in society. His indefeasible rights must be enforceable under the law even against the supreme powers, whether they be personal or anonymous. The true answer to the threat of bureaucracy as a source of abuse of power is to create spheres of arbitrary freedom protected by unbreakable rules. For, however generously devolution of power is practised, there will be strengthening of power at the center, and, therefore, danger to individual freedom. This is true even in respect to the organs of democratic communities themselves, as well as the professional and trade unions whose function it is to protect the rights of each individual member. Their very size might make him feel helpless, even though he had no reason to suspect ill-will on their part. The more so, if his views or actions were such as to offend the susceptibilities of those who wield power. No mere declaration of rights can suffice: institutions are required to make the rights effective. *Habeas corpus* need not be the last constitutional device by which personal freedom was anchored in law. Rights of the citizen hitherto unacknowledged must be added to the Bill of Rights. They must be made to prevail against all authorities, whether State, municipal or professional. The list should be headed by the right of the individual to a job under approved conditions, irrespective of his or her political or religious views, or of color and race. This implies guarantees against victimization however subtle it be. Industrial tribunals have been known to protect the individual member of the public even from such agglomerations of arbitrary power as were represented by the early railway companies. Another instance of possible abuse of power squarely met by tribunals was the Essential Works Order in England, or the "freezing of labor" in the United States, during the emergency, with their almost unlimited opportunities for discrimination. Wherever public opinion was solid in upholding civic liberties, tribunals or courts have always been found capable of vindicating personal freedom. It should be upheld at all cost—even that of efficiency in production, economy in consumption or rationality in administration. An industrial society can afford to be free.

The passing of market-economy can become the beginning of an era of unprecedented freedom. Juridical and actual freedom can be made wider and more general than ever before; regulation and control can achieve freedom not only for the few, but for all. Freedom not as an appurtenance of privilege, tainted at the source, but as a prescriptive right extending far beyond the narrow confines of the political sphere into the intimate organization of society itself. Thus will old freedoms and civic rights be added to the fund of new freedom generated by the leisure and security that industrial society offers to all. Such a society can afford to be both just and free.

Yet we find the path blocked by a moral obstacle. Planning and control are being attacked as a denial of freedom. Free enterprise and private ownership are declared to be essentials of freedom. No society built on other foundations is said to deserve to be called free. The freedom that regulation creates is denounced as unfreedom; the justice, liberty and welfare it offers are decried as a camouflage of slavery. In vain did socialists promise a realm of freedom, for means determine ends: the U.S.S.R., which used planning, regulation and control as its instruments, has not yet put the liberties promised in her Constitution into practice, and, probably, the critics add, never will. . . . But to turn against regulation means to turn against reform. With the liberal the idea of freedom thus degenerates into a mere advocacy of free enterprise—which is today reduced to a fiction by the hard reality of giant trusts and princely monopolies. This means the fullness of freedom for those whose income, leisure and security need no enhancing, and a mere pittance of liberty for the people, who may in vain attempt to make use of their democratic rights to gain shelter from the power of the owners of property. Nor is that all. Nowhere did the liberals in fact succeed in re-establishing free enterprise, which was doomed to fail for intrinsic reasons. It was as a result of their efforts that big business was installed in several European countries and, incidentally, also various brands of fascism, as in Austria. Planning, regulation and control, which they wanted to see banned as dangers to freedom, were then employed by the confessed enemies of freedom to abolish it altogether. Yet the victory of fascism was made practically unavoidable by the liberals' obstruction of any reform involving planning, regulation, or control.

Freedom's utter frustration in fascism is, indeed, the inevitable result of the liberal philosophy, which claims that power and compulsion are evil, that freedom demands their absence from a human community. No such thing is possible; in a complex society this becomes apparent. This leaves no alternative but either to remain faithful to an illusionary idea of freedom and deny the reality of society, or to accept that reality and reject the idea of freedom. The first is the liberal's conclusion; the latter the fascist's. No other seems possible.

Inescapably we reach the conclusion that the very possibility of freedom is in question. If regulation is the only means of spreading and strengthening freedom in a complex society, and yet to make use of this means is contrary to freedom per se, then such a society cannot be free.

Clearly, at the root of the dilemma there is the meaning of freedom itself. Liberal economy gave a false direction to our ideals. It seemed to approximate the fulfilment of intrinsically utopian expectations. No society is possible in which power and compulsion are absent, nor a world in which force has no function. It was an illusion to assume a society shaped by man's will and wish alone. Yet this was the result of a market-view of society which equated economics with contractual relationships, and contractual relations with freedom. The radical illusion was fostered that there is nothing in human society that is not derived from the volition of individuals and that could not, therefore, be removed again by their volition. Vision was limited by the market which "fragmentated" life into the producers' sector that ended when his product reached the market, and the sector of the consumer for whom all goods sprang from the market. The one derived his income "freely" from the market, the other spent it "freely" there. Society as a whole remained invisible. The power of the State was of no account, since the less its power, the smoother the market mechanism would function. Neither voters, nor owners, neither producers, nor consumers could be held responsible for such brutal restrictions of freedom as were involved in the occurrence of unemployment and destitution. Any decent individual could imagine himself free from all responsibility for acts of compulsion on the part of a State which he, personally, rejected; or for economic suffering in society from which he, personally, had not benefited. He was "paying his way," was "in nobody's debt," and was unentangled in the evil of power and economic value. His lack of responsibility for them seemed so evident that he denied their reality in the name of his freedom.

But power and economic value are a paradigm of social reality. They do not spring from human volition; nonco-operation is impossible in regard to them. The function of power is to ensure that measure of conformity which is needed for the survival of the group; its ultimate source is opinion—and who could help holding opinions of some sort or other? Economic value ensures the usefulness of the goods produced; it must exist prior to the decision to produce them; it is a seal set on the division of labor. Its source is human wants and scarcity —and how could we be expected not to desire one thing more than another? Any opinion or desire will make us participants in the creation of power and in the constituting of economic value. No freedom to do otherwise is conceivable.

We have reached the final stage of our argument.

The discarding of the market utopia brings us face to face with the reality of society. It is the dividing line between liberalism on the one hand, fascism and socialism on the other. The difference between these two is not primarily economic. It is moral and religious. Even where they profess identical economics, they are not only different but are, indeed, embodiments of opposite principles. And the ultimate on which they separate is again freedom. By fascists and socialists alike the reality of society is accepted with the finality with which the knowledge of death has molded human consciousness. Power and compulsion are a part of that reality; an ideal that would ban them from society must be invalid. The issue on which they divide is whether in the light of this knowledge the idea of freedom can be upheld or not; is freedom an empty word, a temptation, designed to ruin man and his works, or can man reassert his freedom in the face of that knowledge and strive for its fulfillment in society without lapsing into moral illusionism?

This anxious question sums up the condition of man. The spirit and content of this study should indicate an answer.

We invoked what we believed to be the three constitutive facts in the consciousness of Western man: knowledge of death, knowledge of freedom, knowledge of society. The first, according to Jewish legend, was revealed in the Old Testament story. The second was revealed through the discovery of the uniqueness of the person in the teachings of Jesus as recorded in the New Testament. The third revelation came to us through living in an industrial society. No one great name attaches to it; perhaps Robert Owen came nearest to becoming its vehicle. It is the constitutive element in modern man's consciousness.

The fascist answer to the recognition of the reality of society is the rejection of the postulate of freedom. The Christian discovery of the uniqueness of the individual and of the oneness of mankind is negated by fascism. Here lies the root of its degenerative bent.

Robert Owen was the first to recognize that the Gospels ignored the reality of society. He called this the "individualization" of man on the part of Christianity and appeared to believe that only in a co-operative commonwealth could "all that is truly valuable in Christianity" cease to be separated from man. Owen recognized that the freedom we gained through the teachings of Jesus was inapplicable to a complex society. His socialism was the upholding of man's claim to freedom *in such a society*. The post-Christian era of Western civilization had begun, in which the Gospels did not any more suffice, and yet remained the basis of our civilization.

The discovery of society is thus either the end or the rebirth of freedom. While the fascist resigns himself to relinquishing freedom and glorifies power which is the reality of society, the socialist resigns himself to that reality and upholds the claim to freedom, in spite of it. Man becomes mature and able to exist as a human being in a complex society. To quote once more Robert Owen's inspired words: "Should any causes of evil be irremovable by the new powers which men are about to acquire, they will know that they are necessary and unavoidable evils; and childish, unavailing complaints will cease to be made."

Resignation was ever the fount of man's strength and new hope. Man accepted the reality of death and built the meaning of his bodily life upon it. He resigned himself to the truth that he had a soul to lose and that there was worse than death, and founded his freedom upon it. He resigns himself, in our time, to the reality of society which means the end of that freedom. But, again, life springs from ultimate resignation. Uncomplaining acceptance of the reality of society gives man indomitable courage and strength to remove all removable injustice and unfreedom. As long as he is true to his task of creating more abundant freedom for all, he need not fear that either power or planning will turn against him and destroy the freedom he is building by their instrumentality. This is the meaning of freedom in a complex society; it gives us all the certainty that we need.

1

BALANCE OF POWER AS POLICY, HISTORICAL LAW, PRINCIPLE, AND SYSTEM

1. *Balance-of-power policy.* The balance-of-power *policy* is an English national institution. It is purely pragmatic and factual, and should not be confused either with the balance-of-power *principle* or with the balance-of-power *system.* That policy was the outcome of her island position off a continental littoral occupied by organized political communities. "Her rising school of diplomacy, from Wolsey to Cecil, pursued the *Balance of Power* as England's only chance of security in face of the great Continental states being formed," says Trevelyan. This policy was definitely established under the Tudors, was practiced by Sir William Temple, as well as by Canning, Palmerston, or Sir Edward Grey. It antedated the emergence of a balance-of-power system on the Continent by almost two centuries, and was entirely independent in its development from the Continental sources of the doctrine of the balance of power as a principle put forward by Fénélon or Vattel. However, England's national policy was greatly assisted by the growth of such a system, as it eventually made it easier for her to organize alliances against any power leading on the Continent. Consequently, British statesmen tended to foster the idea that England's balance-of-power policy was actually an expression of the balance-of-power principle, and that England, by following such a policy, was only playing her part in a system based upon that principle. Still, the difference between her own policy of self-defense and any principle which would help its advancement was not purposely obscured by her statesmen. Sir Edward Grey wrote in his *Twenty-five Years* as follows: "Great Britain has not, in theory, been adverse to the predominance of a strong group in Europe, when it seemed to make for stability and peace. To support such a combination has generally been the first choice. It is only when the dominant power becomes aggressive and she feels her own interests to be threatened that she, by an instinct of self-defence if not by deliberate policy, gravitates to anything that can be fairly described as a Balance of Power."

It was thus in her own legitimate interest that England supported the growth of a balance-of-power system on the Continent, and upheld its principles. To do so was part of her policy. The confusion induced by such a dovetailing of two essentially different references of the balance of power is shown by these quotations: Fox, in 1787, indignantly asked the government, "whether England were no longer in the situation to hold the balance of power in Europe and to be looked up to as the protector of her liberties?" He claimed it as England's due to be accepted as the guarantor of the balance-of-power system in Europe. And Burke, four years later, described that system as the "public law of Europe" supposedly in force for two centuries. Such rhetorical identifications of England's national policy with the European system of the balance of power would naturally make it more difficult for Americans to distinguish between two conceptions which were equally obnoxious to them.

2. *Balance of power as a historical law.* Another meaning of the balance of power is based directly on the nature of power units. It has been first stated in modern thought by Hume. His achievement was lost again during the almost total eclipse of political thought which followed the Industrial Revolution. Hume recognized the political nature of the phenomenon and underlined its independence of psychological and moral facts. It went into effect irrespective of the motives of the actors, as long as they behaved as the embodiments of power. Experience showed, wrote Hume, that whether "jealous emulation or cautious politic" was their motive, "the effects were alike." F. Schuman says: "If one postulates a States System composed of three units, A, B, and C, it is obvious that an increase in the power of any one of them involves a decrease in the power of the other two." He infers that the balance of power "in its elementary form is designed to maintain the independence of each unit of the State System." He might well have generalized the postulate so as to make it applicable to all kinds of power units, whether in organized political systems or not. That is, in effect, the way the balance of power appears in the sociology of history. Toynbee in his *Study of History* mentions the fact that power units are apt to expand on the periphery of power groups rather than at the center where pressure is greatest. The United States, Russia, and Japan as well as the British Dominions expanded prodigiously at a time when even minor territorial changes were practically impossible of attainment in Western and Central Europe. A historical law of a similar type

is adduced by Pirenne. He notes that in comparatively unorganized communities a core of resistance to external pressure is usually formed in the regions farthest removed from the powerful neighbor. Instances are the formation of the Frankish kingdom by Pipin of Heristal in the distant North, or the emergence of Eastern Prussia as the organizing center of the Germanies. Another law of this kind might be seen in the Belgian De Greef's law of the buffer state which appears to have influenced Frederick Turner's school and led to the concept of the American West as "a wandering Belgium." These concepts of the balance and imbalance of power are independent of moral, legal, or psychological notions. Their only reference is to power. This reveals their political nature.

3. *Balance of power as a principle and system.* Once a human interest is recognized as legitimate, a principle of conduct is derived from it. Since 1648, the interest of the European states in the *status quo* as set up by the Treaties of Münster and Westphalia was acknowledged, and the solidarity of the signatories in this respect was established. The Treaty of 1648 was signed by practically all European Powers; they declared themselves its guarantors. The Netherlands and Switzerland date their international standing as sovereign states from this treaty. Henceforward, states were entitled to assume that any major change in the *status quo* would be of interest to all the rest. This is the rudimentary form of balance of power as a principle of the family of nations. No state acting upon this principle would, on that account, be thought of as behaving in a hostile fashion towards a power rightly or wrongly suspected by it of the intention of changing the *status quo.* Such a condition of affairs would, of course, enormously facilitate the formation of coalitions opposed to such change. However, only after seventy-five years was the principle expressly recognized in the Treaty of Utrecht when "ad conservandum in Europa equilibrium" Spanish domains were divided between Bourbons and Hapsburgs. By this formal recognition of the principle Europe was gradually organized into a *system* based on this principle. As the absorption (or domination) of small powers by bigger ones would upset the balance of power, the independence of the small powers was indirectly safeguarded by the system. Shadowy as was the organization of Europe after 1648, and even after 1713, the maintenance of all states, great and small, over a period of some two hundred years must be credited to the balance-of-power system. Innumerable wars

were fought in its name, and although they must without exception be regarded as inspired by consideration of power, the result was in many cases the same as if the countries had acted on the principle of collective guarantee against acts of unprovoked aggression. No other explanation will account for the continued survival of powerless political entities like Denmark, Holland, Belgium, and Switzerland over long stretches of time in spite of the overwhelming forces threatening their frontiers. Logically, the distinction between a principle and an organization based upon it, *i.e.*, a system, seems definite. Yet we should not underrate the effectiveness of principles even in their suborganized condition, that is, when they have not yet reached the institutional stage, but merely supply a directive to conventional habit or custom. Even without an established center, regular meetings, common functionaries, or compulsory code of behavior, Europe had been formed into a system simply by the continuous close contact between the various chancelleries and members of the diplomatic bodies. The strict tradition regulating the inquiries, *démarches*, aide-mémoirs—jointly and separately delivered, in identical or in nonidentical terms—were so many means of expressing power situations without bringing them to a head, while opening up new avenues of compromise or, eventually, of joint action, in case negotiations failed. Indeed, the right to joint intervention in the affairs of small states, if legitimate interests of the Powers are threatened, amounted to the existence of a European directorium in a suborganized form.

Perhaps the strongest pillar of this informal system was the immense amount of international private business very often transacted in terms of some trade treaty or other international instrument made effective by custom and tradition. Governments and their influential citizens were in innumerable ways enmeshed in the varied types of financial, economic, and juridical strands of such international transactions. A local war merely meant a short interruption of some of these, while the interests vested in other transactions that remained permanently or at least temporarily unaffected formed an overwhelming mass as against those which might have been resolved to the enemy's disadvantage by the chances of war. This silent pressure of private interest which permeated the whole life of civilized communities and transcended national boundaries was the invisible mainstay of international reciprocity, and provided the balance-of-power principle with effective sanctions, even when it did not take up the organized form of a Concert of Europe or a League of Nations.

BALANCE OF POWER AS HISTORICAL LAW:

Hume, D., "On the Balance of Power," *Works*, Vol. III (1854), p. 364. Schuman, F., *International Politics* (1933), p. 55. Toynbee, A. J., *Study of History*, Vol. III, p. 302. Pirenne, H., *Outline of the History of Europe from the Fall of the Roman Empire to 1600* (Engl. 1939). Barnes-Becker-Becker, on De Greef, Vol. II, p. 871. Hofmann, A., *Das deutsche Land and die deutsche Geschichte* (1920). Also Haushofer's Geopolitical School. At the other extreme, Russell, B., *Power*. Lasswell's *Psychopathology and Politics; World Politics and Personal Insecurity*, and other works. Cf. also Rostovtzeff, *Social and Economic History of the Hellenistic World*, Ch. 4, Part I.

BALANCE OF POWER AS PRINCIPLE AND SYSTEM:

Mayer, J. P., *Political Thought* (1939), p. 464. Vattel, *Le droit des gens* (1758). Hershey A. S., *Essentials of International Public Law and Organization* (1927), pp. 567–69. Oppenheim, L., *International Law*. Heatley, D. P., *Diplomacy and the Study of International Relations* (1919).

HUNDRED YEARS' PEACE:

Leathes, "Modern Europe," *Cambridge Modern History*, Vol. XII, Ch. 1. Toynbee, A. J., *Study of History*, Vol. IV(C), pp. 142–53. Schuman, F., *International Politics*, Bk. I, Ch. 2. Clapham, J. H., *Economic Development of France and Germany, 1815–1914*, p. 3. Robbins, L., *The Great Depression* (1934), p. 1. Lippmann, W., *The Good Society*. Cunningham, W., *Growth of English Industry and Commerce in Modern Times*. Knowles, L. C. A., *Industrial and Commercial Revolutions in Great Britain during the 19th Century* (1927). Carr, E. H., *The 20 Years' Crisis 1919–1939* (1940). Crossman, R. H. S., *Government and the Governed* (1939), p. 225. Hawtrey R. G., *The Economic Problem* (1925), p. 265.

BAGHDAD RAILWAY:

The conflict regarded as settled by the British-German agreement of June 15, 1914: Buell, R. L., *International Relations* (1929). Hawtrey, R. G., *The Economic Problem* (1925). Mowat, R. B., *The Concert of Europe* (1930), p. 313. Stolper, G., *This Age of Fable* (1942). For the contrary view: Fay, S. B., *Origins of the World War*, p. 312. Feis, H., *Europe, The World's Banker, 1870–1914*, (1930), pp. 335 ff.

CONCERT OF EUROPE:

Langer, W. L., *European Alliances and Alignments* (*1871-1890*) (1931). Sontag, R. J., *European Diplomatic History* (*1871-1932*) (1933). Onken, H., "The German Empire," *Cambridge Modern History*, Vol. XII. Mayer, J. P., *Political Thought* (1939), p. 464. Mowat, R. B., *The Concert of Europe* (1930), p. 23. Phillips, W. A., *The Confederation of Europe 1914* (2d ed., 1920). Lasswell, H. D., *Politics*, p. 53. Muir, R., *Nationalism and Internationalism* (1917), p. 176. Buell, R. L., *International Relation* (1929), p. 512.

> To Chap.
> 1

2

HUNDRED YEARS' PEACE

1. *The facts.* The Great Powers of Europe were at war with one another during the century 1815 to 1914 only during three short periods: for six months in 1859, six weeks in 1866 and nine months in 1870–71. The Crimean War, which lasted exactly two years, was of a peripheric and semicolonial character, as historians including Clapham, Trevelyan, Toynbee, and Binkley agree. Incidentally, Russian bonds in the hands of British owners were honored in London during that war. The basic difference between the 19th and previous centuries is that between occasional general wars and complete absence of general wars. Major General Fuller's assertion that there was no year free of war in the nineteenth century appears as immaterial. Quincy Wright's comparison of the number of war years in the various centuries irrespective of the difference between general and local wars seems to by-pass the significant point.

2. *The problem.* The cessation of the almost continuous trade wars between England and France, a fertile source of general wars, stands primarily in need of explanation. It was connected with two facts in the sphere of economic policy: (a) the passing of the old colonial empire, and (b) the era of free trade which passed into that of the international gold standard. While war interest fell off rapidly with the new forms of trade, a positive peace interest emerged in consequence of the

new international currency and credit structure associated with the gold standard. The interest of whole national economies was now involved in the maintenance of stable currencies and the functioning of the world markets upon which incomes and employment depended. The traditional expansionism was replaced by an anti-imperialist trend which was almost general with the Great Powers up to 1880. (Of this we deal in Chapter 18.)

There seems, however, to have been a hiatus of more than half a century (1815–80) between the period of trade wars when foreign policy was naturally assumed to be concerned with the furtherance of gainful business and the later period in which foreign bondholders' and direct investors' interests were regarded as a legitimate concern of foreign secretaries. It was during this half century that the doctrine was established which precluded the influence of private business interests on the conduct of foreign affairs; and it is only by the end of this period that chancelleries again consider such claims as admissible but not without stringent qualifications in deference to the new trend of public opinion. We submit that this change was due to the character of trade which, under nineteenth century conditions, was no longer dependent for its scope and success upon direct power policy; and that the gradual return to business influence on foreign policy was due to the fact that the international currency and credit system had created a new type of business interest transcending national frontiers. But as long as this interest was merely that of foreign bondholders, governments were extremely reluctant to allow them any say; for foreign loans were for a long time deemed purely speculative in the strictest sense of the term; vested income was regularly in home government bonds; no government thought it as worthy of support if its nationals engaged in the most risky job of loaning money to overseas governments of doubtful repute. Canning rejected peremptorily the importunities of investors who expected the British Government to take an interest in their foreign losses, and he categorically refused to make the recognition of Latin-American republics dependent upon their acknowledgment of foreign debts. Palmerston's famous circular of 1848 is the first intimation of a changed attitude, but the change never went very far; for the business interests of the trading community were so widely spread that the Government could hardly afford to let any minor vested interest complicate the running of the affairs of a world empire. The resumption of foreign policy interest in business ventures abroad was mainly the outcome of the passing of free trade and the consequent return to the methods of the eighteenth century. But as trade had now become closely linked with foreign investments of a nonspeculative but entirely normal character, foreign policy reverted to its traditional lines of being serviceable to the trading interests of the community. Not this latter fact, but the cessation of such interest during the hiatus stood in need of explanation.

> *To Chap.*
> 2

3

THE SNAPPING OF THE GOLDEN THREAD

The breakdown of the gold standard was precipitated by the forced stabilization of the currencies. The spearhead of the stabilization movement was Geneva, which transmitted to the financially weaker states the pressures exerted by the City of London and Wall Street.

The *first* group of states to stabilize was that of the defeated countries, the currencies of which had collapsed after World War I. The *second* group consisted of the European victorious states who stabilized their own currencies mainly after the first group. The *third* group consisted of the chief beneficiary of the gold standard interest, the United States.

I. DEFEATED COUNTRIES		II. VICTORIOUS EUROPEAN COUNTRIES		III. UNIVERSAL LENDER
	Stabilized	*Stabilized*	*Went off gold*	*Went off gold*
Russia	1923	Great Britain 1925	1931	U. S. A...... 1933
Austria	1923	France 1926	1936	
Hungary	1924	Belgium 1926	1936	
Germany	1924	Italy 1926	1933	
Bulgaria	1925			
Finland	1925			
Esthonia	1926			
Greece	1926			
Poland	1926			

The imbalance of the *first* group was carried for a time by the second. As soon as this *second* group likewise stabilized its currency, they also were in need of support, which was provided by the third. Ultimately, it was this *third* group, consisting of the United States, which was most hard hit by the cumulative imbalance of European stabilization.

> *To Chap.*
> *2*

4

SWINGS OF THE PENDULUM AFTER WORLD WAR I

The swing of the pendulum after World War I was general and swift, but its amplitude was small. In the great majority of countries of Central and Eastern Europe the period 1918–23 merely brought a conservative restoration following upon a democratic (or socialist) republic, the outcome of defeat; several years later almost universally one-party governments were established. And again, the movement was fairly general.

Country	Revolution	Counter-revolution	One-party govern-ment
Austria ....Oct.	1918 soc. dem. republic	1920 middle-class republic	1934
Bulgaria ...Oct.	1918 radical agrarian reform	1923 fascist counter-revolution	1934
Esthonia	1917 socialist republic	1918 middle-class republic	1926
Finland ....Feb.	1917 socialist republic	1918 middle-class republic	——
Germany ..Nov.	1918 soc. dem. republic	1920 middle-class republic	1933
Hungary ...Oct.	1918 dem. rep.	1919 counter-revolution	——
	Mar. 1919 soviets		
Jugoslavia	1918 democratic federation	1926 authoritarian military state	1929
Latvia	1917 socialist republic	1918 middle-class republic	1934
Lithuania	1917 socialist republic	1918 middle-class republic	1926
Poland	1919 soc. dem. republic	1926 authoritarian state	——
Roumania	1918 agrarian reform	1926 authoritarian regime	——

To Chap.
2

5

FINANCE AND PEACE

On the political role of international finance in the last half century hardly any material is available. Corti's book on the Rothschilds covers only the period previous to the Concert of Europe. Their participation in the Suez share deal, the offer of the Bleichroeders to finance the French War indemnity of 1871 through the issuance of an international loan, the vast transactions of the Oriental Railway period are not included. Historical works like Langer and Sontag give but scant attention to international finance (the latter in his enumeration of peace factors omits the mentioning of finance) ; Leathes' remarks in the *Cambridge Modern History* are almost an exception. Liberal freelance criticism was either directed to show up the lack of patriotism of the financiers or their proclivity to support protectionist and imperialist tendencies to the detriment of free trade, as in the case of writers such as Lysis in France, or J. A. Hobson in England. Marxist works, like Hilferding's or Lenin's studies, stressed the imperialistic forces emanating from national banking, and their organic connection with the heavy industries. Such an argument, besides being restricted mainly to Germany, necessarily failed to deal with international banking interests.

The influence of Wall Street on developments in the twenties appears too recent for objective study. There can be hardly any doubt that, on the whole, its influence was thrown into the scales on the side of international moderation and mediation, from the time of the Peace Treaties to the Dawes Plan, the Young Plan, and the liquidation of reparations at and after Lausanne. Recent literature tends to separate off the problem of private investments, as in Staley's work which expressly excludes loans to governments, whether proffered by other governments or by private investors, a restriction which practically excludes any general appraisal of international finance in his interesting study. Feis' excellent account, on which we have profusely drawn, comes near to covering the subject as a whole, but also suffers from the inevitable dearth of authentic material, since the archives of *haute finance* have not yet been made available. The valuable work done by Earle, Remer, and Viner is subject to the same unavoidable limitation

To Chap.
4

6

SELECTED REFERENCES TO "SOCIETIES AND ECONOMIC SYSTEMS"

The nineteenth century attempted to establish a self-regulating economic system on the motive of individual gain. We maintain that such a venture was in the very nature of things impossible. Here we are merely concerned with the distorted view of life and society implied in such an approach. Nineteenth century thinkers assumed, for instance, that to behave like a trader in the market was "natural," any other mode of behavior being artificial economic behavior—the result of interference with human instincts; that markets would spontaneously arise, if only men were let alone; that whatever the desirability of such a society on moral grounds, its practicability, at least, was founded on the immutable characteristics of the race, and so on. Almost exactly the opposite of these assertions is implied in the testimony of modern research in various fields of social science such as social anthropology, primitive economics, the history of early civilization, and general economic history. Indeed, there is hardly an anthropological or sociological assumption—whether explicit or implicit—contained in the philosophy of economic liberalism that has not been refuted. Some citations follow.

(a) *The motive of gain is not "natural" to man.*

"The characteristic feature of primitive economics is the absence of any desire to make profits from production or exchange" (Thurnwald, *Economics in Primitive Communities*, 1932, p. xiii). "Another notion which must be exploded, once and forever, is that of the Primitive Economic Man of some current economic textbooks" (Malinowski, *Argonauts of the Western Pacific*, 1930, p. 60). "We must reject the *Idealtypen* of Manchester liberalism, which are not only theoretically, but also historically misleading" (Brinkmann, "Das soziale System des Kapitalismus." In *Grundriss der Sozialökonomik*, Abt. IV, p. 11).

(b) *To expect payment for labor is not "natural" to man.*

"Gain, such as is often the stimulus for work in more civilized communities, never acts as an impulse to work under the original native conditions" (Malinowski, *op. cit.*, p. 156). "Nowhere in uninfluenced primitive society do we find labor associated with the idea of payment" (Lowie, "Social Organization," *Encyclopedia of the Social Sciences*, Vol. XIV, p. 14). "*Nowhere* is labor being leased or sold" (Thurnwald, *Die menschliche Gesellschaft*, Bk. III, 1932, p. 169). "The treatment of labor as an obligation, not requiring indemnification . . ." is general (Firth, *Primitive Economics of the New Zealand Maori*, 1929). "Even in the Middle Ages payment for work for strangers is something unheard of." "The stranger has no *personal* tie of duty, and, therefore, he should work for honor and recognition." Minstrels, while being strangers, "accepted payment, and were consequently despised" (Lowie, *op. cit.*).

(c) *To restrict labor to the unavoidable minimum is not "natural" to man.*

"We can not fail to observe that work is never limited to the unavoidable minimum but exceeds the absolutely necessary amount, owing to a natural or acquired functional urge to activity" (Thurnwald, *Economics*, p. 209). "Labor always tends beyond that which is strictly necessary" (Thurnwald, *Die menschliche Gesellschaft*, p. 163).

(d) *The usual incentives to labor are not gain but reciprocity, competition, joy of work, and social approbation.*

Reciprocity: "Most, if not all economic acts are found to belong to some chain of reciprocal gifts and countergifts, which in the long run balance, benefiting both sides equally. . . . The man who would persistently disobey the rulings of law in his economic dealings would soon find himself outside the social and economic order—and he is perfectly well aware of it" (Malinowski, *Crime and Custom in Savage Society*, 1926, pp. 40–41).

Competition: "Competition is keen, performance, though uniform in aim, is varied in excellence. . . . A scramble for excellence in reproducing patterns" (Goldenweiser, "Loose Ends of Theory on the Individual, Pattern, and Involution in Primitive Society." In *Essays in Anthropology*, 1936, p. 99). "Men vie with one another in their speed, in their thoroughness, and in the weights they can lift, when bringing big poles to the garden, or in carrying away the harvested yams" (Malinowski, *Argonauts*, p. 61).

Joy of work: "Work for its own sake is a constant characteristic of Moari industry" (Firth, "Some Features of Primitive Industry," *E.J.*, Vol. I, p. 17). "Much time and labor is given up to aesthetic purposes, to making the gardens tidy, clean, cleared of all debris; to building fine, solid fences, to providing specially strong and big yam-poles. All these things are, to some extent, required for the growth of the plant; but there can be no doubt that the natives push their conscientiousness far beyond the limit of the purely necessary" (Malinowski, *op. cit.*, p. 59).

Social approbation: "Perfection in gardening is the general index to the social value of a person" (Malinowski, *Coral Gardens and Their Magic*, Vol. II, 1935, p. 124). "Every person in the community is expected to show a normal measure of application" (Firth, *Primitive Polynesian Economy*, 1939, p. 161). "The Andaman Islanders regard laziness as an antisocial behavior" (Ratcliffe-Brown, *The Andaman Islanders*). "To put one's labor at the command of another is a social service, not merely an economic service" (Firth, *op. cit.*, p. 303).

(e) *Man the same down the ages.*

Linton in his *Study of Man* advises caution against the psychological theories of personality determination, and asserts that "general observations lead to the conclusion that the total range of these types is much the same in all societies. . . . In other words, as soon as he [the observer] penetrates the screen of cultural difference, he finds that these people are fundamentally like ourselves" (p. 484). Thurnwald stresses the similarity of men at all stages of their development: "Primitive economics as studied in the preceding pages is not distinguished from any other form of economics, as far as human relations are concerned, and rests on the same general principles of social life" (*Economics*, p. 288). "Some collective emotions of an elemental nature are essentially the same with all human beings and account for the recurrence of similar configurations in their social existence" ("Sozialpsychische Abläufe im Völkerleben." In *Essays in Anthropology*, p. 383). Ruth Benedict's *Patterns of Culture* ultimately is based on a similar assumption: "I have spoken as if human temperament were fairly constant in the world, as if in every society a roughly similar distribution were potentially available, and, as if the culture selected from these, according to its traditional patterns, had moulded the vast majority of individuals into conformity. Trance experience, for example, according to this interpretation, is a potentiality of a certain number of individuals in any population. When it is honored and rewarded, a considerable proportion will achieve or simulate it . . ." (p. 233). Malinowksi consistently maintained the same position in his works.

(f) *Economic systems, as a rule, are embedded in social relations; distribution of material goods is ensured by noneconomic motives.*

Primitive economy is "a social affair, dealing with a number of persons as parts of an interlocking whole" (Thurnwald, *Economics*, p. xii). This is equally true of wealth, work, and barter. "Primitive wealth is not of an economic but of a social nature" (*ibid.*). Labor is capable of "effective work," because it is *"integrated into an organized effort by social forces"* (Malinowski, *Argonauts*, p. 157). "Barter of goods and services is carried on mostly within a standing partnership, or associated with definite social ties or coupled with a mutuality in non-economic matters" (Malinowski, *Crime and Custom*, p. 39).

The two main principles which govern economic behavior appear to be reciprocity and *storage-cum-redistribution:*

"The whole tribal life is permeated by a constant give and take" (Malinowski, *Argonauts*, p. 167). "Today's giving will be recompensed by tomorrow's taking. This is the outcome of the principle of reciprocity which pervades every relation of primitive life. . ." (Thurnwald, *Economics*, p. 106). In order to make such reciprocity possible, a certain "duality" of institutions or "symmetry of structure will be found in every savage society, as the indispensable basis of reciprocal obligations" (Malinowski, *Crime and Custom*, p. 25). "The symmetrical partition of their chambers of spirits is based with the Banaro on the structure of their society, which is similarly symmetrical" (Thurnwald, *Die Gemeinde der Bánaro*, 1921, p. 378).

Thurnwald discovered that apart from, and sometimes combined with, such reciprocating behavior, the practice of storage and redistribution was of the most general application from the primitive hunting tribe to the largest of empires. Goods were centrally collected and then distributed to the members of the community, in a great variety of ways. Among Micronesian and Polynesian peoples, for instance, "the kings as the representatives of the first clan, receive the revenue, redistributing it later in the form of largesse among the population" (Thurnwald, *Economics*, p. xii). This distributive function is a prime source of the political power of central agencies (*ibid.*, p. 107).

(g) *Individual food collection for the use of his own person and family does not form part of early man's life.*

The classics assumed the pre-economic man had to take care of himself and his family. This assumption was revived by Carl Buecher in his pioneering work around the turn of the century and gained wide currency. Recent research has unanimously corrected Buecher on this point. (Firth, *Primitive Economics of the New Zealand Moari*, pp. 12, 206, 350; Thurnwald, *Economics*, pp. 170, 268, and *Die menschliche Gesellschaft*, Vol. III, p. 146; Herskovits, *The Economic Life of Primitive Peoples*, 1940, p. 34; Malinowski, *Argonauts*, p. 167, footnote).

(h) *Reciprocity and redistribution are principles of economic behavior which apply not only to small primitive communities, but also to large and wealthy empires.*

"Distribution has its own particular history, starting from the most primitive life of the hunting tribes." ". . . The case is different with societies with a more recent and more pronounced stratification. . . ." "The most impressive example is furnished by the contact of herdsmen with agricultural people." ". . . The conditions in these societies differ considerably. But the distributive function increases with the growing political power of a few families and the rise of despots. The chief receives the gifts of the peasant, which have now become 'taxes,' and distributes them among his officials, especially those attached to his court."

"This development involved more complicated systems of distribution. . . . All archaic states—ancient China, the Empire of the Incas, the Indian kingdoms, Egypt, Babylonia—made use of a metal currency for taxes and salaries but relied mainly on payments in kind stored in granaries and warehouses . . . and distributed to officials, warriors, and the leisured classes, that is, to the non-producing part of the population. In this case distribution fulfills an essentially economic function" (Thurnwald, *Economics*, pp. 106–8).

"When we speak of feudalism, we are usually thinking of the Middle Ages in Europe. . . . However, it is an institution, which very soon makes its appearance in stratified communities. The fact that most transactions are in kind and that the upper stratum claims all the land or cattle, are the economic causes of feudalism . . ." (*ibid.*, p. 195).

7

SELECTED REFERENCES TO "EVOLUTION OF THE MARKET PATTERN"

Economic liberalism labored under the delusion that its practices and methods were the natural outgrowth of a general law of progress. To make them fit the pattern, the principles underlying a self-regulating market were projected backward into the whole history of human civilization. As a result the true nature and origins of trade, markets, and money, of town life and national states were distorted almost beyond recognition.

(a) *Individual acts of "truck, barter, and exchange" are only exceptionally practiced in primitive society.*

"Barter is originally completely unknown. Far from being possessed with a craving for barter primitive man has an aversion to it" (Buecher, *Die Entstehung der Volkswirtschaft*, 1904, p. 109). "It is impossible, for example, to express the value of a bonito-hook in terms of a quantity of food, since no such exchange is ever made and would be regarded by the Tikopia as fantastic. . . . Each kind of object is appropriate to a particular kind of social situation" (Firth, *op. cit.*, p. 340).

(b) *Trade does not arise within a community; it is an external affair involving different communities.*

"In its beginnings commerce is a transaction between ethnic groups; it does not take place between members of the same tribe or of the same community, but it is, in the oldest social communities an external phenomenon, being directed only towards foreign tribes" (M. Weber, *General Economic History*, p. 195). "Strange though it may seem, medieval commerce developed from the beginnings under the influence, not of local, but of export trade" (Pirenne, *Economic and Social History of Medieval Europe*, p. 142). "Trade over long distances was responsible for the economic revival of the Middle Ages" (Pirenne, *Medieval Cities*, p. 125).

(c) *Trade does not rely on markets; it springs from one-sided carrying, peaceful or otherwise.*

Thurnwald established the fact that the earliest forms of trade simply consisted in procuring and carrying objects from a distance. Essentially it is a hunting expedition. Whether the expedition is warlike as in a slave hunt or as in piracy, depends mainly on the resistance that is encountered (*op. cit.*, pp. 145, 146). "Piracy was the initiator of maritime trade among the Greeks of the Homeric era, as among the Norse Vikings; for a long time the two vocations developed in concert" (Pirenne, *Economic and Social History*, p. 109).

(d) *The presence or absence of markets not an essential characteristic; local markets have no tendency to grow.*

"Economic systems, possessing no markets, need not on this account have any other characteristics in common" (Thurnwald, *Die menschliche Gesellschaft*, Vol. III, p. 137). On the early markets "only definite quantities of definite objects could be bartered for one another" (*ibid*, p. 137). "Thurnwald deserves special praise for his observation that primitive money and trade are essentially of social rather than of economic significance" (Loeb, "The Distribution and Function of Money in Early Society." In *Essays in Anthropology*, p. 153). Local markets did not develop out of "armed trade" or "silent barter" or other forms of foreign trade, but out of the "peace" maintained on a meeting place for the limited purpose of neighborhood exchange. "The aim of the local market was to supply the provisions necessary for daily life to the population settled in the districts. This explains their being held weekly, the very limited circle of attraction and the restriction of their activity to small retail operations" (Pirenne, *op. cit.*, Ch. 4, "Commerce to the End of the Twentieth Century," p. 97). Even at a later stage local markets, in contrast to fairs, showed no tendency to grow: "The market supplied the wants of the locality and was attended only by the inhabitants of the neighborhood; its commodities were country produce and the wares of every-day life" (Lipson, *The Economic History of England*, 1935, Vol. I, p. 221). Local trade "usually developed to begin with as an auxiliary occupation of peasants and persons engaged in house industry, and in general as a seasonal occupation . . ." (Weber, *op. cit.*, p. 195). "It would be natural to suppose, at first glance, that a merchant class grew up little by little in the midst of the agricultural population. Nothing, however, gives credence to this theory" (Pirenne, *Medieval Cities*, p. 111).

(e) *Division of labor does not originate in trade or exchange, but in geographical, biological, and other noneconomic facts.*

"The division of labor is by no means the result of complicated economics, as rationalistic theory will have it. It is principally due to physiological differences of sex and age" (Thurnwald, *Economics*, p. 212). "Almost the only division of labor is between men and women" (Herskovits, *op. cit.*, p. 13). Another way in which division of labor may spring from biological facts is the case of the symbiosis of different ethnic groups. "The ethnic groups are transformed into professional-social ones" through the formation of "an upper layer" in society. "There is thus created an organization based, on the one hand, on the contributions and services of the dependent class, and, on the other, on the power of distribution possessed by the heads of families in the leading stratum" (Thurnwald, *Economics*, p. 86). Herein we meet one of the origins of the state (Thurnwald, *Sozialpsyschische Abläufe*, p. 387).

(f) *Money is not a decisive invention; its presence or absence need not make an essential difference to the type of economy.*

"The mere fact that a tribe used money differentiated it very little economically from other tribes who did not" (Loeb, *op. cit.*, p. 154). "If money is used at all, its function is quite different from that fulfilled in our civilization. It never ceases to be concrete material, and it never becomes an entirely abstract representation of value" (Thurnwald, *Economics*, p. 107). The hardships of barter played no role in the "invention" of money. "This old view of the classical economists runs counter to ethnological investigations" (Loeb, *op. cit.*, p. 167, footnote 6). On account of the specific utilities of the commodities which function as money as well as their symbolic significance as attributes of power, it is not possible to regard "economic possession from a one-sided rationalistic point of view" (Thurnwald, *Economics*). Money may, for instance, be in use for the payment of salaries and taxes only (*ibid.*, p. 108) or it may be used to pay for a wife, for blood money, or for fines. "We can thus see that in these examples of pre-state conditions the evaluation of objects of value results from the amount of the customary contributions, from the position held by the leading personages, and from the concrete relationship in which they stand to the commoners of their several communities" (Thurnwald, *Economics*, p. 263).

Money, like markets, is in the main an external phenomenon, the significance of which to the community is determined primarily by trade relations. "The idea of money [is] usually introduced from outside" (Loeb, *op. cit.*, p. 156). "The function of money as a general medium of exchange originated in foreign trade" (Weber, *op. cit.*, p. 238).

(g) *Foreign trade originally not trade between individuals but between collectivities.*

Trade is a "group undertaking"; it concerns "articles obtained collectively." Its origin lies in "collective trading journeys." "In the arrangements for these expeditions which often bear the character of foreign trade the principle of collectivity makes its appearance" (Thurnwald, *Economics*, p. 145). "In any case the oldest commerce is an exchange relation between alien tribes" (Weber, *op. cit.*, p. 195). Medieval trade was emphatically not trade between individuals. It was a "trade between certain towns, an *inter-communal* or *inter-municipal* commerce" (Ashley, *An Introduction to English Economic History and Theory*, Part I, "The Middle Ages," p. 102).

(h) *The countryside was cut out of trade in the Middle Ages.*

"Up to and during the course of the fifteenth century the towns were the sole centers of commerce and industry to such an extent that none of it was allowed to escape into the open country" (Pirenne, *Economic and Social History*, p. 169). "The struggle against rural trading and against rural handicrafts lasted at least seven or eight hundred years" (Heckscher, *Mercantilism*, 1935, Vol. I, p. 129). "The severity of these measures increased with the growth of 'democratic government'. . . ." "All through the fourteenth century regular armed expeditions were sent out against all the villages in the neighborhood and looms or fulling-vats were broken or carried away" (Pirenne, *op. cit.*, p. 211).

(i) *No indiscriminate trading between town and town was practiced in the Middle Ages.*

Intermunicipal trading implied preferential relationships between particular towns or groups of towns, such as, for instance, the Hanse of London and the Teutonic Hanse. Reciprocity and retaliation were the principles governing the relationships between such towns. In case of nonpayment of debts, for instance, the magistrates of the creditor's town might turn to those of the debtor's and request that justice be done in such manner as they would wish their folk to be treated "and threaten that, if the debt is not paid, reprisal will be taken upon the folk of that town" (Ashley, *op. cit.*, Part I, p. 109).

(j) *National protectionism was unknown.*

"For economic purposes it is scarcely necessary to distinguish different countries from one another in the thirteenth century for there were fewer barriers to social intercourse within the limits of Christendom than we meet today" (Cunningham, *Western Civilization in Its Economic Aspects,* Vol. I, p. 3). Not until the fifteenth century are there tariffs on the political frontiers. "Before that there is no evidence of the slightest desire to favor national trade by protecting it from foreign competition" (Pirenne, *Economic and Social History*, p. 92). "International" trading was free in all trades (Power and Postan, *Studies in English Trade in the Fifteenth Century*).

(k) *Mercantilism forced freer trade upon towns and provinces within the national boundaries.*

The first volume of Heckscher's *Mercantilism* (1935) bears the title *Mercantilism as a Unifying System.* As such, mercantilism "opposed everything that bound down economic life to a particular place and obstructed trade within the boundaries of the state" (Heckscher, *op. cit.*, Vol. II, p. 273). "Both aspects of municipal policy, the suppression of the rural countryside and the struggle against the competition of foreign cities, were in conflict with the economic aims of the state" (*ibid.*, Vol. I, p. 131). "Mercantilism 'nationalized' the countries through the action of commerce which extended local practices to the whole territory of the state" (Pantlen, "Handel." In *Handwörterbuch der Staatswissenschaften*, Vol. VI, p. 281). "Competition was often artificially fostered by mercantilism, in order to organize markets with automatic regulation of supply and demand" (Heckscher). The first modern author to recognize the liberalizing tendency of the mercantile system was Schmoller (1884).

(l) *Medieval regulationism was highly successful.*

"The policy of the towns in the Middle Ages was probably the first attempt in Western Europe, after the decline of the ancient world, to regulate society on its economic side according to consistent principles. The attempt was crowned with unusual success. . . . Economic liberalism or *laissez-faire,* at the time of its unchallenged supremacy, is, perhaps, such an instance, but in regard to duration, liberalism was a small, evanescent episode in comparison with the persistent tenacity of the policy of the towns" (Heckscher, *op. cit.,* p. 139). "They accomplished it by a system of regulations, so marvellously adapted to its purpose that it may be considered a masterpiece of its kind. . . . The city economy was worthy of the Gothic architecture with which it was contemporaneous" (Pirenne, *Medieval Cities,* p. 217).

(m) *Mercantilism extended municipal practices to the national territory.*

"The result would be a city policy, extended over a wider area—a kind of municipal policy, superimposed on a state basis" (Heckscher, *op. cit.,* Vol. I, p. 131).

(n) *Mercantilism, a most successful policy.*

"Mercantilism created a masterful system of complex and elaborate want-satisfaction" (Buecher, *op. cit.,* p. 159). The achievement of Colbert's *Reglements,* which worked for high quality in production as an end in itself, was "tremendous" (Heckscher, *op. cit.,* Vol. I, p. 166). "Economic life on a national scale was mainly the result of political centralization" (Buecher, *op. cit.,* p. 157). The regulative system of mercantilism must be credited "with the creation of a labor code and a labor discipline, much stricter than anything that the narrow particularism of medieval town governments was able to produce with their moral and technological limitations" (Brinkmann, "Das soziale System des Kapitalismus." In *Grundriss der Sozialökonomik,* Abt. IV).

To Chap.
7

8

THE LITERATURE OF SPEENHAMLAND

ONLY AT THE BEGINNING and the end of the age of liberal capitalism do we find a consciousness of the decisive importance of Speenhamland. There was, of course, both before and after 1834 constant reference to the "allowance system" and the "maladministration of the Poor Law" which were, however, usually dated not from Speenhamland, 1795, but from Gilbert's Act, 1782, and the true characteristics of the Speenhamland system were not clearly established in the minds of the public.

Nor are they even today. It is still widely held that it simply meant indiscriminate poor relief. Actually, it was something entirely different, namely, systematic aid-in-wages. It was only partially recognized by contemporaries that such a practice was in head-on collision with the principles of Tudor law, nor was it realized by them at all that it was completely incompatible with the emerging wage system. As to the practical effects, it remained unnoticed until later that—in conjunction with the Anti-Combination Laws, 1799–1800—it tended to depress wages, and to become a subsidy to employers.

The classical economists never stopped to investigate into the details of the "allowance system" as they did in the case of rent and currency. They lumped all forms of allowances and outdoor reliefs with the "Poor Laws," and pressed for their abolishment root and branch. Neither Townsend, Malthus, nor Ricardo advocated a reform of the Poor Law; they demanded its repeal. Bentham, who alone had made a study of the subject, was on this matter less dogmatic than on others. Burke and he understood what Pitt had failed to see, that the truly vicious principle was that of aid-in-wages.

Engels and Marx made no study of the Poor Law. Nothing, one would imagine, should have suited them better than to show up the pseudo humanitarianism of a system which was reputed to pander to the whims of the poor, while actually depressing their wages under the subsistence level (powerfully assisted in this by a special anti-trade union law), and handing public money to the rich in order to help them to make more money out of the poor. But by their time the New Poor Law was *the* enemy, and Cobbett and the Chartists tended to idealize the Old. Moreover, Engels and Marx were rightly convinced that if capitalism was to come, the reform of the Poor Law was inevitable. So they missed not only some first-class debating points, but also the argument with which Speenhamland reinforced their theoretical system, namely, that capitalism could not function without a free labor market.

For her lurid descriptions of the effects of Speenhamland, Harriet Martineau drew profusely on the classic passages of the Poor Law Report (1834). The Goulds and Barings who financed the sumptuous little volumes in which she undertook to enlighten the poor about the inevitability of their misery—she was deeply convinced that it was inevitable and that knowledge of the laws of political economy alone could make their fate bearable to them—could not have found a more sincere and, on the whole, better-informed advocate of their creed. (*Illustrations to Political Economy*, 1831, Vol. III; also *The Parish* and *The Hamlet* in *Poor Laws and Paupers*, 1834.) Her *Thirty Years' Peace, 1816–1846* was composed in a chastened mood and showed more sympathy towards the Chartists than towards the memory of her master, Bentham (Vol. III, p. 489, and Vol. IV, p. 453). She concluded her chronicle with this significant passage: "We have now the best heads and hearts occupied about this great question of the rights of labor with impressive warnings presented to us from abroad that it cannot be neglected under a lighter penalty than ruin to all. Is it possible that the solution should not be found? This solution may probably be the central fact of the next period of British history; and then better than now it may seem that in preparation for it lies the chief interest of the preceding Thirty Years' Peace." This was delayed-action prophecy. In the next period of British history the labor question ceased to exist; but it came back in the seventies, and another half century later it did spell "ruin to all." Obviously, it was easier to discern in the 1840's than in the 1940's that the origins of that question lay in the principles governing the Poor Law Reform Act.

Right through the Victorian Age and after, no philosopher or historian dwelled on the petty economics of Speenhamland. Of the three historians of Benthamism, Sir Leslie Stephen did not trouble to inquire into its details; Elie Halevy, the first to recognize the pivotal role of the Poor Law in the history of philosophic radicalism, had only the haziest notions on the subject. In the third account, Dicey's, the

omission is even more striking. His incomparable analysis of the relations between law and public opinion treated *"laissez-faire"* and
"collectivism" as the woof and warp of the texture. The pattern
itself, he believed, sprang from the industrial and business trends of
the time, that is, from the institutions fashioning economic life. No one
could have stressed more strongly than Dicey the dominant role played
by pauperism in public opinion nor the importance of the Poor Law
Reform in the whole system of Benthamite legislation. And yet he was
puzzled by the central importance assigned to the Poor Law Reform
by the Benthamites in their legislative scheme and actually believed
that the burden of the rates on industry was the point in question.
Historians of economic thought of the rank of Schumpeter or Mitchell
analyzed the concepts of the classical economists without any reference
to Speenhamland conditions.

With A. Toynbee's lectures (1881) the Industrial Revolution became a subject of economic history; Toynbee made Tory Socialism
responsible for Speenhamland and its "principle of the protecting of
the poor by the rich." About this time William Cunningham turned
to the same subject and as by miracle it came to life; but his was a
voice in the wilderness. Though Mantoux (1907) had the benefit
of Cunningham's masterpiece (1881) he referred to Speenhamland
as just "another reform" and curiously enough credited it with the
effect of "chasing the poor into the labor market" (*The Industrial
Revolution in the Eighteenth Century*, p. 438). Beer, whose work
was a monument to early English socialism, hardly mentioned the Poor
Law.

It was not until the Hammonds (1911) conceived the vision of a
new civilization ushered in by the Industrial Revolution that Speenhamland was rediscovered. With them it formed a part not of economic but of social history. The Webbs (1927) continued this work,
raising the question of the political and economic preconditions of
Speenhamland, conscious of the fact that they were dealing with the
origins of the social problems of our own time.

J. H. Clapham endeavored to build up a case against what might
be called the institutionalist approach to economic history such as
Engels, Marx, Toynbee, Cunningham, Mantoux, and, more recently,
the Hammonds, represented. He refused to deal with the Speenhamland system as an institution and discussed it merely as a trait in the
"agrarian organization" of the country (Vol. I, Ch. 4). This was
hardly adequate since it was precisely its extension to the towns which

brought down the system. Also, he divorced the effect of Speenhamland on the rates from the wage issue and discussed the former under "Economic Activities of the State." This, again, was artificial and omitted the economics of Speenhamland from the point of view of the employers' class which benefited by low wages as much or more than it lost on the rates. But Clapham's conscientious respect for the facts made up for his maltreatment of the institution. The decisive effect of "war enclosures" on the area in which the Speenhamland system was introduced, as well as the actual degree to which real wages were depressed by it, was shown for the first time by him.

The utter incompatibility of Speenhamland with the wage system was permanently remembered only in the tradition of the economic liberals. They alone realized that, in a broad sense, every form of the protection of labor implied something of the Speenhamland principle of interventionism. Spencer hurled the charge of "make-wages" (as the allowance system was called in his part of the country) against any "collectivist" practices, a term which he found no difficulty in extending to public education, housing, the provision of recreation grounds, and so on. Dicey, in 1913, summed up his criticism of the Old Age Pensions Act (1908) in the words: "It is in essence nothing but a new form of outdoor relief for the poor." And he doubted whether economic liberals ever had a fair chance of bringing their policy to a successful issue. "Some of their proposals have never been carried into effect; outdoor relief, for example, has never been abolished." If such was Dicey's opinion, it was only natural that Mises maintained "that as long as unemployment benefit is paid, unemployment must exist" (*Liberalisms,* 1927, p. 74); and that "assistance to the unemployed has proved to be one of the most effective weapons of destruction" (*Socialism,* 1927, p. 484; *Nationalökonomie,* 1940, p. 720). Walter Lippmann in his *Good Society* (1937) tried to dissociate himself from Spencer, but only to invoke Mises. He and Lippmann mirrored liberal reaction to the new protectionism of the 1920's and 30's. Undoubtedly, many features of the situation now recalled Speenhamland. In Austria unemployment benefit was being subsidized by a bankrupt Treasury; in Great Britain "extended unemployment benefit" was indistinguishable from the "dole"; in America WPA and PWA had been launched; actually Sir Alfred Mond, head of Imperial Chemical Industries, vainly advocated in 1926 that British employers should receive grants from the unemployment fund in order to "make up" wages and thus help to increase employment. On the unemployment issue as on the currency issue, liberal capitalism in its death throes was faced with the still unsolved problems bequeathed to it by its beginnings.

CONTEMPORARY LITERATURE ON PAUPERISM AND THE OLD POOR LAW

Acland, *Compulsory Savings Plans* (1786)

Anonymous, *Considerations on Several Proposals Lately Made for the Better Maintenance of the Poor.* With an Appendix. (2nd ed., 1752)

Anonymous, *A New Plan for the Better Maintenance of the Poor of England* (1784)

An Address to the Public from the Philanthropic Society, instituted in 1788 for the Prevention of Crimes and the Reform of the Criminal Poor (1788)

Applegarth, Rob., *A Plea for the Poor* (1790)

Belsham, Will, *Remarks on the Bill for the Better Support and Maintenance of the Poor* (1797)

Bentham, J., *Pauper Management Improved* (1802)

———, *Observation on the Restrictive and Prohibitory Commercial System* (1821)

———, *Observations on the Poor Bill, introduced by the Right Honorable William Pitt;* written February 1797

Burke, E., *Thoughts and Details on Scarcity* (1795)

Cowe, James, *Religious and Philanthropic Trusts* (1797)

Crumple, Samuel, M.D., *An Essay on the Best Means of Providing Employment for the People* (1793)

Defoe, Daniel, *Giving Alms No Charity, and Employing the Poor a Grievance to the Nation* (1704)

Dyer, George, *A Dissertation on the Theory and Practice of Benevolence* (1795)

———, *The Complaints of the Poor People of England* (1792)

Eden, *On the Poor* (1797), 3 vols.

Gilbert, Thomas, *Plan for the Better Relief and Employment of the Poor* (1781)

Godwin, William, *Thoughts Occasioned by the Perusal of Dr. Parr's Spiritual Sermon, Preached at Christ Church April 15, 1800* (London, 1801)

Hampshire, *State of the Poor* (1795)

Hampshire Magistrate (E. Poulter), *Comments on the Poor Bill* (1797)

Howlett, Rev. J., *Examination of Mr. Pitt's Speech* (1796)

James, Isaac, *Providence Displayed* (London, 1800), p. 20

Jones, Edw., *The Prevention of Poverty* (1796)

Luson, Hewling, *Inferior Politics: or, Considerations on the Wretchedness and Profligacy of the Poor* (1786)

M'Farlane, John, D.D., *Enquiries Concerning the Poor* (1782)

Martineau, H., *The Parish* (1833)

————, *The Hamlet* (1833)

————, *The History of the Thirty Years' Peace* (1849), 3 vols.

————, *Illustrations of Political Economy* (1832–34), 9 vols.

Massie, J., *A Plan . . . Penitent Prostitutes. Foundling Hospital, Poor and Poor Laws* (1758)

Nasmith, James, D.D., *A Charge, Isle of Ely* (1799)

Owen, Robert, *Report to the Committee of the Association for the Relief of the Manufacturing and Labouring Poor* (1818)

Paine, Th., *Agrarian Justice* (1797)

Pew, Rich., *Observations* (1783)

Pitt, Wm. Morton, *An Address to the Landed Interest of the defic. of Habitation and Fuel for the Use of the Poor* (1797)

Plan of a Public Charity, A (1790), "On Starving," a sketch

First Report of the Society for Bettering the Condition and Increasing the Comforts of the Poor

Second Report of the Society for Bettering the Condition of the Poor (1797)

Ruggles, Tho., *The History of the Poor* (1793), 2 vols.

Sabatier, Wm., Esq., *A Treatise on Poverty* (1797)

Saunders, Robert, *Observations*

Sherer, Rev. J. G., *Present State of the Poor* (1796)

Spitalfields institution, *Good Meat Soup* (1799)

St. Giles in the Field, Vestry of the United Parishes of, *Criticism of "Bill for the Better Support and Maintenance of the Poor"* (1797)

Suffolk Gentleman, *A Letter on the Poor Rates and the High Price of Provisions* (1795)

[Townsend, Wm.], *Dissertation on the Poor Laws 1786 by A Well-Wisher of Mankind*

Vancouver, John, *Causes and Production of Poverty* (1796)

Wilson, Rev. Edw., *Observations on the Present State of the Poor* (1795)
Wood, J., *Letter to Sir William Pulteney* (on Pitt's Bill) (1797)
Young, Sir W., *Poor Houses and Work-houses* (1796)

SOME MODERN WRITINGS:

Ashley, Sir W. J., *An Introduction to English Economic History and Theory* (1931)
Belasco, Ph. S., "John Bellers, 1654–1725," *Economics,* June, 1925
——, "The Labour Exchange Idea in the 17th Century," *Ec. J.,* Vol. I, p. 275
Blackmore, J. S. and Mellonie, F. C., *Family Endowment and the Birthrate in the Early 19th Century,* Vol. I
Clapham, J. H., *Economic History of Modern Britain,* Vol. I, 1926
Marshall, Dorothy, "The Old Poor Law, 1662–1795," *The Ec. Hist. Rev.,* Vol. VIII, 1937–38, p. 38
Palgrave's *Dictionary of Political Economy,* Art. "Poor Law," 1925
Webb, S. and B., *English Local Government,* Vol. 7–9, "Poor Law History," 1927–29
Webb, Sidney, "Social Movements," *C.M.H.,* Vol. XII, pp. 730–65

> To Chap.
> 7

9

SPEENHAMLAND AND VIENNA

THE AUTHOR WAS first drawn to the study of Speenhamland and its effects on the classical economists by the highly suggestive social and economic situation in Austria as it developed after the Great War.

Here, in a purely capitalistic surrounding, a socialist municipality established a regime which was bitterly attacked by economic liberals. No doubt some of the interventionist policies practiced by the municipality were incompatible with the mechanism of a market economy. But purely economic arguments did not exhaust an issue which was primarily social, not economic.

The main facts about Vienna were these. During most of the fifteen years following the Great War, 1914–18, unemployment insurance in Austria was heavily subsidized from public funds, thus extending outdoor relief indefinitely; rents were fixed at a minute fraction of their former level, and the municipality of Vienna built large tenement houses on a nonprofit basis, raising the required capital by taxation. While no aid-in-wages was given, all-round provision of social services, modest though they were, might have actually allowed wages to drop excessively, but for a developed trade union movement which found, of course, strong support in extended unemployment benefit. Economically, such a system was certainly anomalous. Rents, restricted to a quite unremunerative level, were incompatible with the existing system of private enterprise, notably in the building trade. Also, during the earlier years, social protection in the impoverished country interfered with the stability of the currency—inflationist and interventionist policies had gone hand in hand.

Eventually Vienna, like Speenhamland, succumbed under the attack of political forces powerfully sustained by the purely economic arguments. The political upheavals in 1832 in England and 1934 in Austria were designed to free the labor market from protectionist intervention. Neither the squire's village nor working-class Vienna could indefinitely isolate itself from its environment.

Yet obviously there was a very big difference between the two interventionist periods. The English village, in 1795, had to be sheltered from a dislocation caused by economic progress—a tremendous advance of urban manufactures; the industrial laboring class of Vienna, in 1918, had to be protected against the effects of economic retrogression, resulting from war, defeat, and industrial chaos. Eventually, Speenhamland led to a crisis of the organization of labor which opened up the road to a new era of prosperity; while the *Heimwehr* victory in Austria formed part of a total catastrophe of the national and social system.

What we wish to stress here is the enormous difference in the cultural and moral effect of the two types of intervention: the attempt of Speenhamland to prevent the coming of market economy and the experiment of Vienna trying to transcend such an economy altogether.

While Speenhamland caused a veritable disaster of the common people, Vienna achieved one of the most spectacular cultural triumphs of Western history. The year 1795 led to an unprecedented debasement of the laboring classes, which were prevented from attaining the new status of industrial workers; 1918 initiated an equally unexampled moral and intellectual rise in the condition of a highly developed industrial working class which, protected by the Vienna system, withstood the degrading effects of grave economic dislocation and achieved a level never surpassed by the masses of the people in any industrial society.

Clearly, this was due to the social, as distinct from the economic, aspects of the matter. But did the orthodox economists have a proper grasp of the economics of interventionism? The economic liberals were, in effect, arguing that the Vienna regime was another "maladministration of the Poor Law," another "allowance system," which needed the iron broom of the classical economists. But were not these thinkers themselves misled by the comparatively lasting conditions created by Speenhamland? They were often correct about the future, which their deep insight helped to shape, but utterly mistaken about their own time. Modern research has proved their reputation for sound practical judgment to have been undeserved. Malthus misread the needs of his time completely; had his tendentious warnings of overpopulation been effective with the brides to whom he delivered them personally, this "might have shot economic progress dead in its tracks," says T. H. Marshall. Ricardo misstated the facts of the currency controversy as well as the role of the Bank of England, and failed to grasp the true causes of currency depreciation which, as we know today, consisted primarily in political payments and difficulties of transfer. Had his advice on the Bullion Report been followed, Britain would have lost the Napoleonic War, and "the Empire would not exist today."

Thus the Vienna experience and its similarities to Speenhamland, which sent some back to the classical economists, turned others doubtful of them.

To Chap.
8

10

WHY NOT WHITBREAD'S BILL?

THE ONLY ALTERNATIVE to the Speenhamland policy seemed to have been Whitbread's Bill, brought in in the winter of 1795. It demanded extension of the Statute of Artificers of 1563, so as to include the fixing of minimum wages by yearly assessment. Such a measure, its author argued, would maintain the Elizabethan rule of wage assessment, while extending it from maximum to minimum wages, and thus prevent starvation in the countryside. Undoubtedly, it would have met the needs of the emergency, and it is worth noting that members for Suffolk, for instance, supported Whitbread's Bill, while their magistrates had also endorsed the Speenhamland principle in a meeting at which Arthur Young himself was present; to the lay mind the difference between the two measures could not have been strikingly great. This is not surprising. One hundred and thirty years later when the Mond Plan (1926) proposed to use the unemployment fund to supplement wages in industry, the public still found it difficult to comprehend the decisive economic difference between aid to the unemployed and aid-in-wages to the employed.

However, the choice, in 1795, was between minimum wages and aid-in-wages. The difference between the two policies can be best discerned by relating them to the simultaneous repeal of the Act of Settlement of 1662. The repeal of this Act created the possibility of a national labor market, the main purpose of which was to allow wages "to find their own level." The tendency of Whitbread's Minimum Wage Bill was contrary to that of the repeal of the Act of Settlement, while the tendency of the Speenhamland Law was not. By extending the application of the Poor Law of 1601 instead of that of the Statute of Artificers of 1563 (as Whitbread suggested), the squires reverted to paternalism primarily in respect to the village only and in such forms as involved a minimum of interference with the play of the market, *while actually making its wage-fixing mechanism inoperative.* That this so-called application of the Poor Law was in reality a complete overthrow of the Elizabethan principle of enforced labor was never openly admitted.

With the sponsors of the Speenhamland Law pragmatic considerations were paramount. The Rev. Edward Wilson, Canon of Windsor, and J. P. for Berkshire, who may have been the proponent, set out his views in a pamphlet in which he declared categorically for *laissez-faire.* "Labor, like everything else brought to the market, had in all ages found its level, without the interference of law," he said. It might have been more appropriate for an English magistrate to say, that, on the contrary, never in all the ages had labor found its level without the intervention of law. However, figures showed, Canon Wilson went on, that wages did not increase as fast as the price of corn, whereupon he proceeded respectfully to submit to the consideration of the magistracy "A Measure for the *quantum* of relief to be granted to the poor." The relief added up to five shillings a week for a family of man, wife, and child. An "Advertisement" to his booklet ran: "The substance of the following Tract was suggested at the County Meeting at Newbury, on sixth of last May." The magistracy, as we know, went further than the Canon: it unanimously allowed a scale of five shillings and sixpence.

| *To Chap.* |
| *13* |

11

DISRAELI'S "TWO NATIONS" AND THE PROBLEM OF COLORED RACES

SEVERAL AUTHORS have insisted on the similarity between colonial problems and those of early capitalism. But they failed to follow up the analogy the other way, that is, to throw light on the condition of the poorer classes of England a century ago by picturing them as what they were—the detribalized, degraded natives of their time.

The reason why this obvious resemblance was missed lay in our belief in the liberalistic prejudice which gave undue prominence to the economic aspects of what were essentially noneconomic processes. For neither racial degradation in some colonial areas today nor the analogous dehumanization of the laboring people a century ago was economic in essence.

(a) *Destructive culture contact is not primarily an economic phenomenon.*

Most native societies are now undergoing a process of rapid and forcible transformation comparable only to the violent changes of a revolution, says L. P. Mair. Although the invaders' motives are definitely economic, and the collapse of primitive society is certainly often caused by the destruction of its economic institutions, the salient fact is that *the new economic institutions fail to be assimilated by the native culture* which consequently disintegrates without being replaced by any other coherent value system.

First among the destructive tendencies inherent in Western institutions stands "peace over a vast area," which shatters "clan life, patriarchal authority, the military training of the youth; it is almost prohibitive to migration of clans or tribes" (Thurnwald, *Black and White in East Africa; The Fabric of a New Civilization,* 1935, p. 394). "War must have given a keenness to native life which is sadly lacking in these times of peace. . . ." The abolition of fighting decreases population, since war resulted in very few casualties, while its absence means the loss of vitalizing customs and ceremonies and a consequent unwholesome dullness and apathy of village life (F. E. Williams, *Depopulation of the Suan District,* 1933, "Anthropology" Report, No. 13, p. 43). Compare with this the "lusty, animated, excited existence" of the native in his traditional cultural environment (Goldenweiser, *Loose Ends,* p. 99).

The real danger, in Goldenweiser's words, is that of a "cultural in-between" (Goldenweiser, *Anthropology,* 1937, p. 429). On this point there is practical unanimity. "The old barriers are dwindling and no kind of new guiding lines are offered" (Thurnwald, *Black and White,* p. 111). "To maintain a community in which the accumulation of goods is regarded as anti-social and integrate the same with contemporary white culture is to try to harmonize two incompatible institutional systems" (Wissel in Introduction to M. Mead, *The Changing Culture of an Indian Tribe,* 1932). "Immigrant culture-bearers may succeed in extinguishing an aboriginal culture, but yet fail either to extinguish or to assimilate its bearers" (Pitt-Rivers, "The Effect on Native Races of Contact with European Civilization." In *Man,* Vol. XXVII, 1927). Or, in Lesser's pungent phrase of yet another victim of industrial civilization: "From cultural maturity as Pawnee they were reduced to cultural infancy as white men" (*The Pawnee Ghost Dance Hand Game,* p. 44).

This condition of living death is not due to economic exploitation in the accepted sense in which exploitation means an economic advantage of one partner at the cost of the other, though it is certainly intimately linked with changes in the economic conditions connected with land tenure, war, marriage, and so on, each of which affects a vast number of social habits, customs, and traditions of all descriptions. When a money economy is forcibly introduced into sparsely populated regions of Western Africa, it is not the insufficiency of wages which results in the fact that the natives "cannot buy food to replace that which has not been grown, for nobody else has grown a surplus of food to sell to them" (Mair, *An African People in the Twentieth Century*, 1934, p. 5). Their institutions imply a different value scale; they are both thrifty and at the same time non-market-minded. "They will ask the same price when the market is glutted as prevailed when there was great scarcity, and yet they will travel long distances at considerable cost of time and energy to save a small sum on their purchases" (Mary H. Kingsley, *West African Studies*, p. 339). A rise in wages often leads to absenteeism. Zapotec Indians in Tehuantepec were said to work half as well at 50 centavos as at 25 centavos a day. This paradox was fairly general during the early days of the Industrial Revolution in England.

The economic index of population rates serves us no better than wages. Goldenweiser confirms the famous observation Rivers made in Melanesia that culturally destitute natives may be "dying of boredom." F. E. Williams, himself a missionary working in that region, writes that the "influence of the psychological factor on the death rate" is easily understood. "Many observers have drawn attention to the remarkable ease or readiness with which a native may die." "The restriction of former interests and activities seems fatal to his spirits. The result is that the native's power of resistance is impaired, and he easily goes under to any kind of sickness" (*op. cit.*, p. 43). This has nothing to do with the pressure of economic want. "Thus an extremely high rate of natural increase may be a symptom either of cultural vitality or cultural degradation" (Frank Lorimer, *Observations on the Trend of Indian Population in the United States*, p. 11).

Cultural degradation can be stopped only by social measures, incommensurable with economic standards of life, such as the restoration of tribal land tenure or the isolation of the community from the influence of capitalistic market methods. "Separation of the Indian from his land was the ONE *death blow*," writes John Collier in 1942.

The General Allotment Act of 1887 "individualized" the Indian's land; the disintegration of his culture which resulted lost him some three-quarters, or ninety million acres, of this land. The Indian Reorganization Act of 1934 reintegrated tribal holdings, and saved the Indian community, *by revitalizing his culture.*

The same story comes from Africa. Forms of land tenure occupy the center of interest, because it is on them that social organization most directly depends. What appear as economic conflicts—high taxes and rents, low wages—are almost exclusively veiled forms of pressure to induce the natives to give up their traditional culture and thus compel them to adjust to the methods of market economy, *i.e.,* to work for wages and procure their goods on the market. It was in this process that some of the native tribes like the Kaffirs and those who had migrated to town lost their ancestral virtues and became a shiftless crowd, "semidomesticated animals," among them loafers, thieves, and prostitutes—an institution unknown amongst them before—resembling nothing more than the mass of the pauperized population of England about 1795–1834.

(b) *The human degradation of the laboring classes under early capitalism was the result of a social catastrophe not measurable in economic terms.*

Robert Owen observed of his laborers as early as 1816 that "whatever wage they received the mass of them must be wretched. . . ." (*To the British Master Manufacturers,* p. 146). It will be remembered that Adam Smith expected the land-divorced laborer to lose all intellectual interest. And M'Farlane expected "that the knowledge of writing and accounts will every day become less frequent among the common people" (*Enquiries Concerning the Poor,* 1782, p. 249–50). A generation later Owen put down the laborers' degradation to "neglect in infancy" and "overwork," thus rendering them "incompetent from ignorance to make a good use of high wages when they can procure them." He himself paid them low wages and raised their status by creating for them artificially an entirely new cultural environment. The vices developed by the mass of the people were on the whole the same as characterized colored populations debased by disintegrating culture contact: dissipation, prostitution, thievishness, lack of thrift and providence, slovenliness, low productivity of labor, lack of self-respect and stamina. The spreading of market economy was destroying the traditional fabric of the rural society, the village community, the family, the old form of land tenure, the customs and standards that supported life within a cultural framework. The protection afforded by Speenhamland had made matters only worse. By the 1830's the social catastrophe of the common people was as complete as that of the Kaffir is today. One and alone, an eminent Negro sociologist, Charles S. Johnson, reversed the analogy between racial debasement and class degradation, applying it this time to the latter: "In England, where, incidentally, the Industrial Revolution was more advanced than in the rest of Europe, the social chaos which followed the drastic economic reorganization converted impoverished children into the 'pieces' that the African slaves were, later, to become. . . . The apologies for the child serf system were almost identical with those of the slave trade" ("Race Relations and Social Change." In E. Thompson, *Race Relations and the Race Problem*, 1939, p. 274).

Additional Note

12

POOR LAW AND THE ORGANIZATION OF LABOR

No inquiry has yet been made into the wider implications of the Speenhamland system, its orgins, its effects and the reasons of its abrupt discontinuance. Here are a few of the points involved.

1. To what extent was Speenhamland a war measure?

From the strictly economic point of view, Speenhamland can not truly be said to have been a war measure, as has often been asserted. Contemporaries hardly connected the wages position with the war emergency. In so far as there was a noticeable rise in wages, *the movement had started before the war*. Arthur Young's *Circular Letter* of 1795, designed to ascertain the effects of the failure of crops on the price of corn contained (point IV) this question: "What has been the rise (if any) in the pay of the agricultural laborers, on comparison with the preceding period?" Characteristically, his correspondents failed to attach any definite meaning to the phrase "preceding period." References ranged from three to fifty years. They included the following stretches of time:

3 years	..	..	J. Boys, p. 97.
3–4 "	..	..	J. Boys, p. 90.
10 "	..	..	Reports from Shropshire, Middlesex, Cambridgeshire.
10–15 "	..	..	Sussex and Hampshire.
10–15 "	..	..	E. Harris.
20 "	..	..	J. Boys, p. 86.
30–40 "	..	..	William Pitt.
50 "	..	..	Rev. J. Howlett.

No one set the period at two years, the term of the French War, which had started in February, 1793. In effect, no correspondent as much as mentioned the war.

Incidentally, the usual way of dealing with the increase in pauperism caused by a bad harvest and adverse weather conditions resulting in unemployment consisted (1) in local subscriptions involving doles and distribution of food and fuel free or at reduced cost; (2) in the providing of employment. Wages remained usually unaffected; during a similar emergency, in 1788–9 additional employment was actually provided locally at *lower* than the normal rates. (Cf. J. *Harvey,* "Worcestershire," in *Ann. of Agr.,* v, XII, p. 132, 1789. Also E. Holmes, "Cruckton," *l.c.,* p. 196.)

Nevertheless, it has been assumed with good cause that the war had, at least, an indirect bearing on the adoption of the Speenhamland expedient. Actually, two weaknesses of the rapidly spreading market system were being aggravated by the war and contributed to the situation out of which Speenhamland arose: (1) the tendency of corn prices to fluctuate, (2) the most deleterious effect of rioting on these fluctuations. The cornmarket, only recently freed, could hardly be expected to stand up to the strain of war and threats of blockade. Nor was the cornmarket proof against the panics caused by the habit of rioting which now took on an ominous import. Under the so-called regulative system, "orderly rioting" had been regarded by the central authorities more or less as an *indicator* of local scarcity which should be handled leniently; now it was denounced as a *cause* of scarcity and an economic danger to the community at large, not least to the poor themselves. Arthur Young published a warning on the "Consequences of rioting on account of the high prices of food provisions" and Hannah More helped to broadcast similar views in one of her didactic poems called "The Riot, or, Half a loaf is better than no bread" (to be sung to the tune of "A Cobbler there was"). Her answer to the housewives merely set in rhymes what Young in a fictitious dialogue had expressed thus: " 'Are we to be quiet till starved?' Most assuredly you are not—you ought to complain; but complain and act in such a manner as shall not aggravate the very evil that is felt." There was, he insisted, not the slightest danger of a famine "*provided we are free of riots.*" There was good reason for concern, the supply of corn being highly sensitive to panic. Moreover, the French Revolution was giving a threatening connotation even to orderly riots. Though fear of a rise in wages was undoubtedly the economic cause of Speenhamland, it may be said that, as far as the war was concerned, the implications of the situation were far more social and political than economic.

2. *Sir William Young and the relaxation of the Act of Settlement.*

Two incisive Poor Law measures date from 1795: Speenhamland and the relaxation of "parish serfdom." It is difficult to believe that this was a mere coincidence. On the mobility of labor their effect was up to a point opposite. While the latter made it more attractive for the laborer to wander in search of employment, the former made it less imperative for him to do so. In the convenient terms of "push" and "pull" sometimes used in studies on migration, while the "pull" of the place of destination was increased, the "push" of the home village was diminished. The danger of a large-scale unsettlement of rural labor as a result of the revision of the Act of 1662 was thus certainly mitigated by Speenhamland. From the angle of Poor Law administration, the two measures were frankly complementary. For the loosening of the Act of 1662 involved the risk which that Act was designed to avoid, namely the flooding of the "better" parishes by the poor. But for Speenhamland, this might have actually happened. Contemporaries made but little mention of this connection, which is hardly surprising once one remembers that even the Act of 1662 itself was carried practically without public discussion. Yet the conviction must have been present in the mind of Sir William Young, who twice sponsored the two measures conjointly. In 1795, he advocated the amendment of the Act of Settlement while he was also the mover of the 1796 Bill by which the Speenhamland principle was incorporated in law. Once before, in 1788, he had in vain sponsored the same two measures. He had moved the repeal of the Act of Settlement almost in the same terms as in 1795, sponsoring at the same time a measure of relief of the poor which proposed to establish a living wage, two-thirds of which were to be defrayed by the employer, one-third to be paid from the rates (Nicholson, *History of the Poor Laws*, Vol. II). However, it needed another bad failure of the crops plus the French War to make these principles prevail.

3. Effects of high urban wages on the rural community.

The "pull" of the town caused a rise in rural wages and at the same time it tended to drain the countryside of its agricultural labor reserve. Of these two closely connected calamities, the latter was the more significant. The existence of an adequate reserve of labor was vital to the agricultural industry which needed many more hands in spring and October than during the slack winter months. Now, in a traditional society of organic structure the availability of such a reserve of labor is not simply a matter of the wage level, but rather of the institutional environment which determines the *status* of the poorer part of the population. In almost all known societies we find legal or customary arrangements which keep the rural laborer at the disposal of the landowner for employment at times of peak demand.

Here lay the crux of the situation created in the rural community by the rise in urban wages, once *status* gave way to *contractus*. Before the Industrial Revolution there were important reserves of labor in the countryside: there was domestic or cottage industry which kept a man busy in winter while keeping him and his wife available for work in the fields in spring and autumn. There was the Act of Settlement which held the poor practically in serfdom to the parish and thereby dependent upon the local farmers. There were the various other forms under which the Poor Law made the resident laborer a pliable worker such as the labor rate, billeting or the roundsmen system. Under the charters of the various Houses of Industry a pauper could be punished cruelly not only at discretion, but actually in secret; sometimes the person seeking relief could be apprehended and taken to the House if the authorities who had the right of forcibly entering his place of abode in day-time found that he "was in want, and ought to be relieved" (31 Geo. III. *c.* 78). The death rate at such houses was appalling. Add to this the condition of the hind or borderer of the North, who was paid in kind and was compelled to help at any time in the fields, as well as the manifold dependencies that went with tied cottages and the precarious forms of land tenure on the part of the poor, and one can gauge the extent to which a latent reserve army of docile labor was at the disposal of rural employers. Quite apart from the wage issue, there was, therefore, the issue of the maintenance of an adequate agricultural labor reserve. The relative importance of the two issues may have varied at different periods. While the introduction of Speenhamland was intimately connected with the farmers' fear of rising wages, and while the rapid spread of the allowance system during the later years of the agricultural depression (after 1815) was probably determined by the same cause, the almost unanimous insistence of the farming community in the early thirties on the need for the retention of the allowance system, was due not to fear of rising wages, but to their concern about an adequate supply of readily disposable labor. This latter consideration cannot, however, have been quite absent from their minds at any time, especially not during the long period of exceptional prosperity (1792–1813) when the average price of corn was soaring and outstripped by far the rise in the price of labor. Not wages, but labor supply was the permanent underlying concern at the back of Speenhamland.

It might seem somewhat artificial to try and distinguish between these two sets of motives seeing that a rise in wages would be expected to attract a larger supply of labor. In some cases, however, there is proof positive which of the two concerns was uppermost in the farmer's mind.

First there is ample evidence that even in case of the resident poor the farmers were hostile to any form of outside employment which made the laborer less available for occasional agricultural employment. One of the witnesses of the 1834 Report accused the resident poor of going "herring and mackerel fishing and earning as much as one pound a week while their families are left to the care of the parish. On return they are sent to gaol but they do not mind as long as they are out again for the well paid work . . ." (p. 33). That is, the same witness complains, why "farmers are frequently unable to find a sufficient number of laborers for their Spring and October work" (Henry Stuart's Report, App. A, Pt. I, p. 334A).

Secondly, there was the crucial question of allotments. Farmers were unanimous that nothing would keep a man and his family as surely off the rates as a plot of his own. Yet not even the burden of the rates would induce them to agree to any form of allotment which might make the resident poor less dependent on occasional farmwork.

The point deserves attention. By 1833 the farming community was stolidly in favor of retaining Speenhamland. To quote some passages from the Poor Law Commissioners Report: The allowance system meant "cheap labor, expeditious harvests" (Power). "Without the allowance system the farmers could not possibly continue to cultivate the soil" (Cowell). "The farmers like that their men should be paid from the poor-book" (J. Mann). "The great farmers in particular, I do not think want them (the rates) reduced. Whilst the rates are as they are, they can always get what hands they want extra, and as soon as it's raining they can turn them all on to the parish again . . ." (a farmers' witness). Vestry persons are "averse to any measure that would render the laborer independent of parish assistance which, by keeping him to its confines, retains him always at their command when wanted for urgent work." They declare that "high wages *and* free laborers would overwhelm them" (Pringle). Stolidly they opposed all proposals to invest the poor with allotments which would make them independent. Plots which would save them from destitution and keep them in decency and self-respect would also make them independent and remove them from the ranks of the reserve army needed by the agricultural industry. *Majendie*, an advocate of allotments recommended plots of ¼ acre, anything above that he thought hopeless, since "the occupiers are afraid of making laborers independent." *Power*, another friend of allotments, confirmed this. "The farmers object very generally, he said, to the introduction of the allotments. They are jealous of such deductions from their holdings; they have to go farther for their manure; and they object to the increased independence of their laborers." *Okeden* proposed allotments of ¹⁄₁₆ acre, for, he said, "this would almost exactly use up as much spare time as the wheel and the distaff, the shuttle and the knitting needles" used up when they were in full activity in every industrial cottage family!

This leaves but scant room for doubt about the true function of the allowance system from the point of view of the farming community, which was to ensure an agricultural reserve of resident poor available at any time. Incidentally, Speenhamland in this way created the semblance of a rural surplus population, where in reality there was none.

4. The allowance system in the industrial towns.

Speenhamland was primarily designed as a measure of alleviation of rural distress. This did not mean restriction to villages since market towns, too, belonged to the countryside. By the early thirties in the typical Speenhamland area most towns had introduced the allowance system proper. The county of Hereford, for instance, which was classed from the point of view of surplus population as "good," showed six out of six towns owning up to Speenhamland methods (four "definitely," four "probably"), while the "bad" Sussex showed out of twelve reporting towns three without and nine with Speenhamland methods, in the strict sense of the term.

The position in the industrial towns of the North and North-West was of course, very different. Up to 1834 the number of dependent poor was considerably smaller in the industrial towns than in the countryside, where even before 1795 the nearness of manufactures tended to increase the number of paupers greatly. In 1789, the Rev. John Howlett was arguing convincingly against "the popular error that the proportion of poor in large cities and populous manufacturing towns is higher than in mere parishes, whereas the fact is just the contrary" (*Annals of Agriculture*, v, XI, p. 6, 1789).

What the position in the new industrial towns was, is unfortunately not exactly known. The Poor Law Commissioners appeared disturbed about the allegedly imminent danger of the spreading of Speenhamland methods to the manufacturing towns. It was recognized that the "Northern counties are least infected by it," yet it was still asserted that "even in the towns it exists in a very formidable degree." The facts hardly bear this out. True, in Manchester or Oldham relief was occasionally given to persons in health and full employment. In Preston at ratepayers meetings, so Henderson wrote, a pauper was vocal who had "thrown himself on the parish his wages having been reduced from one pound to 18 shillings weekly." The township of Salford, Padiham, and Ulverston also were classed as practising the method of aid-in-wages "regularly"; similarly Wigan, in so far as weavers and spinners were concerned. In Nottingham stockings were sold under prime cost "with a profit" to the manufacturer obviously owing to subsidies to wages paid from the rates. And Henderson, reporting on Preston, was already seeing in his mind's eye this nefarious system "creeping in and enlisting private interests in its defence." According to the Poor Law Commissioners' Report the system prevailed less in the towns, merely "because the manufacturing capitalists form a small proportion of the rate-payers and consequently have less influence in the vestries than the farmers in the country places."

However this may have been in the short run, it seems probable that in the long run there were several reasons militating against a general acceptance of the allowance system on the part of industrial employers.

One was the inefficiency of pauper labor. The cotton industry was mainly run on piece work or task work, as it was called. Now, even in agriculture "the degraded and inefficient pensions of the parish" worked so badly that "4 or 5 of them amounted to one in task work." (Select Committee on Laborers' Wages, H. of C. 4, VI, 1824, p. 4.) The Poor Law Commissioners' Report remarked that piece work might allow the use of Speenhamland method, without necessarily destroying "the efficiency of the manufacturing laborer"; the manufacturer might thus "really obtain cheap labor." The implication was that the low wages of the agricultural laborer need not mean cheap labor since the inefficiency of the laborer may outweigh the low price of his labor for the employer.

Another factor which tended to turn the *entrepreneur* against the Speenhamland system was the danger of competitors who might be producing at a considerably lower wage-cost as a result of aid-in-wages. This threat left the farmer unmoved who was selling in an unrestricted market, but might have greatly disturbed the urban factory owner. The P.L.C. Report argued that "a Macclesfield manufacturer may find himself undersold and ruined in consequence of the maladministration of the Poor Law in Essex." William Cunningham saw the importance of the 1834 Act mainly in its "nationalizing" effect upon the administration of the Poor Law, thus removing a serious obstacle from the path of the development of national markets.

A third objection to Speenhamland, and the one which may have carried the greatest weight with capitalist circles, was its tendency to withhold the "vast, inert mass of redundant labor" (Redford) from the urban labor market. By the end of the twenties the demand for labor on the part of urban manufacturers was great; Doherty's trade unions gave rise to large-scale unrest; this was the beginning of the Owenite movement which led to the biggest strikes and lock-outs England had yet experienced.

From the employers' angle, therefore, three strong arguments militated, in the long run, against Speenhamland: its deleterious effect on the productivity of labor; its tendency to create cost differentials as between the various parts of the country; its encouragement of "stagnant pools of labor" (Webb) in the countryside, thus propping up the urban workers' monopoly of labor. None of these conditions would carry much weight with the individual employer, or even with a local group of employers. They might easily be swayed by the advantages of low labor cost, not only in ensuring profits, but also in assisting them to compete with manufacturers of other towns. However, *entrepreneurs* as a class would take a very different view, when, in the course of time, it appeared that what benefited the isolated employer or groups of employers formed a danger to them collectively. Actually, it was the spreading of the allowance system to Northern industrial towns in the early thirties, even though in an attenuated form, that consolidated opinion against Speenhamland, and carried a reform on a national scale.

The evidence points to an urban policy more or less consciously directed towards the building up of an industrial reserve army in the towns, mainly in order to cope with the sharp fluctuations of the economic activity. There was not, in this respect, much difference between town and countryside. Just as the village authorities preferred high rates to high wages, the urban authorities also were loth to remove the non-resident pauper to his place of settlement. There was a sort of competition between rural and urban employers for the share in the reserve army. Only in the severe and prolonged depression of the middle forties did it become impracticable to bolster up the reserve of labor at the cost of the rates. Even then rural and urban employers behaved in a similar fashion: large scale removal of the poor from the industrial towns set in, and was paralleled by the "clearance of the village" on the part of the landowners, in both cases with the aim of diminishing the number of resident poor (cf. Redford, p. 111).

5. Primacy of town against countryside.

Speenhamland, according to our assumption, was a protective move of the rural community in the face of the threat represented by a rising urban wage level. This involves primacy of town against countryside in respect to the trade cycle. In at least one instance—that of the depression of 1837–45—this can be shown to have been the case. A careful statistical investigation made in 1847 revealed that the depression started from the industrial towns of the North-West, then spread to the agricultural counties, where recovery set in distinctly later than in the industrial towns. The figures revealed that "the pressure which had fallen first upon the manufacturing districts was removed last from the agricultural districts." The manufacturing districts were represented in the investigation by Lancashire and the West Riding of Yorkshire with a population of 201,000 (in 584 Poor Law Unions); while the agricultural districts were made up of Northumberland, Norfolk, Suffolk, Cambridgeshire, Bucks, Herts, Berks, Wilts and Devon with a population of 208,000 (similarly, in 584 Poor Law Unions). In the manufacturing districts the improvement started in 1842 with a slowing down of the increase in pauperism from 29.37 per cent. to 16.72 per cent., followed by a positive decrease, in 1843, of 29.80 per cent., in 1844 of 15.26 per cent. and, in 1845, of a further 12.24 per cent. In striking contrast to this development, improvement in the agricultural districts began only in 1845 with a decrease of 9.08 per cent. In each case the proportion of Poor Law expenditure to the head of the population was calculated, the latter having been computed for each county and year separately (J. T. Danson, "Condition of the People of the U.K., 1839–1847," *Journ. of Stat. Soc.*, Vol. XI, p. 101, 1848).

6. Depopulation and overpopulation of the countryside.

England was the only country in Europe with a uniform administration of labor in town and country. Statutes like those of 1563 or 1662 were enforced in rural and urban parishes alike and the J.P.s administered the law equally throughout the country. This was due both to the early industrialization of the countryside and to the subsequent industrialization of urban sites. Consequently there was no administrative chasm between the organization of labor in town and country as there was on the Continent. This again explains the peculiar ease with which labor appeared to flow from village to town and back again. Two of the most calamitous features of Continental demography were thus avoided—namely, the sudden depopulation of the countryside owing to migration from village to town, as well as the irreversibility of this process of migration which thus involved the uprooting of such persons who had taken up work in town. *Landflucht* was the name for this cataclysmic depletion of the countryside which had been the terror of the agricultural community in Central Europe ever since the second half of the nineteenth century. Instead, we find, in England, something like an oscillation of the population between urban and rural employment. It was almost as if a large part of the population had been in a state of suspension, a circumstance which made the movement of internal migration very difficult, if not impossible, to follow. Remember, moreover, the configuration of the country with its ubiquitous ports which made long-distance migration so to speak unnecessary, and the easy adjustment of the administration of the Poor Law to the requirements of the national labor organization becomes understandable. The rural parish often paid outdoor relief to non-resident paupers who had taken up employment in some not too distant town, sending round relief money to their place of abode; manufacturing towns, on the other hand, frequently paid out poor relief to resident poor who had no settlement in the town. Only exceptionally were mass removals carried into effect by the urban authorities as in 1841–1843. Of the 12,628 poor persons at that occasion removed from nineteen manufacturing towns of the North only 1 per cent. had their settlement in the nine agricultural districts, according to Redford. (If the nine "typical agricultural districts" selected by Danson in 1848 are substituted to Redford's counties, the result varies but slightly, i.e. from 1 per cent. to 1.3 per cent.). There was but very little long-distance migration, as Redford has shown, and a large part of the reserve army of labor was kept at the employers' disposal by means of liberal relief methods in village and in manufacturing town. No wonder that there was simultaneous "overpopulation" both in town and country, while actually at times of peak demand Lancashire manufacturers had to import Irish workers in large numbers and farmers were emphatic that they would be unable to carry on at harvest time if any of the village paupers were induced to emigrate.

SUBJECT INDEX

AUTHORS' INDEX